WRESTLING *with the* ANGEL *of* DEMOCRACY

Also by Susan Griffin

Woman and Nature
A Chorus of Stones
The Eros of Everyday Life
What Her Body Thought
The Book of Courtesans

WRESTLING
with the ANGEL *of*
DEMOCRACY

On Being an American Citizen

≪ SUSAN GRIFFIN ≫

TRUMPETER

Boston

2008

TRUMPETER BOOKS
An imprint of
Shambhala Publications, Inc.
Horticultural Hall
300 Massachusetts Avenue
Boston, Massachusetts 02115
www.shambhala.com

© 2008 by Susan Griffin

9 8 7 6 5 4 3 2 1

First Edition
Printed in the United States of America

⊗ This edition is printed on acid-free paper that meets the
American National Standards Institute Z39.48 Standard.

Distributed in the United States by Random House, Inc.,
and in Canada by Random House of Canada Ltd

Designed by James D. Skatges

Library of Congress Cataloging-in-Publication Data
Griffin, Susan, 1943–
Wrestling with the angel of democracy: on being an American citizen /
Susan Griffin.—1st ed.
p. cm.
Includes bibliographical references.
ISBN 978-1-59030-297-2 (hardcover: alk. paper)
1. Democracy—United States. 2. Civil rights—United States.
3. National characteristics, American. 4. Griffin, Susan, 1943–
—Political and social views. 5. Griffin, Susan, 1943– —Diaries. I. Title.
JK1726.G743 2008
323.60973—dc22
2007033776

For my daughter
Chloe Siobhain Andrews

and my grandchildren
Sophie Liberty and Jasper Muir Andrews

The old breath of life, ever new,
Here! I pass it by contract to you, America.

—WALT WHITMAN, "States"

CONTENTS

ACKNOWLEDGMENTS

I would like to thank my extraordinary editor, Eden Steinberg, for her generous support and sagacious insight, and my wonderful agent, Linda Loewenthal, for her continual support and perceptive intelligence. Let me also thank Katinka Matson for her early encouragement. Bokara Legendre, Ty Cashman, and Nancy Kittle gave me support during a difficult period. Mary Watkins, Lori Pye, Nina Simon, Kenny Ausabel, Andrea Lambert, and the late Deborah Tall invited me to speak and provided support in this way. Karin Carrington, Carrie Olson, Mandy Aftel, Nina Wise, Bokara Legendre, Anita Barrows, Joanna and Fran Macy, Dorien Ross, Summer Brenner, Jane White, Terri Jentz, Donna Deitch, Daidie Donnelly, James Hillman, and Margot McLean either read or heard me read sections of the book and provided comments and encouragement. Edward S. Casey, Clyde Thom, Grey Brechin, Chloe Andrews, Alice Walker, and Rebecca Parker gave me important insights. I want to thank Susan Cohan for her fine copyediting. Malcolm Margolin and Marilyn Yalom were very supportive of this project. I am grateful for their insights. I am grateful for the friendship of Jodie Evans throughout this project and for her example of courageous citizenship. Mary and Steve Swig provided another example of deeply committed citizenship, as did Kathleen Thompson and Jenny Hill. I thank Bob McBarton as well as Lee Swenson and Vijaya Nagarajan for the colloquies they have held. I thank Mike Miller for his advice and friendship, both during this project and in earlier days, when I was a student activist. I would also like to thank among many teachers to whom I am grateful Hannah Pitkin and Kay Lawson. Finally, let me thank my former husband, John Levy, for his continuing friendship; and my adoptive family, Geraldine and the late Morton Dimondstein, for all they have taught me.

1

LIBERTY

The people met generally, with anxiety and alarm in their countenances, and the effect of the day, through the whole colony, was like a shock of electricity, arousing every man, and placing him erect and solidly on his centre.

—THOMAS JEFFERSON, *The Autobiography of Thomas Jefferson*

I feel mad, vexed, sick and sorry. Never did I need the voice of a consoling friend more than now. . . . This is a most terrible event. Its consequences are justly to be dreaded.

—GEN. NATHANAEL GREENE, letter to Henry Knox, NOVEMBER 1776, AFTER THE SURRENDER OF FORT WASHINGTON

DECEMBER 2004

Sensing an impending loss, you will be overtaken by many strong emotions. Various forms of torment, remorse, anger, a premature grief, and not the least among these, disquiet, will haunt you. A constant unsettledness, dull in the day, growing more intense at night, will riddle all your thoughts with anxiety.

But if you are fortunate, this storm will have an eye. A wide, even spacious period of calm, a time that seems to arrive as if by some mysterious grace, during which disquiet yields to a gentler state, while you recognize again the virtues, the pleasures, and above all, the astonishing beauty of what you might lose.

Such a realization is, of course, all the more remarkable when what you anticipate losing is so familiar to you that you have ceased to see it clearly. And when what you see again has been so profoundly

embedded in your daily life that you cannot separate it from yourself,
the way you live, and what you think and feel, this recognition is also
a mirror. A glass, as they would have said in a former age, where you
and that which you fear might vanish are pictured as one.

WELL BEFORE I KNEW the meaning of the word, I knew what democracy was. An egalitarian sensibility shaped the first six years of my life, forming not only the way I thought of myself but who I became. What I could think, say, imagine, the nature of my inner life, what some would call my soul, were all marked by the presence of the angel of democracy.

I was born in 1943, my first years marked by the Second World War, a time of intense patriotism. Except that patriotism then was different from what we call by that name now. The crisis we faced at that time seemed to make people come together and tolerate differences, and to intensify rather than diminish a general faithfulness in the idea expressed by the Declaration of Independence, that by right of birth, everyone is entitled to life, liberty, and the pursuit of happiness.

Before I reached the age of reason, this concept would have meant very little to me. Still, though the word was not yet in my vocabulary, I had already had some exposure to democracy. My first understandings came to me almost by osmosis, through what I saw around me, in the way things were done, the way people spoke to one another, laughed, smiled, dressed, even walked, and probably most important in those early years, the way I was raised.

Though I was generally a well-behaved child, I did not fear my parents. They were not by any light progressive, or even liberals, yet, in very simple terms, my mother and father treated my sister and me with a certain measure of respect, as if, at least existentially, they thought of us as equal beings with certain rights of our own. This does not mean we were given free rein. Due to our mother's drinking, my sister and I often suffered neglect, but our household was not overly permissive. Clear limitations were set; we had bedtimes; we were taught table manners; we were expected to behave with respect toward adults. Since my father was a fireman, he made a decent living, but we could afford few luxuries, and thus we were not overly indulged in this way either. The year I was born, 1943, was a time of scarce resources. Until 1946 food was still rationed, a practice that extended the frugal habits of the Great Depression.

Yet in another way entirely, the atmosphere of the postwar period was generous and expansive, a mood that, despite a growing animosity between our parents, infused our household. Dragons overseas had been laid to rest. Life was becoming easier. New houses were being built that working people could afford. We lived in one of them. The dicta of closed worlds and class distinctions had begun to seem old-fashioned.

December

But then the memory of what you have had all your life has another effect. Your mind is suddenly awakened from a certain lethargy. You feel you have been negligent. And now like a lover, seeing the beloved at the door, not only your love but your attention is aroused. As if your life depended on it, you have an urgent desire to know more intimately what threatens to disappear. Is this magical thinking? To describe, enumerate, study, as if this will prevent the loss?

In many households, this leveling spirit had begun to extend to children too. *The Common Sense Book of Baby and Child Care* by Dr. Benjamin Spock, first published in 1946, the year after the war had ended, was swiftly becoming the best-selling book in America. That stern parental voice which once loomed over childhood was being swept away. By the time I was born, in many households, including my own, the notion that children should not speak unless they were spoken to had become antiquated. I am over sixty now, yet I can recall a conversation I had with my father several months before my sixth birthday as clearly as if it had happened yesterday, an interchange that reveals the democratic manner in which I was raised.

If the memory seems commonplace, it was. But that is its virtue. It was one of many similar conversations in which I was given the feeling that I had a right to express myself and to be heard. In this way I was to take in the essence of democracy almost every day. Not just the ideas of freedom and equality, but an intimate experience of both became part of my psyche, an aspect of the way I think and behave that has endured for all of my life.

The year was 1948. We were in the kitchen of our new house, a room filled with windows. It was a warm and sunny day. I remember the quality of light particularly well. I would describe it now as pellucid. Though those who live east of the Rockies do not believe California has seasons, it does. The light grows sharper in the early fall, commanding your eyes to study everything around you.

I had been looking all over the house and our small backyard for my sister. Six and a half years older than me, she was the love of my life then. I shadowed her every step, watched her closely, imitated her gestures, insinuated myself into her company whenever possible. Near noon, growing impatient with my failure to find her, using the name I had given to her when I was still an infant, I demanded of my father, "Where's De De?"

He was sitting at a counter in our kitchen trying to fix some small appliance. "She's with her friends."

"Where?" I asked, excited that I finally had a clue regarding her location.

"I'm not sure," he said. "She told me they might go into the orchard."

We had recently moved from Los Angeles, where we shared a duplex with my mother's parents, to one of many tract houses in the San Fernando Valley built just after the Second World War, and our house was on the corner where the tract ended, across the street from a grove of walnut trees.

I was already racing toward the back door when my father stopped me.

"Wait," he said. "I don't want you to go there."

"Why?" I said, outraged by the idea. The world was safer for children then, and I had always been allowed to go into the orchard in the daytime, alone or with friends.

My father paused, no doubt to consider what to say for a minute.

But I kept repeating the word *why*, until he finally responded, as I knew he would. Whenever my sister or I asked why we were told to do or not do something, we were accustomed to being answered. Rarely were we given the response *Because I said so*.

Finally my father said, "She wants to be alone with her friends this afternoon."

"She does *not*," I said, expressing an imperious confidence, even though I had not really understood what he meant. As far as I was concerned, my father might as well have been speaking Urdu. Regarding my sister, *alone with her friends* was an entirely foreign concept. Solicitous and kind to me, she habitually included me in her activities, taking me with her where she went, often on the back of her bike, never even implying that I was unwelcome.

My petulance continued. Though he explained to me how it could be that sometimes an older child might need to live her own life apart from a much younger child, I remained furious with my father for the next hour, treating him as if he were an evil gatekeeper, thwarting my will out of pure spite. My only defense is that I was just on the periphery of the age of reason, only at its threshold. As with most children of that age, when I really wanted something, neither reason nor reality had any relevance at all.

And yet, looking back over nearly six decades, I realize my father was not wasting his efforts. It is as clear as the light of day to me now that through this conversation and many others like it, he was introducing me to reason. Though I was not yet capable of being reasonable, his attempts to explain the causes of a circumstance that led to a childish but intense grievance were helping me learn.

The blending of private and public life is manifold and endless in its forms. Political theory does not eventuate in legal documents alone but comes to dwell in all of us. And when it does not live there, it cannot survive at all. If by his manner my father was giving me self-respect and the ability to think for myself in granting me the right of free inquiry, he was also teaching me a skill that democracy requires of its citizens. As the Enlightenment philosopher Immanuel Kant wrote, "Reason is . . . the constant condition of all free actions." Since those who cannot reason are dependent on the opinions of those who can, my father was giving me the lesson in reason that both independent thought and independence requires. He may not have been a wealthy man, but in this and many other ways, he handed down to me the rudiments of a great legacy, the inner life of democracy.

DECEMBER

I am following events with increasing urgency. Every day the news eats into me.

In tracing the legacy I inherited, my mind settles on 1776, the year that the American colonies officially declared for their independence from Great Britain. Because it is the inner life I have chosen to explore, instead of armies and battles, it is in fact the Declaration of Independence that draws me. I cannot say when I first heard the words that Thomas Jefferson wrote, nor do I know when exactly I came to understand what they meant. I only know that certain passages are so deeply embedded in my memory that, in the way that time becomes flexible in the mind, they have fused inextricably with who I am.

Thinking of my own nascent democratic consciousness, I realize that it was not only Jefferson's words but the idea that he or anyone wrote them that impressed me. I have a distinct memory of seeing an image, a reproduction of a popular painting that depicted Jefferson sitting at his desk, a candle casting a potent, almost magical, glow across his face, his hands, the parchment on which he had placed his pen. It was a very sentimental glow, yet now it intrigues me, giving me, in a sense, a guideline for my own writing. I want to avoid sentimentality, pierce the glow, and see something more real. And at the same time, that glow itself represents something real in the interior life of democracy, a promise—not just the hope for the private improvements in the conditions of each life that come from freedom and equality, but something more general and less visible. The possibility, perhaps, of achieving the state of mind that can come from living in a world shaped by reciprocity. And from this mutuality, the sense of being kindred with others.

It is not a history I write, nor even an exposition of democracy. I am aiming at neither a definition nor a catalog of qualities. It is the inner states that generate and are generated by democracy that interest me, and the purpose lies in the journey itself too. At this pivotal moment, the idea of navigating my own life as an American citizen seems to satisfy a longing whose meaning I cannot quite fully articulate yet. And at the same time, I am eager to review the history of American democracy that I learned as a child, viewing this with older eyes now, uncovering backstories, motives, moods, psychologies, as well as ambiguities and contradictory grains. All of which are parts of myself too in a sense, since in the mysterious alchemy through which we are all created, we are shaped by histories that we do not know, as much as by those we do.

I was astonished to learn that by most accounts, Jefferson wrote his first draft of the main body of the declaration in roughly two days. I find the details fascinating, as if somewhere in the welter of them I might uncover a clue to how this remarkable document came into being. Aside from errands and brief meetings with colleagues who visited him, Jefferson was sequestered in two rooms while he wrote. He rented these from a bricklayer in Philadelphia. The building was on the south side of Market Street, a stretch of land that had few houses in that period. Originally Jefferson had wanted to stay farther toward the countryside, in a suburb rather than the city. He sought the quiet around him he was used to when he worked at home. Would he pause in his writing, go to the window, look out on a field or a cluster of trees nearby? Or, when he needed to think for a moment, would he just sit and stare nowhere in particular? In any case, the task he was performing would have had little outward manifestation. The greater part of the drama took place in his mind.

Not far away from this deceptively quiet scene, in a more populated area of the city, at the Philadelphia State House on Chestnut Street, delegates to the Second Continental Congress discussed the resolution to dissolve the bonds between the colonies and England that Richard Henry Lee had introduced on June 7. Like Jefferson, Lee was a delegate from Virginia, a colony from which many Revolutionary leaders came. Virginians, including George Mason, had produced crucial bills, legislation, and literature, including Jefferson's eloquent essay *A Summary View of the Rights of British America,* and Mason's Virginia Declaration of Rights, all of which widened the boundaries of the public imagination, bringing what had once seemed reckless and improbable into the realm of reasonable action.

Though there were amendments and compromises to be made to Lee's resolution, everyone knew it would soon be adopted. A severance from Britain was already under way. The first shots had been fired over a year earlier. Colonial armies were being organized. Welcomed by drum rolls, George Washington had just marched his troops into New York City. King George had hired German mercenaries, who were on their way to America. Though no nation existed yet, foreign relations, especially with France, would be crucial to the Revolution. The world had to be told what the American colonists were doing and why.

This was why, three days later, on June 10, the Second Continental Congress appointed a committee to write a document formally declaring the separation of the American colonies from Britain. When, a day later, the committee of seven men, among them Benjamin Franklin and John Adams, convened to discuss what the declaration should say, they made Jefferson their chairman and then, sometime later in the course of the day, asked him to write the document.

Over the next few days, as Jefferson sat in an easy chair in his parlor, laboring over a lap desk of his own design, extraordinary events were still unfolding. Just after Washington's arrival in New York, a group loyal to the king made an attempt on his life. Now Tories were being beaten, forced to ride the rail, and run of town. The air was electric with the possibility of a great transformation.

Yet in the relative quiet of the rooms where Jefferson worked, I imagine the atmosphere was charged in another way. The experience is one many writers have had: the palpable energy generated by words that move beyond small understandings into the shared arena of language. When the music is right, you can almost hear the resonance, as if while they are being written, words travel outward and can already be heard by others who, in some inexplicable way, seem to respond. Whether real or imagined, a response enters your consciousness, bringing more revelations that open the scope of your vision to an even wider circumference.

Since you will be the first reader of your own words, it follows that the same resonance you have sensed will be felt by subsequent readers. Whatever is written or said may one day transmute into action, but words are also actions in themselves. With their music and their meaning, they alter inner moods and at times even restructure consciousness, thus shifting perception and the nature of experience in an instant.

The sentences and phrases that have become such an indelible part of who I am all occur in the beginning of the declaration, a passage consisting of two paragraphs preceding the long list of grievances that the colonists had against the king of England and that justified the American Revolution. As I explore this passage now, it seems that all the fundamental characteristics of democratic consciousness are evident in the first sentence. Not just ideas but attitudes and orientations that were revolutionary are to be found here, and implicit within these are the new ways of knowing, being, and relating that formed the basis for the new psychology and inner life that democracy, if it were to be realized, would demand of us all. This is how the Declaration of Independence begins:

> When in the Course of human events, it becomes necessary for one people to dissolve the political bands which have connected them with another, and to assume among the powers of the earth, the separate and equal station to which the Laws of Nature and of Nature's God entitle them, a decent respect to the opinions of mankind requires that they should declare the causes which impel them to the separation.

As many others have doubtless done, I have often skimmed over this sentence, disregarding its prophetic significance. Though the passage is majestic, auspicious, and eloquent, until recently I have thought of it merely as a grand flourish, the kind of ornament that gives eighteenth-century prose a feel of stately elegance. Yet, looking more closely, now I can see how a democratic consciousness is already manifest here. As the perspective on history is shifted away from the ruling powers, the authority to declare the truth is taken from them too, and what proceeds from this democratized approach to knowledge is the assumption that another kind of authority, the right to take action, belongs to the people.

That I missed the revolutionary significance of this sentence is not surprising. Jefferson never states these principles directly. On the contrary, the genius of the opening words of the Declaration of Independence is that instead of arguing, the voice here embodies them. Many years later, Jefferson was to write that what he aimed for was to express the American mind. But he does more. As has been said of Bob Dylan in a later time, he tapped into the collective American unconscious, an unconscious that contained the seeds of an entirely new way of being.

Jefferson did not, nor did he intend to, express original ideas in the declaration. He conveys the message mandated by the Second Continental Congress and the committee that appointed him. The concepts here had all appeared before in various forms, letters, essays, legislation, and arguments for legislation written by George Mason, Ben Franklin, John Adams, and of course, Jefferson himself, in his great essay *A Summary View*. Thomas Paine's monumental pamphlet *Common Sense,* an essay that everyone at the center of the controversy read, had come out just six months before. It may seem contradictory that in his own terse remarks about the process of writing the declaration, Jefferson claims that he consulted no books, pamphlets, or even notes as he wrote. But this would hardly have been necessary. He had lived for so long and so closely with the ideas he expressed in the declaration, they were permanent fixtures in his mind.

JANUARY 2005

Inauguration of the president again. Not a happy day for me. I am not objective as I write. Not free of opinions. How could it be otherwise? I was raised, after all, to have opinions. And questions. So many have suspicions that the election process was corrupted. Whether this is true or not, the doubt reveals a profound distrust. We are wrestling with the angel of democracy.

Jefferson had been immersed in the thick and fertile atmosphere that created American democracy for many years. Since he was a student at the College of William and Mary under the liberal William Small, he read the works of the Enlightenment philosophers in France, Germany, and England. After studying law with George Wythe, a judge who demanded his students know history and the philosophies behind the law, and who valued Enlightenment philosophy particularly, Jefferson learned to discuss the concepts of John Locke, on the necessity for the consent of the governed, or Montesquieu, on the separation of powers, as clearly as if these ideas were his own. He must have discussed these ideas, as well as their practical implications, when, after sessions of the Virginia House of Burgesses (as the Virginia legislature was then called), he met regularly with Patrick Henry and Richard Henry Lee at the Apollo Room of Raleigh Tavern, where the decision to convene the first Continental Congress was reached.

I like to imagine these gatherings. The word *tavern* has much more pleasant connotations for me than the word *bar,* which pulls up my memories of the dark places where my mother went to drink herself into insensibility. Is it too simplistic of me to think that if somehow these places had hosted conversations of the kind that allow for self-reflections, and even self-revelatory confessions, she might have recovered some sense of herself, enough to grab ahold of her life and put an end to the self-destructive cycle, which eventually came to play such a sorrowful role in my life too? The supposition is not all wishful thinking. I know that my grandparents were not able to give her what, when she was sober, she managed to give to me—the reception that only an attentive listener can provide and that, in its inward development, the soul needs as much as the lungs need air.

Self-knowledge is a complicated process. What may begin as a flicker of intuition; an image; a strange, half-explained desire or discomfort, may evolve into words uttered late at night or early in the morning, spoken in solitude and probably then not even aloud. But without a sympathetic listener, more often than not such insights evaporate and, at least on a conscious level, are forgotten. For this reason, one of the most appealing effects of a political movement is that it encourages what is on the edge of consciousness to be spoken and heard. When they are still fresh and have not sunk yet into ideologies or truisms, political movements create a resonant field. And a fruitful one as well. As observations and insights that have seemed unutterable before are heard, understood, and echoed, new visions come into being.

The effect is catalytic. What John Adams said of an earlier piece written by Jefferson, a proclamation read to the Continental armies on the day that George Washington took command, that "it has Some Mercury in it," can be said of almost any new movement. With wings on his heels, as he flew past all kinds of ordinarily formidable impediments, Mercury could move more swiftly than the other gods. Despite the comforting appeal of tradition and the safety of repetition, when they catch on, new ideas are carried by a force that seems equal to all the gravity and fear of resistance. A shift in consciousness acts like a powerful wind rushing through the social order. Ignoring familiar boundaries, it can travel freely from one nation to another. A new kind of music, an innovative style in literature, a playful way of dressing, new expressions, manners of living, can seem irresistible at times, even to the most conservative among us.

King Louis XV could have had the Enlightenment philosopher Voltaire executed, imprisoned, or exiled for life. Yet after both arresting him and exiling him, he brought him back to court. It is true that he did this partly at the urging of his mistress, Pompadour, who, because the monarch did not like to read, read Voltaire's work to him. Yet this was one of the qualities he loved most in his mistress. She was witty, intelligent, and entertaining, and she entertained him by reporting and reading to him the witty and shocking things being said and written in Paris. He had a dread of boredom. One reason why he loved Pompadour so much is that she helped to relieve the tedium of life at court, which, while it preserved all the old hierarchies and manners, was famously boring. The dread of boredom as a force in politics is often underestimated.

In fact, the nemesis of American democracy, George III, was himself drawn by new ideas. In contrast to Louis XV, he was an avid reader, who assembled one of the largest libraries in Europe. He was especially fascinated by science, which in the eighteenth century was fashionable, and, considering that by implication modern science proposed a radically new approach to knowledge, it was more than a little avant-garde.

Though it is in some ways paradoxical to the self-interest of a ruler to be drawn by the very concepts that undermine the legitimacy of his rule, in another way this interest must have served him well. George was a man as well as an institution, which is to say he was alive. And like all living beings, he had within him the imperative to grow, to evolve, not only in his body but in his mind too.

The mind often expresses its less acceptable desires through metaphor. George III had another passion, one that he shared with Louis XV and Thomas Jefferson, who, along with his own home, Monticello, also designed the University of Virginia. King George loved to build new structures, and for this he sought out the most advanced architects, whose work he preferred to more conventional designs. I have no difficulty imagining him at Kew, where, though possessing countless buildings and rooms inside these buildings, he grows excited by plans for yet another edifice. *Should the columns be Doric or Ionic?* he asks himself. He contemplates installing a garden library with loggia. And perhaps, he thinks, he will extend the White House at Kew. If he does not leap with joy when he sees the Royal Observatory in Richmond Gardens finally completed, it is only because he has been trained for years in the decorum befitting a king. But his spirit leaps. Now he will be able to see the transit of Venus in the night sky. Though sadly, over the years, he will be closed in by his own mind to the point of madness, as he looks at the splendid structure he has commissioned, he must feel an extraordinary spaciousness within himself.

That Jefferson was both an intellectual and a builder, a practical man, may have helped him to craft prose that partakes of both action and thought. Instead of breaking new ground in the realm of revolutionary ideas, his words enact a revolution in consciousness. The tempo of the language, plain and direct by the standards of the times, the graceful but unremitting arc of reason, together with the unvarnished dignity of address evoke a democratic state of mind even before any argument for democracy is made. Indeed, the tone of the first sentence is hardly disputatious at all. Unlike Tom Paine's fiery pamphlet ("I rejected the hardened sullen tempered Pharaoh of England forever," he wrote, "and distain the wretch . . ."), rather than lay out the principles of democracy in contentious statements, the declaration has an air that is, at times, even serene, spoken with a tone of unassailable authority, as if Jefferson were standing on the steps of a structure that had already been built.

And after reading the declaration many times, I have come to believe that not only did democracy already exist in Jefferson's mind, but that he was dwelling there when he wrote the declaration, and this is what gives his prose an extraordinary authority. Indeed, he presents some of his most radical views as assumptions. The first of these occurs in the opening six words, in the simple phrase *When in the Course of human events*. From the vantage of the twenty-first century, it would be easy to miss the meaning here, but scrutinizing the language more closely now, I am startled to find a fundamental shift in epistemology. With a swift verbal stroke, Jefferson has shifted the angle of perception through which the rest of the document, if not the Revolution itself, will be read. With this phrase, he places the American colonies at the center of history. Now in a time when the United States is the most powerful nation on the earth, the audacity of this move may elude us. But in the eighteenth century, when Britain, and indeed all the European empires, considered the American colonies a backwater, existing only at the periphery of significance, this was a startlingly new way to frame the subject.

Whether from London to the American colonies, or Versailles to Paris, or from Washington, D.C., to Bangladesh, relocating the center of significance is never a minor act. To see the events in your own life as important constitutes a bold challenge to those who rule. And by the same token, to be able to see meaning in your own life is fundamental to democratic consciousness. Significance is always allied with power. Political movements occur in the mind as well as in the realm of action, and great transformations of consciousness derive from a shift in perspective. Over time, as democracy has evolved, many old tales have been retold from a fresh point of view, from the eyes of a woman escaping slavery; the eyes of a working person, tired from long hours yet unable to afford a decent meal; the eyes of a woman experiencing rape; or a child, abused in some way. To move a woman, for instance, from the background of a story to the center of it creates a new understanding, both in heart and mind. And this understanding will eventually have consequences. Through a mystery of human psychology as old as humanity itself, to see events from your own perspective will also make you aware of the power you have within yourself to change them.

One can remain suspended between two points of view for years. By listening to what I had to say on the various issues concerning myself that arose in our family, my parents steadily taught me the value of my own perspective. But there were exceptions to this pattern. The sunny memories of my first six years had a shadow side that, before it changed my life, was expressed in occasional eruptions that had the nightmarish quality of injustice. I have carried another memory with me from the time when I was five years old, the full meaning of which it has taken me years to grasp. For a long time, the memory existed in a murky place, in between one point of view and another, my mother's and my own. I was playing on our back patio, the square of concrete my father and his friends poured just after we moved in, during one late afternoon in the fall. The sky was hazy in a way that the sky gets near dusk in Southern California. I had just gotten a new toy; it had not been easy to acquire. After one of my parents helped me fill out and send in a form that had come with a box of cereal, it came in the mail. The long anticipation of its arrival had significantly increased its magic to me; though I cannot remember very clearly what it was, I know I treasured it. It was perhaps a ring, and somehow shaped like the head of Donald Duck, with a compass inside. And what I also know is that on this day I experienced a sudden and overpowering wish to have my ring outside with me so that I could play with it. It was for this reason that I headed inside to look for it. But when I tried to enter the house, I found that the kitchen door, which was never locked, and through which I usually entered, was, on this day, locked.

I remember trying the handle several times in disbelief. When soon it became apparent I could not get in by myself, I began to knock. When no one came, I started to knock more loudly. Then I began to pound and after that to call out as loudly as I could for my mother to let me in. Finally my mother, looking very angry, came to the door, and what surprised me even more than the state of the door was the way she acted toward me. In a severe tone of voice, she told me to stop making so much noise and, even more alarming, told me I could not come in the house. She was resting, she said. And slammed the door.

I waited for a moment in a state of shock before I renewed my efforts, banging and calling again until she returned.

"What did I tell you?" she asked, her voice unmistakably bitter now.

Still, I was not used to such a summary dismissal; I kept on arguing, probably at the top of my voice, that I only needed to come in for a few moments to find my ring.

"I'll throw that ring out if you don't stay outside and be quiet," she shouted at me before slamming the door again.

Her threat threw me into a frenzy of anger. Afraid of retribution, I wept tears of rage alone. By now, my fury had little to do with the ring. Though I did not have the vocabulary to describe it as such then, it was a sense of injustice that enveloped me. I was not used to being treated this way. The house had always been open to me, and in any case, most often I was allowed to express the reasons why I quarreled with the decisions my parents made, even if they rarely agreed with my objections.

What followed is one of many inevitable transmutations that occur in childhood. The bitterness in my mother's tone of voice became mine. I was bitter toward her, of course, but this only intensified the bitterness I felt toward myself, as if her attitude toward me somehow defined me, and my rage toward her only confirmed the justice of that definition.

This was probably what made me ashamed of my tears. Because I did not want anyone to see evidence of the scene that had transpired between my mother and me, which might confirm the nastiness of my character, I waited until the sky had grown dark before I made my way to the house of my best friend, who lived across the street.

Though my tears had dried, I was cold and hungry, and this only added to the dreadful feeling of wrongness that clung to me. So I was surprised by the reception I received. My friend's mother seemed very glad to see me, and after my friend and I played for a while, she invited me to join them for dinner. Because I was not certain I would find dinner at my house, I was relieved to be invited. This was the first time I had tasted dumplings, and I have loved them ever since. The visit restored my composure. But for many years afterward, whenever I remembered that afternoon, I could not fully embrace my own point of view.

It was not until the twentieth century that psychologists and philosophers began to draw a connection between childhood experience and political events. But the connection has been drawn through metaphor for centuries. In the seventeenth century, in his extended argument for the divine right of kings, which he called *Patriarcha,* Sir Robert Filmer associated the authority of monarchs with parental authority. In this work, where he makes the improbable claim that the monarchs of the house of Stuart descended directly from Adam, he asserts that God gave Adam absolute authority over all his children, a right the English kings inherited. "The subjection of children to their parents is the fountain of all regal authority," he writes.

Though he would not be considered a defender of children, the philosopher John Locke certainly paved the way for children's rights in the first of his *Two Treatises on Government*, where he refutes Filmer's ideas. He goes back to biblical texts to find that nowhere did God give to "one man dominion over another, or Adam or his posterity." It is Filmer's thesis regarding absolute parental authority against which Locke frames his own arguments for the idea of a constitutionally limited monarch who is not given the right to rule by God but only by the consent of the governed.

FEBRUARY

The news these days rivals all the stories from history about treacherous court intrigues. It seems that someone in the White House leaked the name of a covert agent to the press. It was done, they say, to undermine her husband, the former ambassador Joe Wilson, who disputed the president's claim that Iraq was importing uranium from Niger— a claim used to justify and build support for the war. An independent counsel has been appointed to investigate.

If monarchy and every sort of tyranny have often been likened to parental authority, what is also true is that the ideas that sustain absolute rule are handed down to children by parents. For this reason, over time, whenever those in power have posited their own point of view as the only legitimate vantage from which to grasp the truth, the process of persuasion takes less and less effort. After successive generations have internalized the perspective of the ruling class, no one has to argue or even assert the validity of it. The assumptions behind most everything a child learns in school and at home, or in the customs and culture of public life, come from the perspective of the powerful.

Born in 1743, when the American colonies were part of the British Empire, Thomas Jefferson was no exception to this rule. The way he was raised could easily have given him a British perspective if not shaped an argument against revolution within him. From a young age he was brought up as a loyal subject of the British crown. The loyalty was handed down through his family. A great part of his ancestry was English. His maternal grandmother, Jane Rogers, had been born and raised in Britain before she married Isham Randolph, in London, at Whitechapel in 1718. Two years later, Jefferson's mother was born in London too. And though his mother's father was from an old and prominent Virginia family, the

Randolphs claimed that their lineage stretched back to the royal houses of Scotland and England. Consistent with this history, the family's wealth, and the station Randolph held as the Master of Dungeness, they retained the patrician manners of the British aristocracy.

Though Jefferson tells us very little about his childhood in his autobiography, it is clear that his mother was proud of her lineage and her station. As for Jefferson's father, by the time he married Jane Randolph, he was a wealthy and prominent man too; a justice of the peace, surveyor of the county, and a member of Virginia's House of Burgesses, Peter Jefferson had acquired the aristocratic manners that characterized British landed gentry. From Thomas Jefferson's way of life, it is clear that he was raised to have the habits of an English lord.

All through his childhood, he was surrounded by British culture. His father's plantation, where he was born and then lived for his first three years, was named Shadwell after the parish near the docks in London where his mother was born. The James River that ran by his grandfather Randolph's plantation, Tuckahoe, where the family moved when Thomas was three years old, was named after the English king, James. That the formal education Jefferson received as a child was British is clear from the name he gave to the small building at Tuckahoe where the tutors his father hired instructed him. He called this wood cabin the "English School." The college he attended is still named after the royal couple, William and Mary.

Before he attended college, along with the Greek, Latin, and classical history, which the children of the British upper class had to learn too, his tutors would have required him to memorize the names of all the English kings: Alfred the Great; Edward the Confessor and William the Bastard, who won the crown at the Battle of Hastings; Edward III and the Henrys of the Tudor dynasty; as well as Elizabeth I; James II, exiled by Cromwell; and William and Mary, who followed Cromwell; and of course, King George II, who ruled when Jefferson was born. His imagination would be sparked by images of the Saxons, one of whose leaders, according to legend, gave his name to the parish of Shadwell. A map of the British Isles would be imprinted on his memory so that he could easily point out where London or Cornwall or Edinburgh lay, and he would have been able to name English flowers, trees, birds too. On his own in his father's library, he read the King James version of the Bible, Shakespeare, Addison, Swift, and Steele.

After the Revolution, Jefferson was to write that Americans "seem to have deposited the monarchical and taken up the republican government with as much ease as would have attended them throwing off an old and putting on a new suit of clothes." But on a deeper level of being, the transition cannot have been that simple, neither for him nor for the rest of Americans. Over two centuries later, our ambivalence about democracy still shows in subtle ways. When I was in grammar school, American children were taught the names of presidents instead of kings. But Britain was prominent in my education. I learned more about Sir Francis Drake, his queen, Elizabeth, and her father, Henry VIII, than I did about the Indian cultures of California. I remember a time when I took Prince Valiant, whom I followed in a Sunday comic strip, as a hero. Though in truth I was also captivated by Davy Crockett and the Indians I read about on the small cards that came with our breakfast cereal, and in high school I read Willa Cather, F. Scott Fitzgerald, and Thornton Wilder. But at the University of California at Berkeley (named after the Irish philosopher), where I majored in English literature, the term then was meant to stand for the literature of Great Britain. For the most part, this canon did not include the greater range of English-speaking writers that exists throughout the world—in Australia, for instance, or Africa, India, or Canada. Even Walt Whitman and Emily Dickinson were treated like warm-up acts to the real show.

In my own family as well, though, along with English ancestors, we had Scotch, Irish, Welch, French, and German progenitors too, a preternaturally strong pull toward British tradition persisted. I remember the slightly awed tone reserved for special topics with which my grandmother and her friends referred to the fine complexion the queen had. I have kept a plate from my childhood that my mother gave me before she died. Commemorating the coronation of George VI in 1937, it is ringed with fading gold leaf and emblazoned with British and heraldic flags, a wreath of laurel, and a crown that surround the profiles of the king and queen. In our family this rather homely souvenir was treated with a reverence reserved only for the most meaningful or valuable objects.

Given the fabric of British traditions in Jefferson's family and the tutelage he received, one might wonder how he ever became a revolutionary, especially considering the insular and self-sufficient world in which he lived, a plantation of twenty-five hundred acres that produced much of its own food, firewood, and candles and bred its own horses. Even when he was sent to live with his tutor, the perspective remained the same, his lessons part of the skein of British allegiance that surrounded him.

Yet there were disruptions in the fabric. And perhaps even a subtle tension in the Jefferson household between Thomas's mother and father, one that subtly mirrored the growing tension between Britain and its colonies. Though, when he married Jane Randolph, Peter Jefferson was a wealthy man, he was not to the manner born. His rise to prominence and relative wealth had come from his own efforts. He was in every way a self-made man. Though his ancestors had been early settlers of America, not only were they Welch but by birth he was privileged to neither wealth nor pedigree. The reason why he insisted that his children receive a formal education was that he had had none himself. He was self-taught. As Jefferson was to write in his autobiography, "My father's education had been quite neglected; but being of a strong mind, sound judgment and eager after information, he read much and improved himself." By the time his son Thomas was born, Peter had become a successful planter with large landholdings, a justice of the peace, an elected member of the House of Burgesses, and a surveyor, who made the first map of Virginia. But the memory of a struggle against penury would have remained in him, the raw edges of a rougher past showing through in small ways, lapses in grammar perhaps, or manners, a way of moving through a room that betrayed a body used to manual labor.

I wonder now if perhaps the pull Jane Randolph felt toward Peter Jefferson was spurred by the not entirely unconscious attraction men and women of different classes frequently feel toward each other. It is as if, in pulling them into union, the erotic force within us all seeks to unify humanity. I can imagine that Peter would have been attracted to Jane for similar reasons. She was a Tidewater Virginian, privileged, refined, part of a powerful clan, everything that a young man born into the hardscrabble life of a frontiersman dreamed of attaining.

My own mother and father came from different backgrounds too. Though the divergence was relatively subtle, it did not seem so within my family. My maternal grandfather was an executive salesman, a title whose meaning I have never been able to decipher, except it made him feel a cut above others. My grandparents were by no means wealthy. But my grandmother used what is thought of as correct grammar, and besides being raised with manners, she studied and followed the etiquette that she believed she ought to have, had she actually been rich. This behavior was forced on the rest of us with an insistent regularity.

By contrast, my father had the air of a workingman. He used a different grammar, saying, for instance, "he don't" instead of "he doesn't"; did not wear striped ties to work; and though he was polite, he was rarely formal. His father had hauled the ice that once kept iceboxes cold to home kitchens in San Pedro, and for a time my father helped him do this. He went to school for two years to study accounting, but nothing came of this. The Depression made it hard to continue school. Instead, he became a fireman. My mother was not disappointed. My father's background was part of what drew her to him. She liked workingmen.

Yet before I was born, the force of attraction between these two began to wane. As I learned much later, my birth was supposed to keep them together. Still, even at the age of five and six, when, at times, I would hear disagreeable shouts coming from the house, I did not notice the deterioration of their marriage. I was distressed when sometimes, while my father was at the firehouse for a forty-eight-hour shift, my mother would disappear, leaving me and my hapless sister to try to find some food. My sister tells me that once when I refused to eat the roast beef she had tried to warm by putting it under a stream of hot water, we went begging in the neighborhood for our dinner. But I did not take my mother's absences as an ominous sign.

I had too many other things on my mind, among them my eager exploration of the small world that surrounded me. In my memory the rows of houses where we lived fade in comparison with the vivid images I still have of the fields and orchards that beckoned me from the borders of our tract. The place where we found ourselves in those years, Van Nuys, in the San Fernando Valley, was changing; our house was a harbinger of the future. What had begun as dry scrubland had been transformed in 1913 by irrigation, after a man named Mulholland engineered the wholesale theft and transportation of water from the Owens Valley and made a fortune in the bargain. (The story is told in the film *Chinatown*.) The farmland had a fleeting existence, providing a pastoral hiatus, before the real business began—a rush of construction, tracts, shopping malls, and millions upon millions of dollars for everyone involved.

But I knew none of this history. When I went to the orchard, which, because it was nearby, I did often, I had the sense of entering what I would call now a hallowed place. I had never been to any church. But the quiet there under the walnut trees, and the simple knowledge that one day I might taste what hung from these trees, threw me into a state of wonderment matched only by the discovery of our cat's kittens after she had just delivered them in our toy box. I knew not to eat the walnuts when they fell. I had been carefully warned that before they were dried they were bitter. But this did not impede the miracle of them for me, that something my mother got from a can and served in a salted mix along with bottles of beer, grew just outside our door.

At the other end of our tract, a daring walk of three blocks away, there was a field where an abandoned and badly weathered red barn stood. Nothing grew in the field but grass, but this grass was hip-high and seemed wild in comparison with the neatly trimmed lawns that fronted all our houses in orderly squares. I remember that one day as I stood with a gaggle of children near the barn, watching a late winter wind rip through this tall green grass (the color of grass in a California winter), I had a distinctly new feeling of exhilaration, that heady sense of freedom a child has at the age of five, when discovering a horizon of existence wider than she has ever encountered before.

Then there were also the secret gardens behind the fences of houses down the road, in front of dwellings far older and larger than ours. These gardens were not sculpted or regimented like their urban counterparts but were instead more like little farms with crops of corn, occasional chickens, and fruit trees. In one of these, a tree laden with ripe peaches stood seductively near the back, peaches that one day, unwisely, I scaled the fence in order to reach. I had been with my sister and her friends in the same territory recently, and they had climbed a fence and gotten fruit. In the back of my mind somewhere, this house seemed the same. But it wasn't. The fruit tree was farther away, the effort more daunting. Screwing up my courage, I made my assault nevertheless, only to be cornered by a snarling dog. All I can remember after that is my tears and my mother's warning never to do that again. But despite the trauma, I never regretted this adventure. Who I was becoming was connected in my young mind to where I was, the place. I felt enlarged by everything I found there.

Peter Jefferson took some pride in his own adventurous background. Though we have none of his words to know him by, a portrait of him can be gleaned from his son's memories. While he wanted his children to have the formal education of which he himself had been deprived, he had still other ideas about what his children should learn. He took Thomas often into the forest, teaching him what he knew: how to survive; to hunt, fish, canoe, forage; and to see through a naturalist's eyes. Wandering first with his father and then alone, in the southwest mountains near Shadwell, Jefferson observed and learned the names of the vast population of birds, insects, plants, flowers, trees.

The land itself and his knowledge of it must have helped Jefferson in his struggle with democracy. If, despite his ties to British traditions, Jefferson was able to embrace an American perspective, he had to be able to perceive the difference between what he actually experienced in America and his British education. The countryside of Virginia did not resemble a British landscape. The name Jefferson gave to his schoolhouse reveals the gap. A child in England would not call his school "English." The designation betrays his awareness, even at a young age, of the divide that existed between his own experience and the lessons he received. He had never been to Europe, seen the king of England, nor even been to London. Both the Rivanna and the James rivers were far more familiar to him than the Thames. Doubtless the river that runs through the city of London had a mythic presence in his mind, as it would to me, two centuries later, when I encountered it in many of the books I read. But he knew the bends and currents of the James as well as he knew the contours of his mother's face; the way that light glints off the water at different hours, the trees that grew along the banks, were closely mingled with his memories of childhood. Sweltering summers; the red color of the soil; all kinds of species; different crops, such as corn and potatoes; and manners of cultivation that were unknown in England were part of his life from an early age.

If a conflict arose within him between what he was learning in school and in the woods, the same predicament also gave him a choice. To see the world as the British did, and thus ignore all that was around him, or to open his eyes directly onto his own existence. The choice would not have required him to repudiate all his education. The same condition of consciousness that has befallen many of those who live in colonized places would have been his too. In his mind the two worlds, empire and colony, must have begun to exist apart, and yet valued, side by side, *separate,* as he writes in the declaration, *and equal.*

In some minds this might have produced an inner dividedness, the ability to ignore logical contradictions or, more seriously, contradictions within the soul, and even to live with two selves who are hardly conversant with each other. In his later years, Jefferson would fall prey to self-contradictions at times. But in this period, when the ideas of democracy were not even fully spoken within him but existed simply as the seeds of who he would become, something else appears to have occurred. In the difference between his formal education and what he actually experienced, he must have sensed, even if unconsciously, a vacuum, a kind of void. So much that he encountered, so much of the life he lived, existed outside the purview of the culture he was taught, not just the fields, but the woods too, the crops, the plants, the trees, the wildlife with which he was intimate. But where there is no guidebook, there is also a greater measure of freedom. He could come to his own conclusions about this world and in this way explore the uncharted dimensions of independent thought.

In an essay that Immanuel Kant wrote one year after the American Revolution succeeded, he defines enlightenment overall as the ability to think "without direction from another," a habit of mind that was required for survival in the American colonies, particularly by those who worked on the land near the frontiers. If the unspoiled landscape around Shadwell was beautiful in the eighteenth century, it was also demanding. Shadwell was set in a wild place. Facing a climate and soil different from Britain, the colonists could not look to British culture for answers to all the contingencies that arose here. Like so many other Americans, both Peter Jefferson and his son faced rough conditions for which new solutions had to be sought continually. Survival required innovation. Throughout his life, Jefferson devised many ingenious inventions, among them a tool for furrowing soil, which is still in use, and the lap desk, of course, which he used as he wrote the Declaration of Independence.

In the famous essay called *A Summary View,* which he wrote two years before the American Revolution, Jefferson complains that since the British never helped build the settlements in America, they should not tax the colonists. But in the end, the relative autonomy of the colonies must have helped to free his imagination. In such circumstances, even failure is a great teacher. To illustrate why so many cannot think independently, Kant uses the example of domesticated animals that have been tied to their carts so long, they become afraid to leave their harnesses for fear of falling. "Actually," he writes, "this danger is not so great for by falling a few times they would finally learn to walk alone."

If an American culture had not yet matured, one that might address the experiences of the colonists, this could also work to open the American imagination to new ways of thinking. Though the absence of the explanations, philosophies, tales, images, lines of poetry, and songs that soften experience and lend form and meaning to life can be unsettling, the lack of a designated significance can also be liberating. It is perhaps part of the thrill of any frontier. Whenever you move beyond the territory culture has described, you will be able to see the world with fresh eyes. And though the Enlightenment idea that human beings can escape the influence of culture appears naive to us now, the fact that in human experience, nature and culture are always intertwined does not refute the more direct and sensual knowledge that comes alive in strange or wilder places, in old-growth forests, in uncultivated lands, on unmined mountains, while wandering fields allowed to grow as they would, or navigating waters that flow freely, unpredictably.

I am thinking now of Jefferson as a boy, making his way up the Rivanna River in a canoe. There are birdcalls, the sound of animals in the underbrush, of branches and leaves falling, of the water that laps at the sides of his boat, and his oars gliding under, through, and out of the river. But taken together, the whole of it enters him as a hush, a quiet, like the quiet he would seek one day in the rooms he rented in the less populated area of Philadelphia. Here on the river, he finds himself in a medium conducive to serenity. Not the silence of the dead but the stillness within any living landscape, vital, quick, and, if at times dangerous, also quickening.

The stillness of nature has given birth to many revelations. The desert hermitage of Christian saints; the shaman's sweat lodge; the garden of Gethsemane, where Jesus prayed; the haiku masters who retreated to the mountains; the Baal Shem Tov and his solitary visions in the forest; the poetic voices of the Koran that came to Muhammad when he was sequestered in the caves near Mecca. It is not just a distance from crowds and conversation, but the more nuanced knowledge of yourself, the nature of your own being, that echoes back to you in the quiet atmosphere of natural places. It is easy to imagine then that as he travels up the Rivanna River or later wanders the Blue Ridge Mountains, Jefferson remembers himself. I am thinking of the self we are so often persuaded to relinquish and replace with a mask made from notions of who we ought to be, what we ought to think and feel. Something of that original self must have returned to him in the wild lands of Virginia.

Was the memory of these journeys with him when Jefferson claimed nature as the final authority for all he proposed in the declaration? These are the words he used: *to assume among the powers of the earth, the separate and equal station to which the Laws of Nature and of Nature's God entitle them.* We cannot know why he chose these words exactly. The term *natural law* had been an element of Enlightenment thought for several decades. Like many other American revolutionaries, Jefferson was fascinated by the science that was revealing nature's laws. Church doctrine notwithstanding, the approach was meeting a wide enthusiasm among thinkers of all kinds. Even George III loved the new vistas on reality that science afforded him.

Yet the leap here is so definite, the landing so stable. Reading the music of his language, I sense no ambivalence, no holding back; Jefferson explains neither natural law nor how it applies to the situation, nor does he defend his argument with historical examples. Had he wished to do so, he could have called upon many elements he had learned about from his British education to serve his arguments: the Magna Carta, granting English people rights; the Glorious Revolution, or Bloodless Revolution, which forced the king to share power with the Parliament, after which it was agreed that the English monarchy governed by consent of the people.

Certainly he called on his knowledge of this history. But he does not rest his arguments on these precedents. Instead of arguing for America's right to independence, the document enacts independence. There is no hint here of the tight and timid tone of those who always look to authority for advice. Embodying certitude, the voice is that of a person who has already placed the ultimate authority regarding what he knows and thinks within himself.

March

I find myself riveted by unfolding events. To reveal the name of a covert agent is against the law. The whole plot, which is being investigated by an independent prosecutor, Patrick Fitzgerald, seems on the verge of being revealed. What is it I want? Not revenge exactly, though I cannot deny some measure of that. No I think it is an equally old wish, and perhaps a need, that keeps me and everyone I know on the edge of our seats. That deep-seated desire I felt even as a child to be told the truth.

There were other experiences too that must have had an influence, glimpses of another world, entirely outside his formal education, that could not have failed to stun Jefferson by presenting him an entirely different worldview than the one he had been taught. Thinking again of his solitary wanderings in the wilder lands of the American colonies, it is interesting to note that he traveled the rivers near his home in a canoe, a vessel that Native Americans had invented. Would Jefferson have known then that the Cherokee considered all rivers to be sacred sites, places to find purification? Close by in the woods of Virginia, there were many Indian tribes. Since, as county colonel, Peter Jefferson was supposed to keep the peace on the frontier between Native American and colonial lands, and because he chose to do this with diplomacy instead of force, he had made many friends among Native Americans, and they were often invited to Shadwell. When he was on his way to Williamsburg, the famous Cherokee warrior and statesman Ostenaco was a guest at Shadwell many times.

Later, during his student years at the College of William and Mary, Jefferson traveled to the Cherokee encampment outside Williamsburg, where he witnessed Ostenaco's farewell speech to his people, the night before he was to depart for England in order to meet George III (who was grateful to him for his bravery during the recent war with the French). While Ostenaco spoke to his people, under a full moon, Jefferson was moved, as he wrote many years later, "to awe and veneration." It was not what the great man said. Jefferson did not understand the language in which he spoke. It was rather the whole moment, the moonlight, Ostenaco's gestures, his sounding voice, the hushed silence of his people, that impressed him so deeply.

I cannot help but wonder if this image managed to migrate into the Declaration of Independence. I am thinking of the extraordinary phrase *Nature's God*. It is the only spiritual authority Jefferson cites, besides the words in the next sentence, to *their Creator*. Later, he would be accused by his opponents, notably John Adams, of being an atheist. But he had a spiritual bent. With the plan of freeing Jesus's teaching from what he saw as the distortions of the church, he wrote his own version of the Gospels. It was not spirituality Jefferson rejected so much as organized religion.

When he was a student at the College of William and Mary, he was inspired by the work of Lord Bolingbroke, an early critic of Christian orthodoxy. As a legislator in Virginia, he would work to end the privileges that the state had granted to the Anglican Church. Despite the many conflicts that had arisen in Europe between various monarchs and the papacy, from Charlemagne to King James to Louis XVI, monarchy had been empowered by organized religion. Jefferson railed against what he called *the loathsome combination of church and state*. He was a passionate advocate of freedom of religion, a right that is inseparable from freedom of speech and independent thought.

Yet something more than this logic must have moved him as he wrote. The language holds a music that acts with considerable power on the soul as well as the mind. As he wrote of nature's God, was Jefferson trying to name the spirit that moved through him, one that reminded him, even if at a great distance, of the woods and rivers he knew, the awe he felt when he witnessed Ostenaco's oration? It would be one among many reasons that he wanted to write in a place that was in a less settled part of Philadelphia, where the atmosphere of countryside could still be felt.

Nature's God. At first glance, the term may seem like a quickly made compromise with religion. By marrying nature with god, he could negotiate an uneasy peace between theology and science. But now, as I focus more deliberately on the term, an entirely different vision of the divine arises. What it conjures is not the image of a god who sits like a monarch on a high throne above earthly life, commanding through an all-powerful will the fate of us all, but a god on level ground with the rest of us. A god who is not only one of us but who is the ground, who is inside us, and outside too, in all that we see, all that surrounds us, a god within whom we dwell, body and soul.

Remembering the tall grass in the field I visited as a child, or the Pacific Ocean, that large, seemingly endless body of water that has been at my side since I was born, if in some sense I would say my experience with nature has been a private affair, often solitary, I have never felt alone in this experience. Whenever I gazed into a field or felt the cool, salty air that came off the sea, it has seemed to me that I have been met by another presence, sensually vivid, touching, joining me in a communion that, like all ineffable exchanges with the divine, defies description.

Speaking of the connection between the human soul and nature, the great theologian Martin Buber writes in his classic work *I and Thou*, "Here the relation vibrates in the dark and remains below language. The creatures stir across from us, but they are unable to come to us, and the You we say to them sticks to the threshold of language." With trees, animals, the kinship can be sensual, profound, responsive, yet it is without words; it is only in the human realm, Buber writes, that "relation is manifest and enters language."

But sometimes it is wordlessness that you want. A dog running excitedly down the path to greet you, birds you observe in a field, directly, without the corrupting barriers of language, without the myriad possibilities inherent in words for hypocrisy, lies, misunderstandings. Yet, in human relations, language is also a vehicle for confession, and with the expression of truth, for another layer of authenticity, and even for a clearer vision of the world, the realm that is, after all, filled with the distant country of others. In the end, words chart the greater dimensions of love.

I am thinking again of the lesson my father taught me that day in our kitchen. The process of reason he was teaching me is not just a necessary precursor for independent thought. It is essential for relationship too. If compassion is an immediate response to the suffering of others, present, some would argue, in the structure of the human nervous system, still something more than compassion is required when your wishes conflict with those of someone else. I wanted to be with my sister that day. But she did not want me to accompany her to the orchard. Kind as she was, she wanted to be with children of her own age, alone, without having to protect or worry about me. It was a new equation I was being asked to learn. Not simple empathy, as in *I feel the same way you do*. But a more nuanced empathy that requires reason to establish a more delicate formula: *If I have the right to want something you do not want, you too must have the right to want what I do not want.* The logic belongs to the complex idea of equality lying at the heart of democracy.

It is the first two sentences of the Declaration of Independence that we all remember. And of these, the second is far more famous: *"We hold these truths to be self-evident,"* it begins, *"that all men are created equal, that they are endowed by their Creator with certain unalienable Rights, that among these are Life, Liberty and the pursuit of Happiness.—That to secure these rights, Governments are instituted among Men, deriving their just powers form the consent of the governed."*

One would not be able to guess from these words alone that their author occupied a very privileged position in a highly hierarchical society. In some ways, the confident tone of his voice should not be surprising.

Jefferson did not suffer from the insecurities commonly rendered by inequality. Within the society of Virginia and the American colonies, he
was born into a position of power. Because his mother's family, the Randolphs, were prominent, all the connections and esteem that prominence yields were his. As the son of a member of the House of Burgesses,
he inherited the entitlement to become a burgess himself. And doubtless
leading to his sense of mastery too was something that he himself understood to be shameful. The plantation he owned was maintained through
the labor of African-American men, women, and children who were
held in bondage and commanded as if they were subjects of the most
despotic sovereign. That he despised the circumstance did not prevent
him from receiving its many benefits. Both as a boy and as a man, he was
used to being served and obeyed.

Yet in the declaration, he does not use his powers of persuasion for
the benefit of his own privilege alone. Clearly to win independence
from Britain was in the economic interest of plantation owners, whose
economies were threatened by British taxes. But in the second sentence of
the declaration, when he writes *all men are created equal,* he has moved
beyond his own interests to include the general good. And now, as I ask
myself why he should do this, still another factor, a not inconsiderable
influence in human consciousness, arises: the force of reason.

Logic is often pictured as a neutral instrument—if not cold and cal-
culated, then above any emotion. But this picture of reason ignores
human nature. In the real life of the mind, reason is colored not only
with desire but with its love of equations and balance; it is itself the goal
of a particular and profound desire, seldom listed among human needs,
though powerfully there nonetheless: the desire for integrity. To tie together actual experience with thought, to make the two columns formed
by experience and thinking come to the same conclusion, is a constant
need of the mind, a need that can be irritating when not met immediately (though over time the irritation can result in pearls of wisdom).

If any age were ever in love with reason, it was the eighteenth century.
The times in which Jefferson wrote and lived would have strengthened
the desire. To a growing intellect, full of curiosity, the elevation of reason
over the dogmas of priests and kings must have felt as if a window had
been opened on a new universe of comprehension. And equality was an
essential part of this mix. From every rank of society, men and women
who were not authorized to determine the truth were making discoveries

that challenged the old doctrines. The air was full of excitement. As crowds gathered to witness Benjamin Franklin's experiments with electricity, they were inwardly electrified by new possibilities, not just in industry but in the mind too.

I look back now on the first six years of my life almost as an idyll—a period filled with light when all the members of my immediate family lived together under one roof. Though my sister was older, and could do things and go places that I could not, we lived in the radiant atmosphere of equality. My mother may have had a subtle preference for my sister as my father preferred me, but none of us was considered a lesser being. We experienced none of the gloomy prejudice or harsh discipline that shadowed Jane Eyre's childhood. My mother, who disliked her mother's snobbery, was not concerned with how we might impress the neighbors. We were immersed in a realm that was casual, direct, easygoing, more impetuous and playful than formal.

Regarding Jefferson's gravitation toward equality, there is one other influence that I am pondering now. I am thinking of the way children can find entry into forbidden chambers of thought that their parents have sealed away and forgotten. When he was not away at school but home, as he wandered the woods and fields, Jefferson was often accompanied by a boy close to his own age, his best friend for many years. Jupiter and he would explore, ride, take a canoe down the river, fish, play childish games together. But this child did not have the same privileges Jefferson enjoyed. He was the son of a man and woman Peter Jefferson counted among his slaves.

I have in mind now an image of the two boys navigating a canoe down the Rivanna River. In the silence, you can hear the lovely sound of their paddles moving in and out of water, in a steady syncopation. Did Jupiter convey to his friend, in the way children do through gesture and attitude, with the inarguable swiftness of feeling, the stark and unbearable injustice of being deprived of liberty? It is hard to imagine that such a transmission did not take place.

To place yourself in another's shoes is not always an act of selflessness. In my own experience, I have found that the line between my needs and another's is ineluctable, and that, like the line between energy and matter, on closer scrutiny, it begins to dissolve. It would take me years to claim my own perspective on what happened between my mother and me the day she locked me out of the house. I learned when I was older that she was having an affair with a man up the street, the father of twins my sister often went to babysit. But it was years after that, and only when I could fully embrace my point of view, that I realized my mother had been drinking that day and was in bed with her lover, which is why she locked me out of the house. And that this was why she had been so angry with me. And there is this too: I must have reminded her of obligations, of the coming loss we would both suffer, the sad price we would both soon pay.

Both personal and private histories are created from a series of small decisions, some made it would seem in an instant. Yet time is an instable measure; since the inner experience of its progress varies according to mood and purpose, one minute does not equal another. In the process of transformation, certain days, weeks, hours, even seconds, seem to carry more weight, as factors and causes that have developed for decades accrue and aggregate, making themselves felt, suddenly, all at once. Above all, the great brilliance of the Declaration of Independence was that it captured an auspicious moment.

In the spirit of change, though this document does not introduce new ideas, it does give them a newly active and vital shape. One of the phrases in the declaration that is most often quoted is the naming of rights described as unalienable in the final version (and which Jefferson called *inherent* in his original draft): the famous, *life, liberty, and the pursuit of happiness.* The concept and most of the language were taken from the second of John Locke's *Two Treatises on Government.* Jefferson did make one change, significant to us even now: where Locke used the word *estate,* Jefferson substituted *the pursuit of happiness.* But the greatest difference between his locution and Locke's is in the music. Where Locke creates a philosophical mood, almost bidding the reader to pause and think, to enter a discursive dialogue, and to argue, Jefferson moves swiftly, with little impediment and great force. It is as if he is riding a wave of history just as it breaks.

What follows the first two paragraphs of the declaration is a long list of the grievances the colonists had against King George III. In Jefferson's draft of the declaration, he included a condemnation of the slave trade, calling it a grave injustice against humanity, blaming its continuation, rather conveniently, on the king rather than on colonists like himself. At the time, he held one hundred men, women, and children in bondage, including Jupiter who had become his manservant for a period and who served him until he was replaced by Robert Hemings. This young man, son of Betty Hemings and most probably Jefferson's father-in-law, John Wayles, (and whose sister was Sally Hemings) accompanied Jefferson to Philadelphia and attended to his needs during the time he wrote the declaration.

It is a pitfall of even the most brilliant mind to be able to avoid the awareness of a contradiction, by inhabiting two separate worlds: one world created by words, in which, for instance, rhetorically, freedom belongs to all of us, and another world of substance, in which freedom is withheld from some of us. And when you add the realm of the unconscious to the mix, including the habit of disguising irrational opinions with a cloak of reason, the pitfall can be wide.

Along with other members of his committee, John Adams made minor corrections to the draft, and it was passed on to the Second Continental Congress, where, after some changes were made, it was approved. Following the insistence of delegates from the southern states filled with slaveholders, the condemnation of slavery was removed. This and other changes, many of them minor, angered Jefferson. Nevertheless most of what he wrote remained unchanged, and on July 4, 1776, it was officially adopted. Four days later on a warm and sunny day, the Liberty Bell rang to gather a crowd to the back of the State House where the declaration was read by John Nixon. The crowd cheered as crowds would do over several months during which it would be read aloud in towns across the colonies, including New York, where on the next day, July 9, as Washington had commanded, it was read in New York to an assembly of his troops. Though the revolution had already begun, now it was official.

Despite the respect my father showed me that day in our kitchen, for many years, whenever I thought of the conversation I had with him, I felt a strange and childish resentment toward him. Only recently did I realize that the reason that anger still tinted the memory was because of what followed, an event that, at least on a logical level, was unrelated, though clearly, on a level of my mind that is not rational, it was deeply connected. Shortly after my sixth birthday, my parents gathered my sister and me together to announce that they were going to divorce each other. They did not tell us about the other decisions that had been made. My maternal grandmother, who was the matriarch of our family, and my grandfather, who invariably deferred to her choices, had met with my father. They were all worried about my mother's drinking. They knew that she had a problem. (The word *alcoholic* was rarely used then except for men living in doorways or women reduced to cheap hotels.) This and the fact that she had gone off and left my sister and me unattended several times for more than a day led them to feel that she should not be trusted with our care. The thought that my father might raise us did not occur to anyone. My grandmother, then in her late sixties, did not think she could handle two children. Since I was the youngest, they decided that I should stay with her in Los Angeles and that my sister would be sent to live with our great-aunt, my grandmother's sister, who lived six hundred miles away, in a town called Davis, just outside Sacramento.

I remember the night my father drove us to Los Angeles. It had turned dark, and I was crying. I had realized too late that we would not be seeing our mother for a long time, and I was sorry that I had not said good-bye to her with this in mind. My sister kindly pointed to my kindergarten, near where we had lived in a duplex with my grandparents, which I had vigorously opposed leaving. "You'll be able to go to your old school again," she told me. We were close to our grandparents' house then. Within a quarter of an hour, my sister and father had gone on their way. Since they still had to drive two hours south to my great-grandmother's house in San Pedro, where my sister and father would live temporarily for a few weeks, they stayed only long enough to leave me and my belongings with my grandparents. I remember no details from that night—except that though, on a conscious level, I did not allow myself to picture this as a permanent separation, even now, every attempt I make to recollect the experience is filled with an unutterable sadness.

Though I did not see my mother again for many months, for a few weeks I visited my sister regularly. My father, who worked at a fire station in Hollywood, would pick me up on weekends at my grandparents' house and take me to San Pedro. My memory of my great-grandmother was that she was very kind. But I was the youngest child. My sister's memory is different. She has told me that Nanny was far harsher with her. We were both, however, enchanted by her garden, which contained corn and vegetables and even chickens. Once, while I was playing with a kitten under her lemon tree, she stood out on her porch with a chicken in her hands, and as she was telling me to be careful of the kitten's sharp claws, she wrung the chicken's neck. The slaughter was for our benefit. She served us the freshly plucked bird for dinner. I cannot remember feeling very sorry about the bird's demise, probably because it had been unapproachable and at times even aggressive, threatening me with its sharp beak. But I was in awe of my great-grandmother's powers.

My great-grandmother lived with her son, my father's father, Grandpa Hal. My great-grandfather had died long before I was born. Nanny and Hal came from Grand Manan, an island off New Brunswick in Canada. They left my grandmother there but took both children, my father, Walden, first and, later, Roland. In their eyes, my grandmother had committed an unpardonable sin, which, years later, I learned probably meant that, just like my mother, she had carried on an affair in the afternoon, when Hal was at work. Compared to California, which for as long as I can remember has always been on the cutting edge of the latest trends, life on the island, Grand Manan, was old-fashioned. I can find much evidence in my memory for my sense that they must have missed the world they had relinquished. It was not only that they would wait for weeks for the supply of seaweed, which they loved to eat raw, to arrive from the island. There were other details that spoke of nostalgia and loss, chief among them a small woodshed in the back that my sister fashioned as a study and where I would go to watch her dip a pen into black ink and write mysterious things. There, on the wall that faced the house, they had hung harnesses and bits, equipment that was essential to their old way of life and that they could not part with, though they had no purpose for it in California.

It seems to me now that an enormous chasm lay between my parents' generation and that of their parents, one that feels far larger to me than the one between my grandchildren and me. Perhaps the difference is that, like my daughter and her children, I was raised in a city, but all my grandparents were raised in rural areas. I encountered what seemed to me a romantic rural past when, the summer after my parents' divorce, my maternal grandparents brought me to visit my grandmother's family on their farm in southern Illinois. It was a child's dream of farm life that was presented to me. My cousin allowed me to ride bareback on one of the horses while he led her around on a rope tied to her bit. My great-grandmother gave me warm milk to drink that had just come from the cow in the barn outside before she showed me her faded collection of photographs you could see through an antique a device known as a stereopticon. One afternoon we all went together down by a stream that ran through the property to pick berries, then ate them in a cobbler that night. I played hide-and-go-seek in the cornfields with cousins I had just met. And then, on the Fourth of July 1949, our family hosted an outdoor cookout.

I still have have many strong images in my mind from this trip: the casinos in Las Vegas where my grandmother finally relented and bought me the belt covered with Indian beads that I had begged for all evening. The communal table at a restaurant in New Mexico where we helped ourselves from serving dishes filled with posole and pork and tortillas. All the strange antique stores my grandmother loved. When we went to Virginia, we visited a plantation, preserved because of a history I knew little of yet. A grand white building with an imposing facade, bearing the first white columns I remember seeing, it was called Monticello.

In pursuit of his own happiness, Jefferson returned to Monticello at the end of September. He had wanted to go home earlier, yielding reluctantly to the demands of the times. He told his fellow delegates that he was worried about the health of his wife, who was pregnant then. Though Martha Wayles Jefferson was a vital, active woman, she was also fragile. Her own mother had died giving birth. And when, eighteen months after the second child she had with Jefferson was born, this child died, her health began to deteriorate. In fact, there was cause for concern. Before the summer was over, she had miscarried.

But there were happier reasons drawing Jefferson home too. By all accounts, Jefferson had more than a loving marriage. They were a passionate couple. During ten years of marriage, Martha Jefferson was pregnant seven times, and that their first child, Martha—or Patsy, as she was often called—was born a bit less than nine months after their wedding on January 1, 1772, suggests either that they were lovers before their wedding or that they plunged into the marriage bed immediately afterward. If they stayed for a few days after the wedding at Martha's father's estate, "The Forest," it was probably because these lodgings were more comfortable. The snow was so heavy on the afternoon they left for Monticello that they had to travel the last eight miles on foot through drifts sometimes two feet deep. By the time they arrived, the servants were asleep and the fires were out, but according to a story that has been handed down, they found a bottle of red wine and began to sing duets. Martha was not only a beautiful woman, with, as her great-granddaughter tells us, "an exquisite shape," but intelligent, well read, and an excellent musician too. According to still another story, during their courtship, two other suitors were so discouraged when, on arriving at Martha's father's house, they heard the couple playing a duet, that they left, forgoing any further attempts. Long after they were married, they still loved to perform together, Jefferson on his violin, Martha at the piano.

And he had other passions drawing him home, Monticello chief among them. In the autumn of 1776, almost five years after he had married Martha, their home was not yet complete. It would take four more decades, during which Jefferson, who designed and redesigned the building continually, often with original, even at times impractical, ideas, saw to every detail, not only adjusting and adding to his plans but participating in the construction himself and carefully scrutinizing all the workmanship and materials. And finally he was drawn by another concern. As a member of what in Virginia had become the House of Delegates, he was deeply involved in building democracy by reforming Virginia's laws so that, in the words of one historian, he might abolish legal barriers to the pursuit of happiness.

When, near the end of the summer, we returned home, I began to realize that the happy life I had known before had ended. I would never again live with my mother, father, and sister under one roof. Though on some level I hoped for my old life to return, and even waited for a miraculous turn of events, the signs were incontrovertible. The first augury was my sister's absence. While I was with my grandparents driving through the deserts of Arizona and New Mexico toward Illinois and Virginia, my father had driven her up the middle of the state to northern California, where she would live with my great-aunt for the next five years. I learned this a few days after our trip "back East," as my grandparents always called it, had ended. I wanted my father to take me with him to San Pedro to visit Nanny and "De De," the name that I still used for my sister. I suppose they tried to tell me. But I could not accept the truth of my loss until I had searched all over the house in San Pedro and in the backyard cottage I thought of as belonging to her.

The other loss was more subtle yet powerful in its own way, a palpably unwelcome change that in hindsight I realize constituted a shift from democracy to monarchy. My grandmother's role as monarch was unquestioned by us all. Even if my mother railed against her occasionally, especially in drunken episodes, and though we complained behind her back, every rebellion was ultimately ineffectual. In the end, we obeyed. The fact that my grandfather had retired made my grandmother's dominance seem more part of the scheme of things. With her constant meals, clean sheets, and comforting domestic order, she was the only evident provider. My grandfather may have driven the car, but he was a terrible driver, and somehow, even as a child, I understood he was allowed to drive only because it gave him a bit of dignity.

But the resemblance of our household to a monarchy had other causes too. My grandparents belonged to an older generation. They did not listen to Dr. Spock but to other authorities, whose methods belonged to an earlier period in which rank was decisive, curtsies were common, when not just white gloves but a semblance of modesty about the female body was required, when children were supposed to obey without question, to be seen but not heard. I soon found that any objection I might make to my grandmother's rules would be quickly categorized as "talking back," which was forbidden.

An especially onerous change in my new routine was the early hour at which I was sent to bed. I had some presentiment of what was to come on our trip back East when, in the various motels where we stopped, I was told to go to sleep well before it turned dark. Unused to such an early bedtime, I lay awake under the weight of an oppressive boredom edged by a disturbingly amorphous gloom. Often I could hear other children still playing outside in a world of easy friendship from which I felt I had been banished. It was on one of these nights that I accidentally scratched my nails against the wall, creating a terrible sensation, which, mixed with grief and foreboding, made me cry inconsolably.

JUNE

I can feel the struggle within myself, whenever I sense a disaster unfolding. I am impeded by a measure of passivity, the desire to please, to conform, to believe everything will turn out all right in the end. Yet there is another desire too: no matter how terrible the possibilities may be, the insistent wish to align what I tell myself with what I sense to be true.

Jefferson believed that a government could be created on American soil that would make its citizens "the happiest and securest on which the sun has ever shone." To this end, for nearly three years, while the superior armies of Cornwallis waged war on an untrained American army whose soldiers lacked winter coats and often shoes, he drafted laws to discourage practices such as entail and primogeniture that had ensured that, through controlled lines of inheritance, large landholdings, and thus an aristocracy, would be preserved. Much of the land in Virginia belonged to a few powerful families, a condition he thought would be harmful to the establishment of a true democracy. Jefferson had a grand plan. He believed true equality could be realized only through an agrarian society. If he agreed with many other founders of the American Republic that owning property should be a requirement for voting, he also imagined that it would be possible one day for every man to own at least a small parcel of land.

I can only imagine the mood that must have captivated him then. It would have been like seeing Monticello rise into three dimensions from the flat pages where he had drafted his designs. The utopian frame of mind is not unlike being in love. Through this lens, many possible worlds take shape, which, though they may not be entirely palpable yet, inspire a palpable passion. In the same way, as he stood in the Virginia House of Delegates, he was already participating in a democracy of a kind. Surrounded by those who shared the general outlines of his vision, every conversation, every exchange, even disagreements, would give him the feeling that all the intimations he had had, the books he loved, the small meetings at Raleigh Tavern, had had a meaning even greater than he had before suspected, were bent to a larger purpose, a prediction that was coming true.

Such a state of mind is both a cause and a result of inspiration. The tired, cold, hungry soldiers in the Continental army were in part sustained by the same vision. Even when battle after battle was lost, this dream of freedom, made even more real by standing ground against His Majesty's troops, came so close it could almost be tasted and touched.

My state of mind worsened considerably after I started school. When young children complain that a teacher is mean, they are usually responding to disposition rather than discipline. I could not complete the reading and writing assignments my teacher gave us to do in class. When

I was younger, I used to write the letters of the alphabet in the crayon drawings I did at home, but after the divorce, I seemed to have forgotten what I had learned, and, though it was not diagnosed at the time, a mild dyslexia that made it difficult to learn to tell time and tie my shoes was also probably to blame. But my teacher blamed me. Believing that I was both stubborn and stupid, she chastised and sometimes punished me, the former being harder to bear than the latter. Among the greatest wounds that children receive in the realm of the psyche are those inflicted through the unkind and limiting ideas that adults express about them. Unfortunately, since I had inherited my father's working-class grammar, the constant disparagement I suffered at school dovetailed perfectly in my mind with the continual corrections that my grandmother made to my grammar almost every time I spoke. Increasingly unhappy with myself, I grew shy and silent.

But I was lucky. I don't know who blew the whistle. I know we had a very liberal principal whom all the children loved. In any case, my teacher must have crossed a line finally, and someone at the school told my grandmother. I had no doubt my grandmother loved me. Though she was strict, domineering, more than a bit paranoid, and always trying to improve me, I was her favorite in the family. She would get angry with me when I broke one of her rules, but if afterward I ran down the long hallway to hide in the corner and cry that no one loved me, she would come after me, hold me in her lap, and rock me against her big, soft breasts until I stopped crying. And now she was to protect me. With all her considerable grandeur, she interrogated my teacher, stared down every bureaucratic hurdle, and got me transferred to another class. My new teacher, an older woman named Mrs. Stone, was kindness incarnate. Instinctively gentle with me, she taught me to draw trees while my grandmother tutored me at home until I could read at the level of my class.

Because Thomas Jefferson believed in the perfectibility of humankind, along with his attempts to reform Virginia's laws, he proposed a system of public education. Doubtless the knowledge that his own father had been deprived of a formal education inspired him. But he was not alone in the opinion that in order to participate responsibly in self-government, citizens would need to know history, learn logic, and be able to read and write.

The idea that human nature is shaped by circumstance was part of Enlightenment philosophy. Yet long after Jean-Jacques Rousseau refuted the idea that evil is inherent and part of the divine plan, the theory that poverty manifests a flaw in the soul persisted, continuing to the end of the nineteenth and even the beginning of the twentieth centuries. This was not an innocent concept. In the kind of childhood that Dickens portrayed in *Oliver Twist, David Copperfield,* and *Great Expectations,* the children of the poor were employed for long hours at starvation wages because it was argued they were inferior morally and mentally. Justification is another shadow side of reason. This exploitation was profitable to manufacturers.

Such attitudes have other consequences too. To be seen as inferior or evil on a daily level, especially by a figure with authority, enters the soul and works a steady erosion. The term *self-esteem* hardly suffices to describe the powerful and yet delicate process by which we see ourselves. Though self-reflection may be associated with philosophers or religious leaders, it is fundamental to all consciousness and most feeling. The idea that you are stupid or lazy will not only undermine your mood but assault your intelligence, your vitality, haunting all that you think and do.

Though he opposed slavery, Thomas Jefferson argued that African-Americans were not fit to participate in democracy fully because he believed they were inherently inferior, unable to reason clearly. He was unable to apply the same logic here that he had summoned regarding those like his father, born in the working class, whom he could see did not lack for intelligence but only education. But like many of the planters who were his colleagues in the legislature, his plantation was dependent on the labor of those he held in bondage.

Though we are all capable of lying to ourselves about the nature of others, some strange justice exists in the mind, the psychological propensity to answer one's own lies with an inward disquiet. Jefferson harbored a nightmare. If, along with other changes to Virginia's laws, he proposed the legalization of what was called manumission—the right of slaveholders to free those they held in bondage—he also argued that freed African-Americans should not be allowed to remain in Virginia. He had visions of a bloody retribution.

In the first two years that I lived with my grandparents, I remember seeing my mother only four times. Soon after the divorce, my father took me to visit her where she worked, behind a lunch counter. She gave me a hot dog, which pleased me, but otherwise, the visit had an oddly strained quality I could not name. I know now that she felt guilty, and this made it difficult for her to act toward me as a mother might, with warmth and happiness at our reunion. She lived in one room, and though I was too young to understand the economics of such an arrangement, it saddened me. The next time I saw her, I visited her at an apartment she shared with two other women. They played jazz records, which I loved, and drank while they fawned over me, let me dance and stay up late. My grandmother disapproved, and though I liked the adventure, I was glad to return with her to a safe haven. The next visit was strained in another way. So many months had gone by that I felt I hardly knew my mother anymore. It was my birthday, but before we celebrated, we went to Woolworth's. While we were there, she asked me if I wanted something. Afraid she had not bought me a present, I looked around in panic, settling on something I hardly liked and had no wish for. In the irrational way that the psyche attempts to protect itself, by ensuring she had a gift for me, I was trying to create the impression that she loved me. Yet the ruse backfired. In the end, my mother did have another gift. Nevertheless, it sickened me so much to look at the one I had chosen at the five-and-dime, I hid it from sight.

Before the fourth visit, one night when I was in the car with my grandparents and my father, my grandmother turned toward us in the backseat to tell us that my mother had married another man. Confused by the concept, I asked, "Will he be my new father?" In the manner no doubt in which she had been raised, my grandmother chastised me immediately for hurting my father's feelings. I could see that this was true and felt so much shame and regret that soon I shut my eyes as if I were asleep. It was a good plan. Whenever I fell asleep in the car, or appeared to sleep, my father would carry me up to my bed, which was, of course, just what I wanted him to do.

Soon I was sent on an overnight visit with my mother in the new house she shared with my stepfather, her new husband. Though I still could not recall her very well as having been my mother, she was sensitive when she was sober, full of humor and a childlike playfulness, and she charmed me. It was during this visit, while I stood in front of a glass door covered with diaphanous white curtains she had just made, admiring her handiwork and the quality of light, that she began to tell me how much she missed me. Wouldn't I like to come to live with her? she asked. Yes, I responded, the way children do, in a moment, from a place deep within that bypasses reason and logic alike and for better or worse goes to the heart of the matter.

While Jefferson carefully crafted legislation that would build democracy in Virginia, to the north, a fierce war was being waged. The consequences of the arguments he made for freedom of religion or a more equitable economy would not depend on his reasoning alone but on the outcome of that war. Despite the most thorough plans, the course of warfare seldom bends to reason. As with those who study the weather, the best military strategists know that in the end they cannot predict what will happen. So many surprises enter the equations: unexpected bravery and betrayals; allies gained and lost; even the weather itself. After the northern army's great victory over the British general Burgoyne at Saratoga, in October 1777, when the American troops retired to Valley Forge, the winter was so cold that the Continental army, ill equipped and ill fed, was nearly lost to the elements. For the next three years, fate seemed to careen recklessly between an American and British victory. If, at the beginning of the next year, the French entered an alliance with America, at the end of 1778, the British seized Savannah. If, in the next year, Spain declared war on Britain, and John Paul Jones captured a major British ship, by the spring of 1780, Charleston had fallen and the British had won a victory at Camden.

It was a difficult moment for Jefferson. In 1779 the General Assembly of Virginia had elected him governor. Already his work was made difficult by wartime privations. Like Patrick Henry who preceded him, he was unable to raise enough militiamen to satisfy the demands of the Continental Congress. Hardscrabble Virginia farmers were wary of leaving their land untended. More prosperous planters were afraid to leave those they held in slavery unsupervised. They might have offered men freedom in exchange for fighting in the Continental Army. But in what remains one of the great ironies of the Revolution, few of them, including Jefferson, made that choice.

In his autobiography Jefferson says little about the progress of the war, referring the reader instead to another history he tells us is far more complete than any he could give. Instead, he gives us an account of changes he made at the College of William and Mary, abolishing grammar and divinity, adding fine arts and natural history. As British troops came closer to home, Jefferson seemed particularly surprised and unprepared. He did well enough with the move inland and away from the battlefields, from Williamsburg to Richmond. Ready to redesign the new capital, he drew up plans for the city and several new buildings. It was as if, since in his mind, the Revolution had already taken place, tending to the architecture was far more important than commanding a militia. But this illusion was to be interrupted. Soon, Cornwallis, together with Benedict Arnold, made a successful siege of Richmond, burning much of the city. Were it not for the cavalryman, Jack Lovett, who rode forty miles overnight at great speed to warn him, Jefferson himself would have been captured. Added to his poor performance, when his term ended but before his successor had taken office, despite the danger of invasion, he simply went home to Monticello, leaving Virginia without a leader. Though later he successfully defended himself against censure by the Virginia Assembly, this temporary vacancy caused a scandal that would forever tarnish his reputation.

JULY

This moment now seems pivotal. So much is in the balance. As more and more aspects of the truth come out, I feel sometimes as if I were holding my breath, hoping for that great yet often terribly slow animal called the public to see. Though there are some hopeful signs.

The same qualities that lead to success often provide the material for failure too. Jefferson had an uncanny ability to remain calm even when violence surrounded him, a composure that is eloquently evident in the Declaration of Independence. It is easy to imagine that he would have developed an uncommon equanimity when, at the age of sixteen, he was faced with his father's death—suddenly bereft, grief-stricken himself, confronting the grief of his mother and his sisters too, not only abandoned by his father but left without a provider, the one who had managed the world he knew, the plantation with all its various livestock and crops, the forest and mountains around, the family, community. He knew the role his father played would soon fall to him. He could have collapsed inwardly from the weight of the responsibility, but he did not. Instead, he worked assiduously to prepare himself for the task.

His remarkable self-possession must have served him again during the preceding years, when he and his wife, Martha, suffered an onslaught of loss. In the year before they were married, Martha had lost her son Jack, born of her first marriage, to a childhood contagion. Just after she married Jefferson, her father, John Wayles, died. Soon after, Jefferson's brother-in-law and his best friend Dabney Carr died too. Patsy Jefferson was born in 1775. But a few years later, their second child, June, died. In the summer when Jefferson wrote the Declaration of Independence, Martha suffered a miscarriage. Then, in the next year, just two weeks after his birth, their only son died. In 1780, while Jefferson was governor, still another child was born who lived only a few months. Certainly death, especially the death of a child, was more common in this period. But even in a time when mortality was a more constant presence, the list was remarkably long. Martha herself buckled under the strain; her health began to deteriorate with the death of her second daughter. By contrast, Jefferson was better able to keep dread and desolation at bay. But this would also be his undoing.

The line between serenity and denial is thin. It can be crossed in an instant of inattention or fatigue. To occupy the mind with other, less troubling issues, or take up ordinary practical details can dull the awful presence of death. If this habit of mind is taught by disaster, it does not always serve as the best response to disaster. Yet to stay calm and aware at the same time is not easy. Denial is often disguised as reason, and underneath a mask of reason it is not unusual to find hysteria.

At seven years of age, I could not have predicted the consequences of the choice I made to live with my mother. The first days were filled with a kind of enchantment for me, as my mother encouraged me to read stories by Hans Christian Andersen aloud to her. She fashioned a little doll after my favorite character, giving me a tiny Thumbelina in a walnut shell on a leaf. That I identified with this small child, an orphan who had been abandoned in the world, cannot have escaped her. She had a quick intelligence and, as my father always did, would sit and talk with me, encouraging me to express my thoughts, listening closely, responding to what I said with a kind of equality, giving me the same respect that she gave to adults. Her regime was far more liberal in other ways too. She allowed me to go outside in my bare feet and to play with the children next door after dinner. Among my greatest thrills was the evening when my stepfather came home with a puppy for me, a standard poodle, who became my confidante.

Vicky grew up quickly. Within a few months she had given birth to a litter of puppies. But by then the idyll of my happy days had ended. After the first few weeks, a sad routine began. In the beginning I told myself the same story my mother told me each time it happened: that it would not be repeated. But it did repeat, almost as regularly as clockwork. About twice a week, when my stepfather failed to return from work by seven in the evening, my mother would grow steadily more and more nervous until finally she would go out in search of him.

Since she did not drive, she would find a friend to take her, go in a cab, or when she was headed for the Copper Bucket, our neighborhood bar, she would walk. Occasionally she even found a babysitter. But usually she believed what she promised me, that she would just be gone for an hour. Over time I learned this was not true. Almost without exception, she would stay out until midnight or early in the morning. When I begged her not to leave, she was apologetic but determined.

In one of the strange paradoxes of fate, that my mother treated me with respect and equality gave me the sense of agency I needed to survive her neglect. By the time she came home, both she and my stepfather would be so drunk they could hardly stand. But because of the strange, sometimes violent way they acted, I was as frightened of their return as I was to be alone. While they were gone, I maintained an alert position between both entrances and by the telephone, often staying in the same place for hours, prepared in case a kidnapper or someone equally frightening might come through one of the doors. But when I finally heard the sound of the car in the driveway, I would run to my bedroom, shut the door, crawl into bed, and pretend to be asleep.

As time went by, I took action in other ways. Even when my tactics failed, they saved me from overwhelming despair. I had learned the names of the bars my mother frequented. On occasion she took me with her, where I would drink Shirley Temples, play the pinball machines, or fall asleep in a Naugahyde booth. I looked for each bar in the yellow pages and then called around to find her, a tactic I had seen her employ to locate my stepfather. More often than not, I would eventually find her. When the bartender called her to the phone, she promised she would come home right away. But she never did. After forty minutes, I would call again. Then, one night when I telephoned, I heard her voice in the background, shouting to the bartender in drunken tones, "Don't tell her I'm here."

In my mother's mind, I had become her mother, against whom she was still in rebellion. My mother struggled in vain for her liberty until just before my grandmother's death. That the greater part of her bondage was imagined made no difference. For years she could not make her life fully her own but remained instead an errant child, trapped in a desperately repetitive mutiny, one which became finally its own kind of prison. When she was sober, we thought of ourselves as allies against my grandmother's draconian dominance. But I loved my grandmother too. It was she to whom I turned in my own desperation in the late hours of the night or the early hours of the morning, when, trembling with fear, fatigue, and on the nights when my mother had not fed me, hunger, I would call to ask if she would come to take me home with her.

Once or twice in the beginning, my grandparents did get up at a late hour and drive from Los Angeles over the hills into the San Fernando Valley, where my mother lived, to take me back with them for the night. But soon, in her own unbending way, my grandmother instituted a new policy. She could no longer rescue me, she said, and, predictably, my grandfather concurred. I had chosen to be with my mother, she told me, and now I had to live with my choice. Indeed, her feelings about my decision tinged my grandmother's resolve with bitterness. No matter how vigorous my pleas or piteous my cries, she would not yield. But in the end, I got what I wanted. My grandmother did not abandon me. Once more, after my grandparents met with my father, still another decision was made. I was to live with my grandparents again.

After the blows to his pride that Jefferson suffered as governor of Virginia, he swore he would never return to politics. He went home to lick his wounds, where he immersed himself in a course of study he had learned from his father, a description of the land and wildlife of Virginia. The project began in response to a series of questions posed by François de Barbé-Marbois, secretary to the French minister at Philadelphia. But the famous *Notes on the State of Virginia* went beyond the scope of these questions, describing Jefferson's political philosophy, his utopian vision of a society of farmers, and arguing at length with the Comte de Buffon, the French naturalist, who had postulated that aboriginal American people and animals were inferior to their European counterparts. As part of his case for the equality of American life, Jefferson asked his friends from every region to measure and weigh the animals they owned or encountered. Enamored of science, he devised a long table comparing European and American examples. He also offers a passionate argument that American Indians are in every way the equals of Europeans. And in the *Notes,* he uses all the power of his genius to inveigh against slavery too: "Can the liberties of a nation be thought secure when we have removed their only firm basis, a conviction in the minds of the people that these liberties are the gift of God?"

Yet, like reason, genius does not provide a direct path to either truth or virtue. Ideas are manipulated, the mind segmented, so that the same man who stands up for equality and against slavery can in another breath express the opinion that those of African descent must be intellectually inferior. And while he wrote, his mind was segmented in another way too. In August of 1781, when he returned to his desk in the study he occupied at Monticello, the Revolutionary War was still waging. Though, in the spring of that year, the battle at Guilford Courthouse in North Carolina had weakened Cornwallis's troops, the British had forced Jefferson to flee Monticello only two months earlier. The outcome of the war was still not certain; the battle of Yorktown, where Cornwallis would surrender, was two months in the future. But the beautifully crafted sentences he wrote in this period bear no scent of danger or death.

Perhaps the design of Monticello, or "little mountain," still under construction as he wrote, yet even then set high on a hill he had constructed thirteen years earlier, with a serene view of the Blue Ridge Mountains, helped him toward a certain detachment. In this regard, one kind of denial would have been wed to another. As he wrote passages against slavery, the arduous labor that made Monticello flourish continued. The gangs of men and women driving plows, the blacksmiths, carpenters, grooms, wagoners, gardeners, and textile workers who lived and worked on top of Monticello mountain or on its slopes, provided an invisible cushion between him and his own daily needs, allowed him to work in ease. In the world he inhabited, bloodshed, sweat, servitude, even mortality and decay, dwelled in a shadowy place, peripheral to the vision on which his mind was trained.

AUGUST

More is being revealed every day. Hints that Libby is connected somehow. Increasingly one has the sense that this case may be what breaks the strange of spell of obedience that seems to have cast a shadow over public life since September 11, 2001.

But in 1782, Jefferson's denial would be shattered. The threat did not come from the British. The American Revolution came to an end before Jefferson completed the last draft of his *Notes*. In the early spring of 1782, King George's minister, Lord North, would resign, and by November of the same year, a preliminary peace treaty would be signed. But just as the American independence Jefferson had helped to envision began to seem inevitable, in the first week of September, he suffered a painful reversal of fortune. In May, his wife, Martha, had given birth to another child, Lucy Elizabeth. But her seventh pregnancy had been difficult. After the birth, she continued, as Jefferson wrote to James Monroe, "very dangerously ill." According to Patsy, their eldest daughter, her father remained at her mother's bedside, "never out of calling," until the day of Martha's death, on September 6 of that year.

Jefferson was inconsolable. As Patsy wrote years later, moments before Martha actually died, he lapsed into a state of insensibility and had to be carried out of the room by his sister. She took him into the library, where he fainted, remaining unconscious for so long "that they feared he would never revive." He did not leave the room for three weeks, pacing incessantly. When finally he emerged, it was only to wander on horseback for several more weeks, aimlessly traveling the back roads and forests around Monticello, occasionally breaking down in sobs, in what Patsy called his ceaseless "melancholy rambles."

When his friends in Congress, worried for his state of mind, asked him to come to Paris to help negotiate the peace, he agreed. "I had . . . rested all prospects of future happiness on domestic and literary projects," he wrote his friend Chastellux. "A single event wiped away all my plans and left a blank which I had not the spirit to fill up."

I came back to my grandparents a changed child. Though my experiences had been harrowing, I was less shy than I had been before and infinitely stronger. As I look back on it now, I can see that the reasons are multiple and complex. Certainly, primary to my new outlook was the fact that I had participated in the decision to leave my mother. Added to which the laxer rules at my mother's house allowed me a critical perspective regarding my grandmother's regime. My own objections began to seem just to me. My mother's more democratic approach to children encouraged this realization. Ironically, in the end, that my perceptions of her neglect had been validated and my efforts to save myself successful gave me more confidence in my own judgments and in my power too.

What also augmented my sense of capability in this period was a shift in the center of gravity from home to school. The classroom became my refuge, a way to escape the sad dramas that continued within my family. Here, I could replace the battle between my mother and my grandmother, my father's visible loneliness, the aching loss of my sister, with other subjects. The drama of American history appealed to me. I loved to imagine myself as Paul Revere, brave beyond measure, riding at a thunderous pace to warn my fellow citizens that the British were coming. Doubtless this passion inspired the request, which was granted, that I made for horseback-riding lessons. Just as important to me was the drama within the classroom. Our fifth-grade teacher had served in World War II and on occasion even wore his uniform to school. He was full of practical wisdom delivered in pithy phrases, which I memorized and repeated at the table so often that the phrase "Mr. Houghton says" became a joke in our family. Along with the drama of American history, he revealed the rudiments of democracy to us, a system for which I developed a fierce enthusiasm, partly because I was so in love with him.

When I moved into the sixth grade, I was loath to change teachers, but soon I fell in love with my next teacher too. It was in Mrs. Seigal's classroom that I became something of a star through my close and thorough knowledge of *Robert's Rules of Order*. She had chosen to demonstrate the life of democracy by holding classroom discussions governed by the accepted rules of debate. One late afternoon, just after she began these lessons, while I was searching through the bookshelves my grandmother kept underneath my bedroom window, I was surprised and exhilarated to find a copy of *Robert's Rules of Order*. My grandmother belonged to at least three different women's clubs that used this book as a manual. I started to read it immediately and, after I finished, read it again and again until I gained a comprehension of the correct procedures few children of my age possessed. I was so fond of raising my hand to call out "Point of order" that finally, in the interest of time, my teacher had to restrain me from this activity.

During this year, we learned also about the Bill of Rights and the Constitution. Though it was not yet entirely conscious, I know that part of the great appeal the study of democracy held for me was the association that had formed in my mind between self-government and the household I shared in earlier years with both my parents and my sister, where an atmosphere of greater equality and freedom prevailed. By contrast, my grandparents' household was run more like a monarchy. I know that

I began to sense this even then because of a yellowing piece of paper I still possess, written in pencil by my own hand when I was ten years old. I do not know whether the idea to write my own constitution came from a classroom assignment or myself. But it is clear that the content and language were entirely my own. In it I ask for certain basic rights, what I would call consistency now, and certain freedoms, to stay after school for club meetings or extracurricular events. But the best part of this document comes at the beginning, when I name the purported signatories. In an earnest but muddled amalgam of childish psychological and political insight, I called my grandmother the "Queen" and my grandfather the "Vice-King." The double entendre of this second name was not intended, but I can imagine the glee it must have caused the adults at the time, since in the years before I was born, my grandfather was famous for going on alcoholic binges, during which he would spend whole weekends carousing with women he picked up in bars. What I was really displaying when I used the word *vice* was my knowledge of who really ruled. And perhaps also, I used that word thinking that since he was by far the more lenient one, he ought to have a title with at least a nod toward democracy.

It would be wrong to conclude from the portrait I have painted thus far of my grandmother that she was rigid, humorless, or puritanical. She did in fact have a wilder side, a love of the theater and poetry, including works by Dorothy Parker and Cornelia Otis Skinner. Sometimes, as I was going to sleep, she used to read me lines from a long poem called "The Highwayman" about a young woman who falls in love with a brigand. It is a vivid poem and florid. As the young woman's lover says goodbye to her at the window, ". . . he scarce could reach her hand, / But she loosened her hair in the casement! His face burnt like a brand / As the black cascade of perfume came tumbling down his breast / And he kissed its waves in the moonlight." I loved to hear my grandmother read this poem; she did it with great passion. Her taste for these lines was not as uncharacteristic as might be imagined. When I was a bit older, my sister told me the story that our grandmother had had a child with my grandfather before they were married. During her pregnancy, she went to stay with relatives in Virginia, where the child was stillborn, or at least that's what everyone was told. Just before my grandmother's death, she gave me an early edition of Walt Whitman's *Leaves of Grass* that she must have owned all her life. It was less morality than the desire to appear respectable that motivated her. Powerful and in many ways fearless, she was inordinately concerned about what the neighbors might say, a concern that contradicted the abiding feeling she emanated that she was by far the superior of all of them.

AUGUST

As I search within myself, in the terrain of grief over what I'm afraid we have already lost, I think again of the phrase "New World." At the edge of hopelessness, an unreasonable hope. Perhaps a new world waits to be born within us.

One of the sources of my grandmother's sense of her own elevation was our lineage. My grandmother's maiden name was Branch, and she was descended from the writer James Branch Cabell. Though on occasion she spoke proudly about this connection, she never discussed his work, perhaps because, in his day, one of his novels, *Jurgen,* was considered pornographic. Cabell's progenitors had fought in the Revolutionary War. And from the same side of the family, in a serpentine way I have never been able to follow, she claimed as another ancestor General Nathanael Greene, Washington's second-in-command, who weakened Cornwallis's troops at Guilford, in North Carolina, so near the border with Virginia, in the battle that turned the tide of the war.

A reasoned approach might have counted my father's ancestry as a disruption in this otherwise commendable patriotic history. His side of the family descended from Loyalists, wealthy New Yorkers who had had to go into exile during the Revolutionary War. They lost all their land when they fled and hence joined the class of those who earn their living by their hands. But neither traitorous acts nor diminished means prevented my grandmother from welcoming the addition of this history to ours. Though she was distressed about my father's working-class origins, she added his early Tory ancestors to a long column of figures that proved our family had been in America for at least two centuries, which, in the middle of the twentieth century, acted as a serviceable enough replacement for a title and, at least by my grandmother's measure, gave a slightly bluer hue to our blood.

Neither my sister nor I were much interested in all of this. Because of the jigs and brogues to which I was exposed in the movies, when I was younger, I was more drawn to the Irish side of our history, the family members who crossed the water in the nineteenth century to escape the potato famine. I longed to have brown skin like my cousin by marriage who had come from Mexico. As for my sister, whenever she came to visit, during the summer or Christmas or Easter vacations, her first request was to make an outing to Oliveira Street, an enclave of Mexican shops and restaurants in downtown L.A. that had an indelible effect on both our sensibilities.

As we grew up, it became more and more clear that my sister and I were leaning further in the direction of democracy than our parents had. Although, at nine years of age, I was entirely unaware of who Senator Joseph McCarthy was and would not have been able to explain the meaning of segregation either, by the time I turned fourteen, I was my sister's accomplice in dinner table discussions where, to the heated disagreement of everyone else in our family, even our more democratically inclined father, we expressed our ardent advocacy for civil liberties and civil rights. But we belonged to another generation, and ours would be a different state of mind.

By the fall of 1782, negotiations for peace between Great Britain and America had begun. Though out of concern and respect for Jefferson, Adams and Franklin had asked him to join them in Paris for the talks, the ship waiting for him was blocked by ice a few miles below Baltimore. Then, a month later and before he was able to sail, word reached him that a provisional treaty had been signed. Always reticent to record his emotions, he says nothing about what he felt. One can only imagine the moment. A slight chill seizes the body when a risky step, a gamble with scarcely even odds, is met with success. Even if everything that has been desired is granted, the ground can suddenly seem startlingly new and unstable; a subtle death accompanies such victories, the loss of the old foundation on which you once stood. I have experienced a few such moments: the joy can be breathtaking, with only the slightest backward glance, and the taste of fear is nearly undetectable.

Indeed, all that Jefferson had dreamed of had been achieved. The United States was an independent nation. The future of America was in the hands of Americans now; only the task of what had been envisioned—a government by the consent of the governed, founded on the rights of life, liberty, and the pursuit of happiness—remained ahead.

2
YOSEMITE

There is a soul at the center of nature. . . .

—Ralph Waldo Emerson, "Spiritual Laws" (1841)

I believe a leaf of grass is the journey-work of the stars.

—Walt Whitman, "Song of Myself" (1855)

The great Tissiack, or Half-Dome, rising at the upper end of the Valley to a height of nearly a mile, is nobly proportioned and life-like, the most impressive of all the rocks, holding the eyes in devout admiration.

—John Muir, *My First Summer in the Sierra* (1911)

We Indians think of the Earth and the whole universe as a never-ending circle . . .

—Jenny Leading Cloud, White River Sioux

August

The weather is in the news so much more often now. A storm approaching Florida has turned into a hurricane.

THERE ARE MEMORIES of wild places that have come to dwell in the most intimate regions of my mind. I am thinking now of that startling and strangely beautiful mountaintop in Yosemite known as Half Dome, a massive granite sphere sliced midway so dramatically that across its face you can trace the path of an ancient glacier. Though I cannot recall when I first encountered this extraordinary sight, over most of my lifetime, it has provided the eastern edge for all my ideas about where I am on this earth, not just geographically but also in the way it evokes a quality of nature, one that, since it seems immeasurably grand and beyond comprehension, bears on the question of existence.

Countless images of Yosemite Valley have tried to capture this grandeur. As I grew up, I saw many photographs taken by Ansel Adams, and I must have also seen that famous painting done by Albert Bierstadt in 1868, which depicts the landscape bathed in the golden light of a setting sun. I can hardly connect this image with the Yosemite I know. The image is inaccurate, and the glow seems sentimental. Yet, as with the depiction of Jefferson surrounded by an aura of candlelight I saw as a child, the light does hold some meaning for me, as if the painter were trying to capture another promise, a sense of being kindred not just with other people but with the land, the stones, the trees, with all of nature.

It is not only Half Dome that has shaped my physical and spiritual parameters. I can no more separate the whole terrain of California from my own story than from my body. California has a distinct and dramatic topography. On one side it forms the western coast of the American continent, looming out over the Pacific Ocean, then curling back into bays and inlets for 3,427 miles. To the east the state is bordered for over 400 miles by the Sierra Nevada. The state of Nevada begins somewhere on the eastern side of the ridge. Yosemite, where Half Dome towers above the eponymous valley, can be found midway on a north-south axis in the same range. Below Bakersfield, if you travel south, past the Sierra, you will find the climate warmer, until, as you keep traveling southeast, you will encounter a wall of heat from the Mojave Desert. Los Angeles and its basin, where I was born and raised, has a climate not unlike the Mediterranean, temperate, mild, sometimes hot, often warm at night, with soft sea breezes the nearer the water you go.

AUGUST

The hurricane has become much stronger. They've named it Katrina, giving it a woman's name of course. It's heading toward Louisiana now.

The whole of California, the land and climate, the quality of light, the ocean that shines early in the morning and when the sun goes down, are mixed with all my memories, becoming part of the weave of who I am. The clearest influence on my emotional life can be traced to the summers I spent, often six weeks at a time, camping at a site north of Yosemite and above Lake Tahoe in the High Sierra.

I cannot say that I remember my first ride up into the woods, but after my first year, I memorized the route, noting certain milestones with growing anticipation. The journey would begin on a bus that, along with all the other girls attending the camp, I boarded in Sacramento. The bus, however, could only go part of the way. No properly paved road led to the camp, which, set in the hills by the side of Lake Rucker, seemed remote and, in the 1950s, to have an astonishing wildness, as if it were set back, not only in space but in time too.

At the end of the paved road, we would all be loaded onto the open bed of a wide truck, a ride that for most of us was thrilling in its own right, above and beyond our destination. But even so, I was fixed intently on our arrival mostly because I knew that I would finally see my sister again. After our consignment to our mother's mother and her sister, my mother's aunt, who each lived in separate halves of the state, we saw each other only at specific times of the year. To celebrate Thanksgiving, my grandparents would drive up to Davis, just outside Sacramento, where my great-aunt lived and where for four days of bliss I spent every moment with my sister. We shared her bed at night, and after we played guessing games about what we had drawn with our fingers on each other's backs, as I dropped off to sleep, she told me stories that, not unlike Winnie-the-Pooh, revolved around a community of forest creatures, birds, squirrels, raccoons, and bears who had distinctly human qualities and problems.

At Christmastime my sister would travel to my grandparents' house on the Southern Pacific train. I can still remember vividly how I intensely suffered waiting for her train to arrive at Union Station with an anxious anticipation that seemed to stretch out interminably, partly because my grandparents nearly always arrived very early for events. After New Year's, when she would return on the same train, I would cry for most of the ensuing week. Since I knew I would not see her again until Easter, a length of time I could hardly imagine, her loss plunged me into a bleak state of grief, as if nothing in the world would ever be set right again.

When the graded soil at the side of the road turned red, I knew we were within a half hour of our destination. Sometimes a lumber truck would come barreling down the road toward us, sending so much dust our way that we would be coated with it. The trees along the road seemed taller and thicker, and, aside from the sound of the truck, you could, if you paid attention, begin to feel a quiet that was enveloping, one that instead of an absence of sound seemed more like some mysterious presence. This was among the first experiences I had that could be called auspicious. Though when I write that, another such memory comes to mind: the evening when, during our journey back across America, my grandmother took me by the hand to lead me to the edge of the Grand Canyon, so that we could watch the sun set together, marveling at the sharp depth below, while cathedrals of rock turned red in the fading light.

When our truck would finally pull into the dusty area where we unloaded, I saw my sister at last, most often wearing her blue jeans, a white shirt, and a red bandana around her neck. We did not look like sisters. While I was blonde, she had my mother's dark hair and the more sharply delineated profile that came from our grandfather. As soon as I was lifted out of the truck, she was by my side. Then, delirious with joy, I would cast myself into her arms. The first time I arrived was the most intense, but every time afterward called up the same emotions, the sense that after months that had felt to me like years of separation, we were finally reunited.

Very soon, however, we would have to separate again. The camp was divided into several different levels, each with its own fire pits and several clusters, each made of five or six cots set up close together, in a flat area cleared of brush. As an older camper, my sister belonged to a more advanced group than I: girls who engaged in some activities exclusively together, took longer hikes or canoe trips that campers my age were too young to join, and who slept together on a different level. I was sent off with two counselors and the other young campers, of whom I was the youngest, to set up our living quarters. I endured the separation partly because I was inside my sister's world now. In my eyes, everything I saw and did reflected her and perhaps, in a deeper sense, returned to me the courage and confidence that had been growing within me just before our parents divorced.

AUGUST

Much trepidation along the gulf. The mayor of New Orleans has ordered evacuation. Massive traffic jam on the roads leading out of town. Fear for those caught on the roads and those staying home who in most cases lack the means to go.

Like all the other girls there, I soon grew proud of the fact that we used neither cabins nor tents but slept out in the open air. The only buildings in the camp were the outhouses, which we cleaned ourselves, and the cookhouse, which we never entered. Even the dining room beside the cookhouse, where we ate when we were not cooking over campfires, was outdoors. We had a splendid amphitheater, with graded log seating in a semicircle around a very large fire pit, which was next to the lake and the docks we used.

Camping here required many skills, some of which, such as chopping wood or whittling, I was only allowed to learn as I grew older. But I learned to lash immediately. This was not just a meaningless craft but a way to weave twigs together to make small shelves on branches on which we might store supplies and treasures.

Another skill I had to learn right away was to find my way from one place to another by following the very narrow paths that formed a network up and down the slopes and sideways through our camp. Though little handmade wooden signs were posted along the way, if you weren't looking carefully, it was still possible to get lost. It is far easier to lose your way in the High Sierra than it might seem. This was a serious danger, one intensified by the way the weather can change very quickly, so that even in the summer, you may suddenly find yourself in cold, wet weather, even occasionally a snowstorm.

The other danger came from the many rattlesnakes that sequestered themselves everywhere in the area. One year the cluster where I slept, which was nestled near huge boulders, had to be moved because a nest of snakes was found in the rocks. We were all taught that snakes gravitate to rocks for the sunlight and heat. That the diamonds on their backs can easily be mistaken for foliage; the S shapes their bodies make when moving, resembling branches; and that a coiled snake was within an instant of striking. We carried snakebite kits with us and learned what was then considered the best procedure for first aid: to lance the wound and suck the potentially fatal poison out. Whenever we hiked in groups off the trails, we each carried a stick with a fork at the bottom. The technique we learned was to extend this stick into brush before stepping there. The fork was supposed to be put over the head of any snake we encountered, to keep it from striking, a move that fortunately I never had to make.

The best defense, however, that all of us had, whether against snakes or disorientation, was observation. I remember clearly the day I realized that manzanita grew just at the point where I needed to take a trail that went up and to the right as I returned to my site. Farther along the same trail, I knew I would find a madrone tree, its roots embedded where I walked, the trunk leaning, as madrones do, back into the woods. Learning the names of trees was less an act of classification for me than a shift in my own consciousness, a gradual sharpening of my own perception, so that I learned to see more than the height or color of the leaves, but the color and kind of bark, whether the needles were in clusters, the pattern and veins of the leaves, if the tree bore acorns or pinecones, and what those looked like too. If the practical skills I was acquiring gave me a heady sense of independence, observation strengthened my ability to think independently. Instead of relying on maps or ideas, what I was learning to do was to see for myself, to enter what Ralph Waldo Emerson called "the thousand-eyed present."

Emerson played a vital role in the longer history of how, like so many others before and after me, I came to spend time in the Sierra. His work had a profound influence on John Muir, the naturalist responsible for conserving so much of the wilderness in California, including Yosemite National Park. He visited Muir in the Sierra once in 1871. But born and raised in Boston, he lived all his life in the far more settled state of Massachusetts. It was to separate himself from society and pursue further what he had called in his first book, *Nature,* "an original relation to the universe" that Emerson settled seventeen miles outside Boston. He moved to Concord with his second wife, Lydia (whom Emerson called Lydian), on the day that they were married. Here in the town where the first shots of the American Revolution had been fired, he would continue to explore transcendentalism, a philosophy that recalled Jefferson's words in the Declaration of Independence, *"Nature and Nature's God."*

A few days before his wedding, on the two hundredth anniversary of incorporation of the town of Concord, at the request of its citizens, Emerson delivered a lengthy address revealing the town's history, for which he had interviewed a few surviving minutemen who had fought in the battle of Concord and were later among those who came to the meetinghouse to hear him speak.

Was he aware that he was continuing the American Revolution in his own way? The windows of the Old Manse, where he wrote his history of Concord, looked out on the river near the field where the fateful battle took place. But now a more subtle battle ensued, an inner conflict, bearing precisely in its own way on where he was, the place, the land, the fields, the sky. As he wrote, he must have been aware of the forces arrayed against his vision, a revolution going in the opposite direction, toward modern life, invention, industry, and development.

Not even quiet Concord was immune. By 1850, the woodlands that just fifty years before had made up over a quarter of the town had been reduced to less than half that size. Emerson was not indifferent to the costs of progress. If, inviting a friend to visit, he promised that being on the major coach route between New York and Boston, this town was not hard to reach, he had other feelings about this kind of traffic. "Civilized man," he lamented, "has built a coach, but has lost the use of his feet. He is supported on crutches, but lacks much support of muscle. . . . A Greenwich nautical almanac he has, and so being sure of the information when he wants it, the man in the street knows not a star in the sky."

Almost every night when I was in the Sierra, I would look up to see a sky full of stars, dazzling, mysterious, and plentiful. A sight that was especially wondrous to me, since, when I was home in Los Angeles, there were rarely more than a few stars visible at night. It was not just the city lights dimming the heavens. Set in a basin between low mountains, the city trapped all the smog that was produced from the steadily increasing number of cars clogging its streets and newly constructed freeways. I never thought much about the curious relationship our family had to this phenomenon. My grandfather was an executive salesman who sold automobiles. His life and the life of my grandmother had followed a trajectory common in midcentury America. In White Heath, Illinois, the small town where they were both born and raised, his father had been a butcher and hers a farmer. But though my grandmother inherited a parcel of land, my grandfather was not a farmer, and since my great-grandfather's butcher shop went to an older son, my grandparents had few prospects for success in that part of the country. Thus, when a big car company offered my grandfather employment, they had moved west to a big city, as so many others in their generation did.

My grandmother loved the sophistication of city life, but nevertheless, she kept up her farm ways, always buying fresh produce, sometimes from roadside stands just outside the city, doing all her own baking from scratch, and just as the growing season came to an end, canning tomatoes, strawberries, and whatever else was at hand. My grandfather was not interested in produce. By the time I came to live with him, he had already been forced into retirement because of his drinking. His days were slow and governed by a series of habits, one of which was to oversee the family car. He did not wash or polish it himself, but he went out every afternoon to survey every inch of it, flicking away dust or debris, kicking the tires, and generally admiring it. We had a new Dodge sedan every year.

This stable life had an appealing aspect, yet the countryside, which might have offered a domain of adventure to a child, was missing from the scene. Whenever I went to summer camp, I felt as if I were retrieving a lost part of myself, an exhilaration, astonishment, and vitality that I felt had been mine all along. I was thrilled to go out with a small party at night, armed with forked sticks, as we hiked through brush and climbed the boulder where we lay on our backs to gaze at the constellations, each of which our counselor named for us. There are memories from these days that I still have in my body, the quickening shock, for instance, of jumping into the glacially cold waters of a Sierra pool, formed by a congregation of gray-white rocks, very clear, deep for some reason, and because of this colored a brilliant emerald green. There were other days that we spent exploring meadows. I learned to name the wildflowers, lupine and poppy, lavender against orange, among them. On Sundays a nondenominational service was held in the meadow closest to our camp. We sang various songs together and pondered some scripture. But whatever spiritual moments existed in those texts paled next to the powerful feelings that came to me when I saw those stars, plunged into those ice-cold waters, or let my eyes follow dragonflies and monarchs as they hovered, then floated over the meadow, then glided away, not out of sight so much as into the greater whole of creation that I could feel around me and to which undeniably I belonged.

A century before I was born, when Emerson wrote "Self-Reliance," and neither the automobile nor electric lights had been invented yet, stars could still be seen from most American cities. But technical progress was on the horizon. The path to Edison's invention had been laid before the Declaration of Independence was signed, when Benjamin Franklin published a book describing a series of experiments by which he proposed to reveal the nature of electricity: *Experiments and Observations on Electricity, Made at Philadelphia.* Released first in London, where it quickly went through five editions, it caused a great sensation through-out Europe. Just outside Paris, on a stormy night, Thomas-François d'Al-ibard, performing one of Franklin's experiments, drew sparks from the sky. He reported his success immediately to the Académie royale des sci-ences. The idea of electricity, suddenly irresistible, captivated European consciousness. Even Louis XV's physician repeated the experiment, drawing sparks in the king's gardens at the Hotel de Noailles. The British scientist Joseph Priestley, the man who discovered oxygen, described Franklin's achievement as the most important contribution to philoso-phy since Newton. When electricity joined gravity as a major force, "na-ture's most fearsome phenomenon," to quote the historian Phillip Dray, had been stripped "of its mystical provenance."

AUGUST

Good news early this morning. The storm did not do as much damage to the city as predicted. I am so relieved. There is no other city quite like it anywhere.

The pursuit of the truth is rarely more dramatic than with scientific ex-periment. Though a concept may be persuasively argued with words and logic, its apotheosis lies in reality. Even the church, with its reliance on sacred texts and deductive reasoning, understood the need for an earthly dimension. Ritual; the priest's robes; the choir; the great cathedrals, some taking decades to build; miracles; the stigmata; the presence of the host; God's body in the communion bread and wine. The wish to see thought take a material shape is as intense as any desire.

Though in hindsight the night would seem portentous, the evening began almost comically. A portly middle-aged man and a boy, both soaked in rain, struggling to get a kite aloft in a storm. The famous painting by Benjamin West that is enshrined in the iconography of the Enlightenment, shows a heroically windblown Franklin, a burgundy silk cape swirling about him, catching the light that illuminates his forehead too and toward which he points, reminding us of God in Michelangelo's *Creation of Adam,* an effect heightened not only by the perfectly framed bolt of lightning above Franklin, but by the angels who surround him, as they pull on the kite string and play with a large gyroscope. Yet despite an air of romantic excess, the painting captures something inward. No matter how shabby or ridiculous the rain-soaked

Franklin might have seemed to a casual witness, it was a large passion that drove him out into the storm. Word that his experiments had already been conducted successfully in France had not reached him yet. He had been waiting for weeks, impatient to know if his reasoning had led him to the right conclusions. Would a spark travel from the heavens down the string he held into his hand? Would he be able to feel the charge as he envisioned it? I can imagine that he would have strained toward the clouds, focusing not just his eyes but every cell of his being on the sky. In the painting, his face shows some relief, almost as if the beloved had finally returned, faithful in the end to her promises. But he bears an expression of utter calm and fortitude too. A kind of mastery, as if he knew he was right all along.

In an age when the success of every experiment validated reason, it is easy to understand why, like the Enlightenment itself, the American Revolution went hand in hand with the scientific revolution. There was, of course, the way that Franklin's reputation as a scientist made him an effective ambassador to France when he served during the Revolution, a role that, given France's pivotal military contribution to the war with Britain, was particularly significant. That his discovery of electricity had made him a popular figure was only part of the story. By association, the success of his experiments could not help but rub off on the experiment in democracy he was representing. He and his ideas seemed to have the power to transform life. During the Revolution, the British apparently believed he possessed such extraordinary powers that, strategically placed, just across the water in France, he might be able to send a cataclysmic electrical storm to let loose its fury on the British Isles.

The real power, of course, lay in the electricity of ideas about both nature and society. The lightning rod Franklin placed on the Pennsylvania State House in 1752 was an augury of more than one kind of change. The excitement must have been consuming. A door was opening within the mind. If ideas about the nature of existence, propagated by centuries of church scholars, were being challenged, this was only part of the story. Consciousness itself was being transformed. The understanding that instead of the earth, the sun is at the center of the solar system; that the stars are not fixed and eternal but constantly changing; that lightning is a natural phenomenon, a form of electricity that, like gravity, is a binding force of earthly existence meant that life itself is understandable through reason. The ability to discover the truth, once the privilege of church and state authorities, belonged now to anyone willing to ask questions, form theories, and perform experiments. What was once a volume of indecipherable signs had become an open book.

That the Declaration of Independence was signed under the same roof that hosted Franklin's lightning rod was no coincidence. The new approach to knowledge was vitally important to democracy. The rise of reason also empowered even the most common citizen, who might be able to observe and report, estimate, weigh evidence, form theories, attempt to prove them. In the realm of ideas, truth no longer emanated from a single center, a dissemination of authority that would be crucial to democracy. Using the power of reason, citizens of the new country called America were to decide who should govern and how.

Yet no matter how welcome, the turn would have cut deeply into the soul as well as the mind. The new world that science had opened could be unsettling. Though Jefferson and Franklin, both Deists, still believed in a Creator, the god of Deism had fallen silent after the creation was finished. In exchange for the great expansion of creativity that science offered, the assurance that a wise Lord and Master oversees the universe, lending even the worst disasters an ultimately moral if not happy meaning, had to be sacrificed.

Since electrical storms are rare in California, I have always been thrilled to encounter the sudden sight of long arrows of light flying across the sky. Even as a child, I did not see lightning as a bolt of fire sent to earth by an angry God. Raised inside the scientific worldview, I was fascinated by the phenomenon. Like all children, I was full of questions. What makes lightning? Why does water pour from the sky? What is electricity? Though the adults in my family were often unable to give me satisfying scientific answers, they never discouraged my curiosity, nor did they give me metaphysical explanations. They were not particularly religious. Neither my parents nor my grandparents ever went to church; and had I not acquired religious beliefs at a certain age, Jesus would only have been mentioned at Christmas, when my sister and I would place a diminutive figure of an infant in a cradle next to Mary and Joseph and the worn wooden animals that made up our crèche under the tree.

AUGUST

The calm was short-lived. The levees are breaking and there is no way to fix them.

Were it not for the crushing fear of death that overtook me at the age of seven, I doubt I would ever have been sent to Sunday school. It was the solution my grandparents chose when, night after night, as the lights were turned off in my room at the end of the hall, I would struggle with the darkness, imagine murderous creatures lurking in the shadows, and then, even if I were certain nothing malevolent was in the room with me, begin to cry with terror at the mere thought that my existence was ultimately bound to come to an end, one way or another.

August

Eighty-five percent of the city is under water now. On the television, one horrifying scene after another. Families stranded on the roofs of their houses, rising up as if in a lake. Dead bodies floating in the water.

Sunday school saved me from this nightly torture. It was not the promise of an afterlife that impressed me. Rather, I replaced my cries with prayers. As I prayed, I could feel a comforting presence come back toward me from the shadows. In Sunday school we read the Bible, and as my skills at reading improved, I became a good student of both the Old and the New Testaments. Although I was earnest enough to actually read through the endless genealogies, nevertheless my favorite passages in the King James translation were the same as many other readers. I loved the book of Genesis, the Psalms, including the Lord's Prayer, which I memorized, Ecclesiastes, the Song of Solomon, and the Gospels, especially the Sermon on the Mount. I did not yet know that Thomas Jefferson had made his own version of the Gospels, featuring the teachings of Jesus. Yet, as I began to learn the basic tenets of democracy, I found the democratic ideal of equality to be reflected in the Christian ideal of compassion.

Soon I had begun to attend the Presbyterian Church, where I went to Sunday school, next to my elementary school; I was excited to be baptized because then I could take communion; the idea of drinking the blood of the lamb especially appealed to me. I did not mind that it was only Welch's grape juice. All I wanted was the drama. As with many shy children, my inner life was intense.

Only later in life did I see that it was a desire for ritual that must have drawn my grandparents to the Masonic orders of which they were members. My grandfather was a Mason, "thirty-third degree," my grandmother explained to me with unconcealed pride, though, to her credit,

she never pronounced the full name to which apparently this rank entitled him: "sovereign grand inspector general." One afternoon I was allowed into a great hall to watch my grandfather, utterly unrecognizable
in his uniform, a saber at his side, a feathered hat such as admirals wore
in the eighteenth century on his head, as he marched toward the most
sovereign and grandest inspector general placed in charge of it all for
some kind of investiture whose purpose I did not grasp.

My grandmother's clubs were more accessible to me. After a brief
meeting, in which *Robert's Rules of Order* was strictly applied, followed
by some marching around the room in geometrical and strange yet ar-
canely meaningful patterns, the mostly middle-aged and older women,
with blue and tightly curled hair, would retire to the next room for lunch
or dinner, where I was the youngest and most favored guest. I was given
so many party favors and candy cups that I always needed at least one
bag to cart them all home with me.

I did not know then that the Masonic order was formed by stonema-
sons, many of whom worked on the great cathedrals. Eventually they
formed a guild and later became associated somehow with the Enlightenment. The idea of religious tolerance was one of the principles of their
organization. Since they allowed members from all religions to belong,
the Masons were basically Deist and took as a core creed reason along
with certain shared and fundamental humanist values, such as the democratic ideal, which is shared with many religions, that you should do to
others what you would like done to you.

But when as an adolescent I joined Job's Daughters, the girls' wing of
the Masonic order, this philosophy remained in only the most perfunctory ways. We used *Robert's Rules of Order* too and elected our president,
but no one ever seemed to notice that everyone in our group was white
and Protestant. I did not know then that since the eighteenth century,
Masons in America had refused membership to black Americans. Even
when a black chapter was formed separately, the Masons refused to recognize it. But Britain finally invested the black organization, which went
on to include many distinguished members, among them Frederick
Douglass and W.E.B. DuBois.

My sister, who during our childhood found herself more often in
open rebellion against our family, took a different spiritual path. At the
age of sixteen, she converted to Catholicism. For a long time I was the
only one in our family who knew this. Despite the Masonic precept of

tolerance, none of my grandparents approved of Catholicism. My grandfather, who had descended on one side of his family from the Protestant Irish, was particularly vociferous on this subject. So it was in secret that my sister showed me the gold-edged pages of her books about saints and discussed various rituals with me. Bit by bit, as she became more and more enthusiastic, she settled on the idea of becoming a nun. Dazzled by her passion and all the beautiful stories she told me, I might have followed in her footsteps were it not for the fact that I already had a church and was fond of our pastor, a very liberal, kind, and handsome young man.

I remained, however, fascinated. My attraction would be tried one summer in Yosemite, where my sister and I were camping with our father, when one morning while he still slept, we rose before dawn to hike toward the center of the valley so we could attend services at the Catholic church there. Because my sister had not told my father about her religious conversion, she believed the trip had to be clandestine. After she left a note claiming we had gone on a hike, she swore me to secrecy. She knew I could keep a secret. When she trusted me enough to smoke an occasional cigarette in front of me, I vowed I would never reveal what I knew, even if tortured.

Though I was never put to this test, it was torturous enough for me to rise so early in the morning and walk for half an hour without breakfast. The occasion was memorable to me not just for the beautiful ritual, which I did find dazzling, but because, while steadfastly imitating my sister, as she knelt and performed her genuflections, I fainted. This, too, we held back from our father, fearing he might deduce our other secret from it.

As I write now, half a century later, if my sister's reasoning seems somewhat confused to me, it is chiefly because our father had no particular prejudice against Catholics. Nevertheless, our covert journey must have added a great deal of drama to the intensity of her devotion, as if she were a brave combatant in some religious war. On my part, I did not feel my morning of worship in a Catholic church had made me at all disloyal to my Protestant church. I had inherited that habit of the American mind through which one is able to entertain many different religions side by side without any sense of serious conflict.

By the middle of the twentieth century, the principle of religious tolerance, so crucial in American history, had evolved into a general acceptance that most of the differences among the great variety of religious beliefs belong to accidents of history and in any case should not be taken too seriously. My grandfather's rancor against Catholics was a case in point. Everyone else in the family looked on his passionate prejudices as strangely anachronistic. Indeed, my grandmother always explained that he had inherited his views from his father, who emigrated from Ireland to America during the potato famine. Being an Orangeman, he brought his enmity toward Catholics with him. Though my grandfather discouraged me from wearing green on Saint Patrick's Day, since I was intrigued with shamrocks and leprechauns, I did so with great enthusiasm.

The tolerant atmosphere toward religious difference that I shared with most of my family and friends has another cause too. In my generation, we became used to hosting two very different worlds of meaning in our minds. We rarely worried about conflicts between religion and science. I read the first words of the Bible, "In the beginning God created the heavens and the earth," so often that I knew them by heart. But when I began to learn and understand the story about the origin of the earth derived from astronomy, geology, biology, and evolutionary theory, I accepted this as an accurate description. When I became old enough to contemplate scientific theories, I also began to grasp the idea of symbolic truth and thus could read the biblical story of creation as metaphorical. But an even more powerful force in my consciousness that allowed these two views to coexist peacefully in my mind was the habit of pluralism I had learned very young.

In a democracy many different points of view about every possible subject will be expressed, and almost all of them must be tolerated. This is one reason why democratic societies are usually pluralistic. But as I reflect on this question, other causes occur to me. Since uniformity, whether in religion or ideology, must almost always be enforced by some form of tyranny and even violence, I am beginning to wonder if, like the environment, human culture naturally tends toward and flourishes with variety.

I have observed the tendency in my own mind. As much as I cherish my opinions, I am drawn, as if by an endless appetite for new tastes, to different perspectives. I notice that my mind loves variety, as if somewhere in my consciousness I were seeking some relief from the old boundaries of what I had imagined to be myself. Despite the ferocity with which I, like most everyone I know, guard my identity, I find that I take a strange yet steady pleasure in contemplating its dissolution. I am thinking not only of the Buddhist idea of the self as an illusion but of something I once heard about Japanese grammar, that in this syntax, the word "I" is rarely used. That I do not exist as a separate entity is a fact that from time to time my mind grasps, as if I were picking up a beautiful glass paperweight filled with colored crystals in the shapes of flowers, feeling the cool, polished surface against my skin, tumbling it in my palm, peering into the mysteries of its beauty.

Yet this pleasure almost always moves beyond dissolution toward reason. What would the experience mean, I ask, to view the cosmos through another grammar? I find myself trying to integrate the meaning of what has seemed disruptive and foreign into my former picture of the world, to balance it against my own experience, to fuse it with all I value, including myself.

September

All those who were not able to leave the city were told to go to the Superdome. But no one seemed to plan for their arrival. There's no more food, no water that is drinkable, and the plumbing has broken down too.

I still have the Bible I studied as a child. Its black leather binding is faded and brittle in places with age, but the gilt edges of the pages shine even now. The gold star and the American flag I pasted inside remain as evidence of an early patriotism. And resting in the Old Testament like a bookmark is a small photograph I have had since I was nine years old. It depicts a river in the High Sierra, somewhere near the summer camp I attended. I remember putting the photograph there as one might place an image of a holy person on an altar.

When several decades later I learned that the hieroglyph for God derived from the flags used to mark off sacred land, I recognized a feeling from my past. Though I had never put words to what I experienced, for years I had experienced the place where I camped as a child in the High Sierra as numinous. It was never a conscious decision to regard that place as sacred, but rather, like the Carlsbad Caverns, which I saw as a younger child, formed over time from discrete moments and memories that gradually crystallized into a tangible forest of brightness in my mind. I am thinking of the time, for instance, before the rest of my fellow campers had arrived at our site under the redwoods, when I stood alone for a few moments, my head thrown back, my eyes traveling up the trunk of one tree, until I was dazzled, not only by the height but by the force of being that met my attention. Seeing the light glance off the surface of Lake Rucker as the sun began its descent only to catch a cluster of pine needles in its brilliance cast me into an intense state of mind, infused with a very particular joy, a kind of rapture, not unlike being in love. And there was also the time when, after a small group of us hiked all day to reach an area above the tree line filled with massive white rocks and sugar pines, the inherent silence of this spare landscape struck a chord of profound quiet inside me. It was as if in this newly discovered territory I had also found an aspect of my own mind.

If years later I came to believe that spirit exists within nature, at that age, though these experiences had had a powerful effect on me, I did not weave them into any particular philosophy. The idea would have been foreign to the small world I inhabited then. Society does not invent experience, but it selects which events and emotions are significant and gives them a context, which shapes meaning. Whenever a perception or an understanding goes unnamed, it tends to be buried or erased in memory, or at least pushed to the margin of consciousness altogether. In the same way, when an experience is named and treated as significant, every outer reflection amplifies its inner importance. In this way, society shapes even the most inward thoughts.

Yet society itself changes, and by a process of coevolution that is still partly mysterious, the ideas on which societies are founded change too. Transformation in the consciousness of a culture, which often occurs the way it does in nature, piecemeal, by a progression of slight variations and slow erosion, is a complex process with countless causes, in which some are evident and some not. Any new insight can claim many seemingly disparate elements as silent ancestors. By challenging the church's ideas, Galileo's discoveries would eventually play a role in undermining clerical authority, including the idea of the divine right of kings to rule, and this pointed to the end of monarchy and the beginning of democracy.

But in the process of change, an effect quickly becomes a cause. If the development of science enabled democracy, the founding of democracy also had an effect on what in the eighteenth century was called natural philosophy. Over time, the idea of equality among citizens was to open the way to experience nature differently. When the hierarchical order that placed monarchs over lords and lords over commoners collapsed, a radical suggestion appeared at the periphery of vision: the notion that realms considered even lower—animals, plants, forests, fields of flowers, and grasses—might be elevated in consciousness too. And at the same time, as gradually the collective attention turned from reciting the poetry of ancient scriptures and peering at beautifully illuminated manuscripts to the direct observation of beetles and their iridescent wings, the flight of butterflies, the cocoons of moths, the tendrils of ferns, skeletons of lemurs and monkeys, bird feathers, seashells, the strata of rocks by the sea, new visions of the cosmos began to appear. And with this in turn a different experience of the human soul was also born.

It is easy to see the potential for revolutionary thought in the conditions of Emerson's birth. Born in 1803, just twenty-six years after the Declaration of Independence was written, Emerson inherited not only the rights of a citizen in a democracy but a frame of mind open to asking questions and seeking change. No wonder, then, that in cities and towns or on farms, well settled but ringed with abundant uncultivated land that afforded intimate and daily relationships with forests, streams, mountains, the American imagination could begin to see nature as an expression of spirit.

Yet, as with every substantial alteration in consciousness, the transformative perception of nature that arose in the nineteenth century was born through a series of smaller steps, sometimes faltering, sometimes fearful, sometimes leaping. I am thinking now of just one of what must have been countless such moments in Emerson's life, a revelation he experienced early in 1838 during a Sunday church service.

As he sits trying to listen to the sermon, he finds it intolerably dull. He bears the minister no ill will. He is a good man, well intentioned, Emerson believes. Nevertheless, he lets his attention wander. He is drawn toward the window. Not just his eyes but his whole soul leans in that direction. While the preacher's monotonous words drone on, he gazes at a patch of the countryside covered in snow. There is a snowstorm outside, and the snow keeps on falling. But all this whiteness, the repetitive, silent motion, which he has doubtless observed since infancy, does not bore him at all. Was there a wind? The passage of clouds? Were there shafts of light striking here and there with sharp points of illumination?

That evening he would write in his journal, "The snowstorm was real, the preacher merely spectral. Vast contrast to look at him and then out of the window." He is near the end of a longer conversion, one that began in 1831 and would continue for seven years, through doubts and decisions followed by waves of insight, until finally he decided to cease his weekly sermons in Lexington before delivering the famous address to the graduating class at the Divinity School at Harvard, the lecture that expressed his harshest criticism of the theological tradition in which he had been schooled. It was because of this address that he would not be invited to speak again at Harvard for thirteen years.

Emerson's career as a minister had been both brilliant and brief. Graduating from Harvard at the age of eighteen, he taught school for several years, until, by twenty-one, unhappy with the mediocrity of his life, he quit teaching in order to devote himself entirely to the study of theology. He entered Harvard Divinity School and, one year later, in 1826, he was approved to preach. It was a rich period in his life. He fell in love with Ellen Tucker, whom he would soon marry. It is an indication of his passionate nature, which the eloquence of his prose tends to soften, that despite the fact that she was seriously ill with tuberculosis he was determined to marry her. Rising as he had, with his mother's efforts, out of poverty, despite bouts of sadness, he must have had the feeling he could meet any circumstance. Even a bout with illness moved him further on his path. During his convalescence he spent his time reading and thinking. He would need to have confidence in his own resilience for many reasons. Gradually his thoughts were turning him toward a second American revolution, a revolution in religious ideas.

In many ways this was a revolution that had started years before. By 1829, the year that Emerson was appointed minister of Boston's Second Church, a dramatic change in the theology preached there had already taken place. The pulpit he was to occupy once belonged to Cotton Mather, who had delivered famously harsh sermons against what he believed to be rampant sin in New England, a place that in its recent pre-colonial past, he argued, had been "the *Devil's* territory" and was still, he declared, riddled with Satanic influences. But the atmosphere was hardly the same by the time Emerson began his ministry. The fire and brimstone had died down. Indeed Emerson would be troubled by something else entirely, not flames, but the absence of heat. He did not want to administer perfunctory rituals or preach a creed that he found to be, in his words, "corpse cold."

Paradoxically, the sight of death would move him to action. Despite the great love between them and their happiness, Ellen died in 1831, just over a year since their wedding. Several months after her burial, propelled by grief for the beautiful young woman he loved, he revisited her tomb and—extraordinary as it may seem today—opened the coffin. It would of necessity have been a bracing moment, a stark realization, even a physical shock. Yet in a strange way, it also seems oddly characteristic of this man that he would go toward that which must have both terrified and wounded him, the sight of the body of the woman he loved, decaying.

My first experience of death was muted and vague. I did not know why the family had assembled outside wearing dark and formal coats in what I mistook as a park. When someone told me that my Grandfather Hal, my father's father, had died, I did not really take in the fact. Since I saw him rarely, his absence was not especially notable to me. Only over time did I realize that I would never see him again.

It is fitting in an unaccountable way that while nature dictates mortality, trees, grass, even a handful of flowers, help the human mind to hold the immensity of death. The finality is difficult to absorb. Like the convulsions of the dying, the efforts within consciousness to come to terms with fatality are similar to those of the body laboring to give birth. The temptation is to impose an order on mortality, some kind of reason or justice, a divine punishment, even a calling. If you do not yield to this urge, your sorrow will be laced with a desolation more vast than ordinary thoughts can subsume, a void untouched by the empty exigencies of an existence that suddenly seems meaningless. Besides mollifying dogmas or denial, there is no relief from this expanse. It must be traversed. But in the journey across your own grief, here and there, along the omnipresent edge between life and death, a new dimension of experience arises, bringing with it, even as you feel the sharpest pain, a wildly strange species of joy.

Is this the state of mind that Emerson described on the day Ellen died? Fresh from her death, he wrote in his journal, "I am alone in the world and strangely happy." Afterward he would live through many despondent months of grief, a process that appeared to lead directly to his admission that he was deeply dissatisfied with the ministry. Now he would call the profession "antiquated." It would be wrong to conclude that he had grown dissatisfied with everything in his life. There is little evidence of such an outlook. The whole movement of his mind is colored now more by passion than depression. "It is the best part of man . . . ," he writes, "that revolts against being the minister. His good revolts from official goodness." He had been wandering in an unfettered wilderness and discovered there a part of himself, intolerant either of dishonesty or mute obedience and the living death that results from both.

But Ellen's death brought him closer to what he did believe too. More and more he began to see divinity in nature. In an entry in his journal dated June 15, 1831, he addresses his late wife, telling her that while walking near Lake Champlain, he found her, "dear Ellen, nowhere and everywhere." Going further in the same direction, he writes that he is gradually able to read "the divine alphabet" now in "mountains, sunshine, thunders, night, birds and flowers."

The course of this particular contemplation would continue until, just months before he was to give up his pulpit in Boston, Emerson began to see a kinship between human consciousness and nature. Writing in his journal again, he compares the development of his own thoughts to the natural process of crystallization. And in the same period, after observing his brother Charles's collection of shells, he comments, "I suppose an entire cabinet of shells would be an expression of the whole mind."

The force of the new ideas evolving within him must have been considerable. The step he finally decided to take would have momentous consequences in his life. For a long time he had felt the weight of meaningless rituals in his ministry, which he began to consider dishonest to administer. Now he acted. In June of 1832, he wrote a letter to the governing committee of Boston's Second Church informing them that he no longer wanted to administer the eucharist. "I think Jesus did not mean to institute a perpetual celebration," he told them. Away in the White Mountains of New Hampshire, where he hoped life might be "reconsidered . . . far from the slavery" of habitual modes, and where "the pinions of thought would be strong," he considered what he would say to his congregation. Soon afterward, he returned to Boston to deliver an eloquent sermon. "Freedom is the essence of Christianity," he argued. "Its institutions should be as flexible as the wants of men." Persuaded or not, the majority of his parishioners wanted to keep him as their minister, but after considering Emerson's position for over a month, the committee decided to dismiss him nevertheless.

As the burden of hypocrisy was lifted from his shoulders, I can imagine that he must have felt a certain release. Unchained from traditions he found empty, he would not even be compelled to argue against them any longer. And yet, it is nearly impossible to move beyond conventional wisdom without feeling some sense of isolation, not the quiet solitude he had chosen in the mountains but the loneliness of an exile, as doors are closed to circles that, viewed from the outside, may suddenly seem more inviting.

Did he think at all of Anne Hutchinson, the seventeenth-century midwife and unofficial Puritan minister, who argued that the word of God could come to anyone, directly, without the aid of a church or clergy? Because of her blasphemies, she was put on trial. I can imagine her ghost might have wandered the edges of Emerson's mind, late at night, when the boundaries between one time or place and another seem to blur. He would not have been comforted by her story. After she was banished from the colony, she and most of her family died in the wilderness.

September

The mayor of New Orleans and the governor of Louisiana ask the federal government for help again and again but nothing happens. Strange disconnect, as if the officials in the White House were living on a different planet.

Daylight would have quickly dispersed such morbid images, and by his own account, Emerson was not particularly afraid of death. Whatever retribution he faced was mild. Yet even without the severe resistance that society so often mounts to new ideas, the process by which a new way of thinking breaks through individual consciousness is protracted and, if at times exhilarating, difficult. It contains many smaller deaths. Blinding insights will be followed by doubt. Arguments arise that seem unanswered, and each objection will be ringed with silent attachments, old loyalties to friends and family, even familiar faces, certainly familiar ways and habits, phrases, voices so intimate you have confused them with your own. If you are to change your own mind, you will have to wrestle not only with authority but with imagined authority, a disguise assumed by the aspect of yourself that resists change. But along the way, as old structures of thought are dismantled, the foundation for a new perspective is being built.

During the long months while he compared the life he was used to living and the one he envisioned, Emerson held up a mirror to his own mind, recording the process of his thinking in his journal. Day by day, his thoughts were growing stronger and more clear. Soon after he delivered his fateful sermon, in a heady mix of democracy and theology, he wrote that Christianity is meant to engender a "critical conscience." A capacity for independent thought would be necessary if each worshipper were to become "the only and absolute judge of every particular form that the established religion presents." But beneath this developing clarity, a conflict raged within him. Though his arguments were forceful, for months after he resigned his ministry, the dramatic struggle within him continued so fiercely that he became bone-thin. Even as his mind expanded, his body grew increasingly weak.

In the process of creating new concepts, the mind must persuade the whole being, body and soul, to concur. And the body is often slow to reconcile change. Yet, as Emerson's body labored, released from habitual patterns, his thoughts too winnowed, shedding all that was inessential until they reached a fine clarity. A month after his dismissal, as if recording the core of his inner dialogue, he wrote words that seem, even now, to lay the foundation for a far more democratic form of worship:

Why must I obey Christ?
Because God sent him.
But how do I know God sent him?
Because your own heart teaches the same thing he taught.
Why then shall I not go to my own heart first?

Even while grief and loss shadowed him and doubt wore at his body, Emerson was preparing for his real work. "I walk firmly," he wrote, "toward a peace and freedom which I plainly see before me."

His inner departure would soon be accelerated. In December of 1832, on a brig called the *Jasper*, Emerson began a voyage across the Atlantic. He planned to begin his tour of Europe where European culture itself began by visiting ancient ruins in Italy. Then he would see Paris and afterward spend time with men he admired, Carlyle, Wordsworth, and the aging Coleridge in England and Scotland. By a strange paradox of travel, in which as your horizons are broadened, you discover yourself, it was to be on this journey that Emerson gained the last shards of courage and reflection he would need to fashion a new American philosophy.

At the Temple of Minerva, impressed by the site that had hosted twenty-five hundred years of worship, he asked if this did not prove the "ineradicableness of the religious principle" and marveled that practices "in these regions everywhere" combined pagan and Christian antiquity. Yet a ceremony in the Sistine Chapel where he witnessed the pope bless the palms, followed by a procession of cardinals in their red robes, seemed to him no more than "millinery and imbecility." Though he was not much impressed by the city of Paris either, he was dazzled by the Cabinet of Natural History in the Jardin des Plantes. Twenty-five years before Darwin would publish *On the Origin of Species,* Emerson described a kinship with other species: "I feel the centipede in me— cayman, carp, eagle, and fox. I am moved by strange sympathies."

The experience was pivotal for him; for a period he thought he might become a naturalist. But though he was drawn by science, the affinity he felt toward the natural world came to him in another way. Like his life-long friend Carlyle, he saw more in nature than the mechanical operations of matter. He knew that what he sensed in the natural world could be neither measured nor proved by the scientific method. But the limitations set by science could no more circumscribe his philosophy than church doctrine could dissuade him from his own perceptions. Claiming the validity of intuition as an essential path to knowledge, like his friends the Romantic poets Coleridge and Wordsworth, he found a mirror of his own soul in the clouds, fields, flowers, and streams he loved.

Emerson was not alone in his inclinations. By slow and subtle increments, since the period known as the Age of Reason, when Thomas Jefferson wrote the Declaration of Independence, the intellectual weather that colors consciousness had changed. The new mood favored not only intuition but a different epistemology altogether, another way of knowing that seemed to arise from a softer focus and the more sensual dimensions of human consciousness. Through this new angle of perception, even the image of freedom was transformed. In 1830, when Delacroix painted a scene from the battles that took place during that year in the streets of Paris over freedom of the press, he depicted an inner transformation too. At the heart of the canvas, Liberty leads the people, and this figure is a woman. Holding up the tricolor flag representing not only the French nation but the dream of democracy, she strides through a scene of violent conflict. There is no mistaking her sex. Her long silken gown, swept downward by her passionate efforts, has fallen below her breasts, their graceful roundness a moving contrast to the dead and injured who lie before her. Her beauty is neither salacious nor decorative but crafted to a different purpose. She is a goddess whose presence announces the deepest level of transformation. She not only leads a revolution but announces a revolution within the revolution. It is as if all the passionate and corporeal knowledge that had been repressed in the name of an eighteenth-century ideal of reason has returned in this body.

Yet though Emerson's travels had deepened his convictions, he found that none of the great men he met were focused on the subject he most cherished, "insight into religious truth." Now, on his return to America, he would craft a new American spirituality, called transcendentalism, a philosophy that reconfigured nature, expanded democracy, and in the process reshaped awareness itself. Over time, the science of ecology, the environmental movement, and the movements for conservation and the preservation of wild places, which would save the mountains where I camped as a child, were nurtured by this new philosophy. It would carry a respect for nature into public consciousness—a respect that would expand the concept of equal rights to include all life-forms. But something else in this new orientation, a shift far closer to the bone, was also occurring. As the circle of empathetic regard established by democracy enlarged, so too did perception itself.

I am thinking of the communion I felt as a child in the Sierra under trees or in fields of wildflowers. I told no one what I felt. In my small world, no one referred to mystical experience, even in the church I attended. The consumption of communion wafers, which had attracted me so much, in the end seemed disappointingly flat. And if there ever had been any mystical content to the Masonic rituals my grandparents performed, this too had vanished. All the symbolic movements they made seemed almost mechanical. I had not yet read Emerson, knew nothing of the ravishments of the oversoul, nor had I heard the story of how, as a young man, when John Muir discovered a cluster of rare orchids, called *Calypso borealis,* growing by the edge of an icy pond, deep in the outback of Ontario, he sat down and wept for joy, feeling that he "was in the presence of superior beings who loved me and beckoned me to come." Still, though I had not yet acquired a vocabulary for what I experienced, something had shifted in the climate of public opinion. I did not believe nor was I ever told that Satan lurked in the woods. Everyone in my family from the oldest to the youngest looked on the treasured mountains of California with a kind of reverence.

It is an angle of vision that has sustained me, returning me again and again to myself. Outside of summer camp, I remember one incident from my younger childhood with the particular clarity one reserves for turning points in a life. I was walking home, following the route I usually took, when suddenly, as I passed the empty lot I had seen so many times, I stopped to look at it. The lot, which was on a hill and was thick with trees and brush, had been empty for so long that it seemed like a small wilderness area. Now I was drawn by a tree that seemed to me as if it would be easy to climb. In the previous weeks, I had been climbing trees with the girl next door, who always seemed to be able to climb higher than I could. But this was a tree I knew I could scale. There were no trails through the lot. I had to persevere through fallen branches and rough weeds. But once I got to the tree, I climbed to one of the higher branches with ease. And that was when something happened to me that transformed me in an inward, invisible way. Realizing suddenly how alone I was, I felt a moment of fear, but this was soon replaced by my awareness of the silence. There were birdsongs and breezes, but no voices, and because this was not a trafficked street, not even the sound of cars. Then, I felt something enter my awareness of this silence that, even today, though I've felt it many times since, I cannot name except to say that I could feel with a sudden sharp intensity the presence of life all around me and that the undeniable force of this presence pierced a habitual barrier and suddenly made me aware of the deepest regions of my own soul. Knowing myself in this way, I was to become far stronger. High in a tree that I had climbed by myself, I found a new source of independence.

Imagining Emerson on the day that he turned his attention away from the preacher whose sermon bored him and began to gaze at the falling snow, I can see that while he entered a communion with the natural world that blazed far brighter than the rituals he had renounced, he was discovering new regions within himself. In a movement that has two directions, leading inward and outward at the same time, as Emerson shifts his attention, the respect he gives to the natural world and the respect he gives to his own soul are conjoined, inseparable as a tree and the soil around its roots.

Of course, a different man might have turned his head away just for a moment and then turned back, blaming himself for his failure to listen to the preacher. To gain the insight he received, Emerson had to be able to respect his own feeling of boredom, an accomplishment more difficult than on the surface it would seem. The weight of the congregation, tradition, his education, would have pressed him to pay more attention to the minister's words. And whenever, despite his best efforts, his attention did lapse, the same pressure would make him feel guilty, as if he were mistaken or even wicked to be bored. He might even feel that, through his innermost thoughts, he is in danger of becoming a pariah, lonely and isolated. But just as he turns his head, he will realize he is not alone. From the other side of the window, his feelings will be answered and met almost immediately. The snow, with its vibrant presence, emanating a brilliant spirituality, comes to his aid, fortifying his trust in his own perceptions.

Paradoxical as this may sound, it is easy to ignore your own perceptions. Whatever is unexpressed retires quickly to dark corners of the mind, often to be forgotten. But if you turn your attention inward and study what is inside, you will be able to remember what you perceived or felt and in this way restore the full scope of your being. In the same way that the observation of nature leads to conservation, reflection is essential to the preservation of the soul. But to know yourself presents a challenge when all around you, you find proscriptions against certain thoughts and models for how you ought to think or feel, even who you should be, an environment that tends to make you reject your own insights.

It was not just by the stricter rules they enforced but by countless other signs too that I knew my grandparents had been born to a world far different than mine. I hardly ever saw my grandmother naked. Though, for a period, when I was young enough to be considered innocent yet strong enough to help her into her corset, I helped her press the round folds of her belly and the long pendulums of breasts into this tight structure, which seemed to mold her in the same way that I had seen her mold cookie dough into stars and circles. Properly pinioned, her body would become hard where it had been soft, and reminded me of the photographs of unnamed ancestors my grandfather and I loved to study, in which the men and women sat up ramrod-straight, with no hint of a slouch nor of a smile nor any expression but the stern look you often see on soldiers in training when they are being inspected.

I do not know if in fact my grandparents were raised by the methods of Dr. Schreiber, the German pedagogue who derived his methods from Prussian military schools, but it seems to me that at the very least, the atmosphere in which they were raised bore the stamp of this influence. At the turn of the last century, his advice was still popular in both Europe and America. My grandmother constantly admonished me to sit up straight, though she never tied a strand of my hair to my waist, to remind me painfully of this advice, as Schreiber advised. Her methods, though strict, had all been tempered. I do not doubt that she was far more lenient with me than my great-grandparents had been with her. In any age, and within all of us, the attitudes and ideas of the present are mixed with those of prior ages—sometimes layered, as when an earlier era can be perceived just beneath the surface, sometimes side by side, expressed at times as odd inconsistencies and at other times as compromises, when, in the inner regions of consciousness, some agreement has been cobbled together between contemporary ways and whatever was followed in the past.

SEPTEMBER

Grief and anger over what is happening. As outside the Superdome stranded people of every age wait for buses that never appear, we watch it all on television. Right in front of our eyes, a baby and then an elderly woman die.

On my desk I have a copy of a photograph of Emerson that was taken in 1877, when he was seventy-four years old. Sitting next to his son Edward, he holds his infant grandson, Charles, on his lap and, placing his cheek against the crown of the boy's head, smiles at the camera. Delight has clearly captivated his face. He has given himself entirely to the pleasure. Though he is not slumped, he is not ramrod-straight either. He sits with his legs casually apart. And Emerson's son stretches his legs out too, as he watches his own son and his father with unconcealed bemusement. What we would say now about the photograph is that it seems *natural*.

Naturalness is less an art than a state of being. The word *natural* suggests that what seems natural in human beings is in fact a state of nature. But since, with the rare exception of children raised by wolves or dogs, human nature has always been shaped by society and culture, it is almost impossible to know what human behavior in a state of nature would actually be. What is usually meant by naturalness is behavior that is less restrained by convention and that seems more authentic. Being *natural,* your expressions seem to mirror what is actually felt more accurately. That those who behave in a manner unembellished by the desire to please or fit in often leave a powerful impression reflects the strong desire all of us must feel to achieve a harmony between inner and outer selves. As Emerson put it, "Only in our easy, simple, spontaneous action are we strong."

By the time I was a born, the American identity was stamped with casualness, a mode that gives the appearance if not the reality of authenticity. Very early my mind was filled with images from films and newsreels in which the strict postures of European soldiers formed a stark contrast to the looser manner of American GIs, waving in friendliness to everyone, offering candy and gum to kids, speaking with an unfettered directness. Despite the rigorous lessons my grandmother gave me from Emily Post about how to sit properly and which fork to use first, I was a child of American culture. I changed to blue jeans and tennis shoes as soon as I came home from school and went out to join my friends as we played on the sidewalk or danced in the sprinklers. When I spent time with my father, he and I would pick up a hot dog at a stand in the park, eating as we strolled. I listened closely to the intimate sounds of Frank Sinatra and Lena Horne; watched Elvis Presley gyrating his hips on *The Ed Sullivan Show;* learned to use a hula hoop and play baseball.

But darker aspects of the American character can be found underneath this easy surface. The obsession for revenge, for instance, that Emerson's friend Melville captured in his story of Captain Ahab and the white whale. On a subtler level, I am reminded of several of the snapshots I have from my childhood that were taken in front of my grandparents' house, where we posed next to one of the neatly pruned junipers that framed the entrance. Our postures seem more natural than those my ancestors assumed. But since the camera my grandparents owned was only brought out for holidays and birthdays, we were wearing our best clothes. And if, instead of the stern expressions assumed by our progenitors, we smiled, these smiles were often forced, at the request of my grandmother, the designated photographer, who was trying her best to make us resemble the new ideal of a happy family.

The truth, of course, was otherwise. Despite all her efforts at concealing the truth, among the photographs I have of our family, there is one my grandmother took in the year my parents divorced that shows my father simultaneously trying to smile and force back tears. And another photograph, a companion piece to the first, shows my mother as she glares angrily at the camera with the wild look she always had in her eyes when she drank too much. Yet despite my fear of her drunkenness, when she was sober, I was deeply drawn to something in my mother, a wild edge, a fire that one could detect even beneath the shyness she displayed with strangers.

Despite every kind of social limitation, the scope of the human mind remains immense. I am thinking now of Copernicus, how he gazed at the night sky until finally, by steady observation and careful calculation, he realized that the sun is the center of the solar system. Did he guess that by challenging the official picture of the heavens rendered by the church, his observations would lead to the downfall of kingdoms and the rise of democracy? By a circuitous but certain path, his vision of the farthest reaches of the universe would also lead to the transformation of inner worlds. But the motion did not end there either. The oscillation in human consciousness that moves from the center of the soul to the far edges of the known universe does not stop anywhere but travels outward and inward continuously, forming one field of perception. And at the heart of this process, what Emerson called "the circle of the eye," there is a quiet but constant reciprocity; the great mystery in the geography of perception is that the way you see the world will either enlarge or limit the scope of your own being.

The idea that a mirror of the human soul can be found in nature fascinated Emerson. The reflection could be interpreted as a postulate of the theory that the senses are deceptive and that what we call reality cannot be proved to exist at all. But it was neither solipsism nor narcissism that drew Emerson. He rejected the arguments of philosophers such as Hume who asserted that truth can never be known. What he means by the circle of the eye belongs to a different impulse entirely. He does not shrink with distrust from his experience of nature but instead leans into it, giving himself to and finding himself in the world.

A host of thinkers and artists within his generation was leaning in the same direction. At the moment when Emerson took his lightning leap, as he let the brilliance of the snow illuminate his own soul, he must have felt this invisible presence hovering in the atmosphere. After he left the pulpit, taking the right to spiritual knowledge with him, distributing this authority freely and equally to every man and woman alike, he was soon to become the leader of a movement that embraced his insights. But he was also being moved. The almost palpable force of a new vision could be felt throughout the nation. Walt Whitman sensed the mood early on. He had already been "simmering, simmering, simmering," he said, before Emerson brought him "to a boil." You can hear a powerful alchemy in the music of his words: "My tongue, every atom of my blood, form'd from this soil, this air . . ." The American speech he uses—plain, direct— seems to charge language with a wild energy, full of hope, as if the voice of democracy itself were speaking. Not many miles away, with a different, more crisp and idiosyncratic American cadence, Emily Dickinson also reports the collaboration she sees between nature and her own soul: "The breaking of the day / Addeth to my Degree." In the same period, adding to the growing onslaught of wonder and change, paintings of wild lands to the west and north, of glassy lakes, formidable waterfalls, and high mountain peaks, arrive to dazzle the eyes with a fusion of natural beauty and the human regard.

And there would be this too, looming as large and majestic as any range of mountains: the whole social body. The processes of democracy widen "the circle of the eye," making us all more keenly aware of other lives. It was not just ideas but events, circumstances, the suffering and courage of others, that shaped and sustained Emerson's revolutionary philosophy. A powerful coalition of concerns inhabited the time and place in human history where he stood, at a crossroad, wondering what to do with the rest of his life.

Did his imagination take him a few hundred miles to the south, a journey of less than three days by coach, where, for instance, one might find a seven-year-old child who has been ordered to stand on her feet all day and for several hours at night, as she does day after day, in case she might be needed for some errand? She has been separated from her mother, sold off along with bales of cotton and one or two farm animals. She still cries at night for her mother, but she does not complain. Even earlier in her young life, she learned a terrible lesson in submission when her older brother was beaten for talking back, struck with a metal rod, lashed sixty times, and then, while the blood still flowed from his wounds, left to crawl back to his flimsy cabin and to lie alone without bedding on a dirt floor for days, their mother forbidden to tend to him, though finally she did sneak in late at night to give him food and wash his wounds, so that her son might survive.

In the volatile chemistry of democratic consciousness, a respect for nature is often allied with a passion for social justice. Emerson had been an abolitionist for years. And his second wife, Lydian, a passionate advocate for emancipation, would have kept him informed. Nevertheless, for years the issue of slavery remained in the background of his thoughts, well beyond his immediate focus. Where the mind goes depends on another kind of geography. There are borders within ourselves we do not cross, confining ideas we have acquired and never questioned. Along with many others who favored abolition, Emerson told himself that those of African descent were inferior. It would take an encounter with an African-American man to free him from this limiting view. The change came less through argument than through example. When Emerson heard Frederick Douglass speak, he was dazzled by his brilliant eloquence; in the presence of a man who shared his own agility of mind, his old prejudice was burned away.

Now he would be fully engaged. No longer marginalized by hazy notions of inferiority, the issue of slavery began to occupy a central position in his mind. Drawn to the subject, he began to read a number of books, including a volume about the slave trade that contained a large foldout diagram of a typical slave ship, dozens of figures, inked in the shapes of bodies, laid out one right next to the other, cheek by jowl, in equally close rows. This was how thousands of men, women, and children had been carried to America, shackled together for weeks in an airless hold.

When any group is diminished in the public imagination, their histories, including the history of their diminishment, will be forgotten, untold, and left, in the wake, unconsidered. I was thirty years old before I first encountered a diagram of a slave ship. The imagery is terrifying. Like the memory of Half Dome, it left a permanent mark in my mind; to include the unspeakable cruelty I witnessed, I had to change the dimensions of all that I had learned about American history. In the classrooms I attended, from grade school through graduate studies, I had never seen this image. I had been active in the civil rights movement before I could even vote myself, but still, I had not seen this diagram before I was raising a child of my own. The story of the middle passage was part of neither the national discourse nor our common memory.

Finally Emerson had come to feel the urgency over abolition that impassioned so many of those around him, not only his wife, Lydian, but Henry David Thoreau and his mother and sisters Helen and Sophia Thoreau—all fervent abolitionists—and his new friend, the feminist and abolitionist Lucretia Mott. On August 1, 1844, he made a speech in Concord calling for emancipation. His condemnation of slavery was fierce. Compelled now by a new and clarifying fury, he could see that the institution was diminishing America's brightest hopes. It was not only religion, but democracy too, that was becoming *corpse cold*. Accordingly he came to believe that the victims of slavery held a key to the future: "The black man carries in his bosom an indispensable element of a new and coming civilization," he declared.

More often than not, whenever you restore what has been excluded or repressed from your mind, you will also rekindle the vitality of your thought. The same principle holds true in the process of democracy. To exclude anyone from this process will have a deadening effect, though the consequences are often concealed. The pattern is as common to human psychology as greed or deceit. In the public mind after the embers of a real passion have died, grief and in fact any awareness of that loss will be avoided when the living phenomenon is replaced with empty symbols, repeating the word *freedom* or waving the flag, for example, while forgetting the real meanings of either. To keep the spirit of democracy alive requires a continual revolution. "You must," Emerson suggested in the speech he gave in 1854 against the Fugitive Slave Law, "be . . . yourselves Declarations of Independence."

Though no one knows for certain how many factors allowed Emerson to cross the borders in his own mind that had prevented him from feeling the terrible realities of slavery, the speech he gave at Concord reveals part of the process. At night in the dark, he reminded his audience, you cannot tell the difference between black and white. *We are all the same,* he said. The perception of equality would have acted as a quickening catalyst in his mind. In no way an inert ingredient, this is perhaps the most important element in the alchemy of democracy. When you sense equality between yourself and another, a level field of consciousness is created, the ground on which you can imagine that whatever someone else has suffered might happen to you too. The shadow of the other's suffering will fall over all your thoughts.

And there is this also adding to the mix: in Emerson's reference to the comprehension of equality, he sets the moment of insight in the night, a time when we are all returned simultaneously to the knowledge of the body and to dreams. Was what he recorded in his journal on February 7, 1843, a foreshadow of his new insight? "Earth spirit, living, a black river like that swarthy stream is thy nature," he wrote, "demoniacal, warm, fruitful, sad, nocturnal."

Perhaps this is among the many reasons why protesting the injustice that others endure can liberate the soul from a different kind of prison. The inclination toward equality that all of us have is discouraged when, as children, we are taught to limit the boundaries of the imagination according to systems of thought that divide society along lines of dominion. So a child born to a title would learn that some of the friends he has loved are considered inferior and that as an aristocrat he is superior to commoners. In this light, as Emerson's outrage intensified, he would have been freed from a cloudy set of deceptive lessons, which no doubt, in subtle but effective ways, had been dividing his own soul. Thus, through his reawakened compassion, he would have reclaimed part of himself.

I suspect that Lydian Emerson well understood how deeply the life of the soul is connected with the lives of others. As her daughter would later describe, she studied the horrors of slavery so closely that it seemed she witnessed daily, "the selling away of little children from their mothers." She made her inner mood manifest when, on July 4, 1850, she protested the continuing institution of slavery by draping the front gate and gateposts of the Emerson home with yards of black cloth. So, when the people of Concord marched along the famous route Paul Revere had taken less than a century before, as they passed by the Emersons' house, they would be moved from a celebration of the birth of democracy to grief over its demise.

Emerson gave many speeches against abolition. The round of appearances fatigued him. Yet though he was eager to return to his own work, he knew his work was tied to the events taking place around him. "It is not possible to extricate oneself from the question in which your age is involved." Is this because, in the deepest region of human consciousness, the soul is inseparable from other lives?

The controversies that surrounded Emerson in nineteenth-century America are threaded throughout his work. Though transcendentalism shared many concepts with the Sanskrit and Buddhist texts and the German idealists he read throughout his life, he created a uniquely American philosophy from the circumstances and conditions to which he was alive and present. Along with the abolition of slavery, Emerson was also sympathetic to the struggle for women's rights, which he learned about from his friends Margaret Fuller and Lucretia Mott. It was, after all, what he had observed firsthand when, since his father's early death, his mother managed to feed her children and give every one of them an education. All his life he knew and valued women who loved to read and think and challenged his own thinking. The pattern began with his aunt Mary Moody Emerson, a major influence. It was from this eccentric, outspoken, and self-educated woman that Emerson first learned of Goethe and Herder, Locke, Plato, Marcus Aurelius, Mary Wollstonecraft, and Rousseau. Occasionally in his essays, instead of using *he* to stand for all humanity, he even writes "he or she" or simply "she."

Democracy has often evolved through men and women who straddled divided worlds, including Thomas Jefferson, descended from wealthy planters on one side and hardscrabble farmers on the other. In this regard it does not seem irrelevant to me now that as a young man within his family, Emerson seems so androgynous. Among his brothers—two who died young, one who was born mentally disabled, two others who suffered breakdowns—he was clearly the caretaker, a role he played with the kindness and solicitude often showed by women. That those who contribute to democratic consciousness would transgress the boundaries of prejudice and assumption is consistent with the deep desire for free speech and thought, not just as tools in the eternal battles for political power that occur in every era but from an even more fundamental democratic impulse, the desire to enlarge consciousness.

And there would have been this too: hovering at the edge of Emerson's awareness, perhaps as a boy while he made his way through the streets of Boston, and certainly when he entered the pulpit where Cotton Mather once preached, as he looked out his window or walked in the woods of Concord, another voice, inaudible and strange yet oddly intoxicating, would have haunted him. If once the surrounding land had been home to thousands of Indians, by the time Emerson was born, the Mohegan, Mahican, Nauset, Pennacook, Pocasset, Pocumtuc, and Massachusett tribes had been decimated, their numbers reduced to a fraction, less than one out of every hundred, by disease and the attrition of constant warfare with European settlers and shrinking territory; their languages forbidden, rapidly being forgotten.

Yet still Native Americans played a vivid role in the white imagination. It seems as if almost every turn of American history has had another history standing beside it. The men who threw containers of tea overboard in the Boston Tea Party dressed as Indians, the influence of the Iroquois Confederacy on the Constitution, even the name of the state where Emerson lived all his life, Massachusetts, had been taken from the first people that flourished there.

A century later, growing up in California, I felt the influence of Native American cultures on my life. Though, in the middle of the twentieth century, the illusion persisted that the Indian tribes that had once lived in the state had all perished, as a small child, I believed that just over the hill, a bit farther than I could walk, lived people who wore feathers and carried bows and arrows. I had a vague picture of tepees arranged around a clearing. Though this was a romantic vision, part of an American mythology I inherited, it reached deep into my psyche, calling up a region of other possibilities in my mind.

In the summer after my parents divorced, I acquired two objects that were talismans of a mysteriously powerful desire within me. I could not name what was emerging in my imagination, but I knew I treasured the piece of petrified wood my grandparents purchased at a roadside stand near the Colorado border as we traveled east. I pondered the fact that I was holding in my hand something so old, older than me or anyone I knew, older even than any human history I had encountered. As I tried to understand how wood could turn into stone, my mind seemed to open to the existence of vast forces, moving and changing all around me.

But the object I loved with an even greater intensity was the belt that, as we made our way back to Los Angeles, my grandparents bought for me from a roadside stand near Las Vegas, along the border between California and Nevada. Covered with turquoise, white, and red beads, it was made by Indians, and this gave it an inestimable value for me.

Like many children my age, I was eager to learn whatever I could about the people who had lived all over America long before European settlers arrived. Is it possible that a kind of ghost dance continues among the descendants of the settlers who pushed Indians from their land? It was as if a part of my own soul were trapped in the cultures my ancestors had tried to erase. I was hungry for any source of knowledge. That was why, each week when my grandfather opened a new box of Shredded Wheat, I would stand nearby waiting to be given the card that came inside the box, where some account was printed describing a different aspect of the Indian way of life. I was thrilled when the card was not a replica of one I already had but instead told me something new about how tepees are made or what a peace pipe is. In my daydreams I identified with the Indian boy the cards pictured as he went about his day. I tried to emulate everything about him, especially the way he walked through a forest without making a sound. To accomplish this feat became my greatest ambition, and for this reason I begged my grandparents for a pair of moccasins.

This was another lure of the summer camp in the Sierra where I would spend my summers as a child, along with my sister, who eventually was to become a counselor there. I could practice my quiet steps over rocks and pine needles and twigs. My efforts were in harmony with the general atmosphere of the camp. Around the campfire or through the activities I joined, I learned fragments of Native American culture: songs, stories, how to paddle a canoe, to carve wood, lash branches together, and build a campfire. It was only recently that I heard, from one of his great-nephews, about the influence of Ernest Thompson Seton, the man who was responsible, near the beginning of the twentieth century, for introducing Indian culture into the practices of the Boy Scouts and in time the Girl Scouts of America. He himself had discovered the beneficial effects of Indian cultures when, as an experiment, he began to teach Native American practices to a group of wayward boys who vandalized his community. After they had broken into his home, he decided to teach them the Indian tales and crafts he had studied and written about: how to build a willow bark structure or a tepee, how to make a drum or a shield, to make a pair of moccasins or decorate a canoe, and the philosophies inherent within all these crafts. When he saw that the boys were tamed by this culture that had been called "savage," he introduced the same teaching to American scouting. There was some tension with the scoutmaster in Britain, Lord Baden-Powell, and his followers in America, who favored a more military model. Writing now, it seems to me that in this, a small but significant battle over democracy was being waged. The story goes that once a friend who had been observing Seton as he taught a group of children how to start a fire with a pair of sticks asked him why he made them struggle over such a primitive method. Seton is said to have answered by placing his hand over the fire and saying, "You are thinking of the fire that is lit here," and then placing his hand over his chest, "while I am thinking of the fire that is kindled here in the heart."

The proverb promising that the sins of the fathers will be visited on the next generation has many levels of meaning. Justice has a secret life among children. An injustice committed by her parents or grandparents can lodge in a child's mind, even if the child knows nothing of the events and all that she feels is a kind of emptiness somewhere in her soul, coupled, at times, with an unexplained longing.

I cannot help but wonder now if, even unconsciously, through things he saw and incidents he witnessed, stories he heard, Native American philosophies must have migrated, even in small ways, into Emerson's thoughts. Just as he came to believe that snow, trees, rocks, are all manifestations of spirit, the Indian peoples who still live in Massachusetts believe that the Creator made people out of the earth and trees. When Emerson wrote his essay entitled "Circles" claiming the circle to be a primary form of consciousness and existence alike, did he know that the circle, including the cycles of life and the seasons, is fundamental to the cosmologies of the Native peoples of Massachusetts? Even Emerson's rejection of what he considered dry scripture in favor of the living lessons of life all around him shares an attitude with a well-known parable ascribed to an anonymous Indian woman. "If you leave *your* Bible outside, it will dry out and disintegrate and one day be carried away by the wind," she said, "but our scripture *is* the wind."

And there is this too: early in his career, just before he decided to break with formal Christianity, Emerson would be profoundly moved by an encounter with a powerful Native American speaker. In 1832 he went to hear the Cherokee leader known as Major Ridge lecture an audience in Boston about the plight of Cherokee who were being threatened by a policy bluntly named "Indian removal." Even before it was formally instituted as a policy of the United States government, the practice had been conducted for well over two hundred years, since the first European settlers came to America. The extensive land the Cherokee lived on—once nearly forty thousand square miles, in what would eventually be called Kentucky, Tennessee, Alabama, Georgia, Virginia and West Virginia, and North and South Carolina—had diminished to one-tenth of the original size, due to campaigns of aggression, pressure, and assault. The conflicts were resolved many times by twenty-eight different treaties, each of which was eventually broken. Now, as more and more white families in Georgia sought to own their own farms, the scattered lands the Cherokee occupied in Georgia, Alabama, Tennessee, and North Carolina were being contested again.

The term *Indian removal* makes no attempt at obfuscation. Yet the strangely exaggerated sense of entitlement the term expresses points to a source that perhaps even today remains unexamined. One catches a glimmer of an older meaning in arguments the state of Georgia put forward in a series of court cases brought by the Cherokee Nation. The state of Georgia argued that it had the right to seize Indian land because European settlers had discovered America. Though the Supreme Court rejected this line of reasoning, if the thread of the argument is followed, it leads to a series of British flags planted in American soil and, through those flags, to a line of British monarchs, and the divine right of these kings to rule.

The evolution of American democracy is not simple. The direction of the motion is not always forward. Like every process of transformation, there are many moments of retreat, contradiction, murky layers of ambivalence, and even frank resistance to change, all this accompanied by the temptations of ambition and power.

I am thinking now of Thomas Jefferson, who was so moved when he witnessed the Cherokee leader Ostenaco speaking to his people. He never forgot a quality he sensed in this man, something he could not entirely explain to himself. He did not believe that Native Americans were inferior. Yet he shared certain assumptions with his age, prejudices most probably made all the more inflexible since in a time of change they provided the illusion of stability.

Jefferson based his idea of the perfect American citizen on an image from the European Enlightenment: an educated man who, if not white, resembled a white man in every way except skin color, and who held property. If Native Americans were to be given equal rights, he argued, they would have to become what he called "civilized," by which he meant they must model their behavior after the manners of prosperous white men, learn to read and write English, and acquire private land.

This reasoning fit well into Jefferson's vision of an agrarian democracy, a dream that, like so many utopian ideas, arose as an answer to a grim reality. Despite the French Revolution and the expansion of democratic rights in England, as the eighteenth century ended and the nineteenth century began, throughout Europe the collapse of peasant economies and the rise of modern industry had created a vast urban population of poor, sporadically employed wage laborers who, despite long hours of work, often went hungry and homeless. The pitiless cities that Charles Dickens would portray in his novels had already come to exist.

But even in the New World, land was not limitless. So in an effort to bend circumstance to his vision, when a dearth of land began to make an agrarian democracy seem impossible, Jefferson aimed his sights at land ceded to Native Americans. If Indians, he argued in a letter to Congress, were growing "more and more uneasy at the constant diminution of the territory they occupy," then the government ought to encourage them to abandon hunting and instead "to apply [themselves] to the raising [of] stock, to agriculture and domestic manufacture, and thereby prove to themselves that less land and labor will maintain them." The advantage of this, he went on to argue, was that then they might be induced more easily to trade their forests "for the means of improving their farms, and of increasing their domestic comforts."

Bold as he was at expressing his motives clearly, he added another more altruistic consideration: "I trust and believe we are acting for their greatest good." If reason can help the mind move in the direction of justice, it can also be used to make almost any action appear to be just.

Can it be that history, as much as a climate or a body of water, aims toward balance through actions that move in opposite directions? Jefferson sent this letter to Congress in January of 1803. Emerson, who would

one day speak out passionately against Indian removal, was born five
months later, and just three weeks before Jefferson would negotiate the
Louisiana Purchase, acquiring the rights to more than eight hundred
thousand square miles of land west of the Mississippi. As if regarding the
question of possession, the long presence of hundreds of Indian nations
in this vast region had little relevance; he bought the land for fifteen million dollars from France.

Still, like a song whose melody repeats itself again and again in memory,
the relevance persisted. So at the same time that American soldiers were
forcing Indians off the lands they had occupied for countless generations, another idealization, a projection perhaps of all that had been left
out of the eighteenth-century idea of what it is to be human, claimed the
white imagination, forming a strange twin within the shared soul of the
nation. Whether in Longfellow's *Hiawatha,* or the novels of James Feni-
more Cooper, Whitman's rolling invocations, or through crude cigar
store statues, or later during my childhood as the Lone Ranger's silent
partner on TV, the personification of a wilder side of being, feathered or
dressed in buckskin, at home in the forest and closer to a state of nature,
endured, forming a stark counterpoint to the choked and constrained
propriety of those who claimed to be closer to perfection.

Born five years before Jefferson wrote the Declaration of Independence, the Cherokee leader who Emerson heard address an audience in
Boston, the man called Major Ridge, or Kah nung da tla geh ("He Who
Walks on the Mountaintop"), was just over sixty years old in 1832, an elegant, powerful man with thick long white hair, burning eyes, and a riv-
eting style of speech. It was this style, filled with vivid stories from his
own life, what Whitman called "the concrete and its heroisms," driven by
the cadence of feeling and shaped by a philosophy consonant with the
land and the community in which he was raised, that would inspire
Emerson to find fault with his own sermons. From the way that new
manners of speaking, with a different music, have entered and shaped
my own thoughts, I can imagine the moment. Emerson hears the words
Ridge speaks clearly, and though he takes in the meaning, and he agrees
with what Ridge is telling his audience, he has not heard anything new.
Yet he senses something beyond his usual understanding that brings him
to listen in a different way: he is captivated by a force that does not depend on words alone; his mind has responded to the music of this vivid

speech with a startling resonance. He is on the verge of discovering a new voice within himself.

For even the simplest of decisions, there is usually more than one cause. Wavering between one course of action and another, the soul can be swayed in an instant by very subtle influences. Was it then entirely a coincidence that just a few months after hearing Ridge speak, Emerson gave up his pulpit at Boston's Second Church? The forfeiture would open the way for his real work, a long life of writing and lecturing during which he explored a new way of seeing, shaped by the sense that all life is connected, that every existence expresses a larger meaning, and that spirit lives in rocks and rivers as well as the human soul.

But Major Ridge would suffer a different fate. In the beginning, his life seemed full of promise. Born near the Hiwassee River at Savannah Ford, an area that belongs to Tennessee now, his birth seems to augur his character. During her labor, his mother, who was bothered by smoke from the fire inside, asked to be carried outside, a practice common among Cherokee women, who preferred to be under the trees and the sky as they gave birth. Nevertheless, because the shaman who was present saw signs of a malevolent force nearby, at his command she was carried back inside.

When, as soon as the boy was born, the midwives placed him at his mother's breast, the shaman pulled him away, warning that the child must drink nothing but the tea he had brewed for seven days, an infusion that would keep him safe from the curses of witches. The shaman said the boy would become a valiant warrior, with extraordinary powers to see what is invisible to others, by changing his shape, and flying like a raven to a higher vantage point. His mother was glad. It was all that she hoped for her son. But she had other concerns. Afraid that her milk might dry up, she waited for the shaman to fall asleep before, ignoring his prohibition, she asked the midwives to bring her the boy so that she could feed him.

Over time Ridge would fulfill the shaman's prophecy. Like a raven flying through the sky or a man standing on top of a mountain, he could see what others around him could not. But like his mother too, he was not afraid to defy authority. As with Emerson, the courage to depart from accepted opinion, together with an ability to see the larger picture, would one day make him a leader. At the age of seventeen, he became a warrior, joining the continuing battles between settlers and the Cherokee over the boundaries set by the Hopewell Treaty, signed in 1785, the first agreement between the Cherokee and the new government of the United States. As the war dragged on year after year, he witnessed many atrocities committed by both sides. In one battle led by the warrior Chief Doublehead, he was horrified to see warriors from another tribe of Cherokee murder two children. Ridge began to wish for an end to war. Many of his fellow warriors shared the same desire. His tribe had been decimated, and he was weary of constant battle. Finally he told his future bride, Susanna, "I will hunt deer, not men."

But even that was not to be. As fate would have it, the area in Georgia called Pine Lodge, where Ridge moved after marrying, had been chosen by the United States government for the introduction of new technology: farm tools, spinning wheels, and cotton combs. It was part of an official policy, begun by Washington and continued by Jefferson, to disseminate the white way of life to Native Americans, in an effort the government called "civilizing," as if only one civilization existed.

One day, after hunting for half the year, Ridge returned home to find that his wife had earned more through weaving cloth than all the pelts he had collected could ever bring. Soon he began to take up farming instead of hunting, using the same methods that his neighbors, some former warriors, and some white settlers, used to great profit.

In this way, his life was being cast into a larger motion made by two cultures, side by side, in conflict but also exchanging ideas, sharing and competing over land, and all the while, leaning toward a future neither could have predicted or imagined. Through one of those strange confluences by which history turns, now Ridge would enter a conflict with Doublehead again, but this time for a very different reason. Doublehead had been double-dealing, cheating his own people by making shady deals in which he accepted bribes from corrupt government agents for parcels of land once held in common by the whole tribe.

This was why, in 1807, Ridge along with two other warriors, assaulted Doublehead one night and murdered him for his crimes. But this act of violence did not solve the problem. Cherokee land was slowly being lost by means of many similar betrayals.

The corruption of the Indian agents proceeded almost naturally from the underside of official policy. It was just one of many shadow strategies played out to feed the ravenous hunger for land that was rapidly developing in this period with no end in sight. By the 1830s the ploy, no longer concealed, became the subject of a popular song whose lyrics declared unashamedly,

> All I ask in this creation
> Is a pretty little wife and
> a big plantation
> Way up yonder in the Cherokee nation.

As with many other tragedies throughout history, it has sometimes been said that the eventual displacement of the Cherokee from their ancestral lands was inevitable. But such judgments are tautological. They reason simply that events occurred in the past because that is the way they happened. It is an argument favored by conquerors, asserted not just as an interpretation of the past but as prophecy. Yet neither interpretations of history nor prophecies of what is to come are impervious to error. In the last century, both Hitler and Stalin boasted that all their victories were inevitable and that accordingly their power would be sustained over generations.

The belief in inevitability serves an inward purpose too. It shields the soul from painful awareness, shame, and even grief. By erasing the possibility of choice, this idea protects the mind from the full weight of whatever injustice has been committed in the name of the future. Yet, in the early nineteenth century, the history of the forced removal of the Cherokee from east of the Mississippi had not yet been written; if one outcome was in the making, others could still be imagined. Unlike the past, the present is always fluid. Even prescience and calculation are simply ingredients in the continual alchemy of change.

Reading various accounts of his life, I am struck by the subtle calibrations Ridge would have needed to navigate the treacherous waters of his time. Along with the Choctaw, Creek, Shawnee, and Seminole, the Cherokee wavered again and again between war and peace with the white settlers around them. Many feared that the trend toward giving up traditional ways for the ways of white people would destroy Indian cultures. Yet there were many others who found these ways attractive. Though the demand from white society that they assimilate must have had some influence, I can also imagine something else. The draw of the exotic is powerful. Ideas and customs that lie outside the boundaries of your culture often seem to hold a mysterious energy, promising life to a part of yourself that perhaps has long been hidden and repressed.

Certainly an attraction existed in the other direction. When he was a boy, the explorer Daniel Boone learned how to hunt with a spear from the friendly Indians in Pennsylvania and on the frontier where he grew up. Like Boone, Davy Crockett often dressed more like an Indian than a white man, in buckskin with a fur hat. And though he was famous as an Indian fighter, after he was elected to Congress, he fought against the policy of Indian removal with a fierce passion.

Though Ridge was drawn to many aspects of white society, still for decades he led a forceful resistance to removal. During the autumn council of 1807, at a pivotal moment not only in his own life but in the life of his people, Ridge spoke out against the transportation of Cherokee to the West. Four powerful chiefs had made a proposal to ask President Jefferson "to remove our people toward the setting sun." All of the men had been swayed to favor the idea by a series of bribes from the U.S. Indian agent Colonel Meigs, one of the men who had once bribed Chief Doublehead. It was the alternative supported by many settlers, especially in Georgia, who did not know the Cherokee very well and feared their presence.

Until Ridge stood to speak, Meigs must have believed he had won a victory. Even in his thirties, Ridge was an impressive man, broad-chested, with a deep voice and a reputation for being above corruption. In a chain of reasoning that resembles the Declaration of Independence, Ridge began by objecting that he had not been consulted about this move. "What are your heads placed on your body for but to think," he said, "and if to think, why should you not be consulted?" Expressing his opposition to exile with an eloquent mix of poetry and reason, he continued, "Look abroad over the face of this country—along the rivers, the creeks and their branches, and you will behold the dwelling of people who repose in contentment and security. Why is this grand scheme projected to lead away to another country the people who are happy here?" Moved by his words, the council declared broken the four chiefs who had put forward the proposal; they were all banished from power. Ridge had prevailed.

Even visionaries cannot always see every consequence of their actions. This victory would change Ridge's life in many ways, influencing the turns he would take far into the future. But one of the effects was immediate. The council had already decided that, in response to requests from the U.S. government, they would institute a more formal democracy and that they would send a delegation to Washington, D.C., to further this process. Thus they chose a new group to make this journey, appointing Ridge as one of six men assigned to meet at the beginning of the next year with the president of the United States, who was, in that year, Thomas Jefferson.

The meeting took place in the last year of Jefferson's second term. The preceding four years had not gone as well as expected. Though his first term ended exultantly with the Louisiana Purchase and the second had begun auspiciously enough with the triumphant return of Lewis and Clark, the agenda he had devised so carefully conjured circumstances he had not predicted. Though war with France had been averted, now there was a threat of war with Britain. And the new territories, so exciting to behold on paper, with the promise of an endless supply of land, presenting the possibility that every citizen might become a landholder, revealed another side now, a reality full of imperfections. The astonishing array of specimens Lewis and Clark had brought back from their expedition—colorful plumage, the remains of various animals, more than 134 vascular plants, a wide range of minerals, artifacts from Indian cultures, including buffalo skins, baskets, bows and arrows—spoke of an unimaginably rich diversity. But this was part of the problem. How could Jefferson wrap his mind around all this, and if he could not comprehend it all with any precision, how would this vast area ever be governed? The son of a surveyor, more than a decade ago, he had authored a bill that mandated the mapping of all the land in the United States east of the Mississippi. Slowly, by careful measurement and geometry, he had divided the new American land into neat squares, each six by six miles, townships whose straight lines wavered only at the banks of the rivers that snaked through the land. But now there were more than eight hundred thousand square miles to consider, much of them unexplored, with uncooperative Indian tribes blocking the way, unfathomable canyons, jagged mountains, bodies of water unheard of, unseen, towering glaciers, and hardly any towns or roads, trading posts, no means of sending a letter, few farms, and beyond the most rudimentary markings, all of it unmapped.

Although Jefferson had been careful in his first term to limit the power of the federal government, since west of the Mississippi there were no states, the federal government was the only possible authority. And could this even be called a democracy in any case, when the seat of governance in these territories consisted of a series of forts, the courts military, the law martial, the men who made and enforced local policies soldiers?

It is easy to imagine, then, that at this moment, when he was weary from eight years of serving as president, a visit from Cherokee leaders would have been a welcome break. Jefferson greeted Ridge and the other five men warmly, telling them that he knew that his own home, Monticello, had been built on former Cherokee land. Did he remember as he spoke with them his early experience, as a child at Shadwell, that silent scene he witnessed, a group of Indians saying a sad good-bye to their ancestral lands? But on this day he had a happier task. The thought that the Cherokee were going to use the United States Constitution as a model for the formalization of their own democracy pleased him. This too was part of his vision: to bring the Indians he admired into the fold. Perhaps this meeting fortified his faith in the bright future for the New World that he had envisioned as a young man.

I wonder now if Jefferson recognized a kindred soul in the Cherokee man with the deep voice who came to meet with him. Ridge was a visionary too, a man who could see into the future, and he was willing to risk change. Looking back on this history, it would be easy at this particular moment to judge him, as if he had been too quick to learn from the white settlers. But no culture remains the same, even over a decade. Native American peoples influenced one another, inspired by the different stories, hunting skills, ways of living, they encountered among strangers. And as the shaman who attended his birth said, Ridge was a shape-changer. He could assume the body of a raven, it was said, and study the terrain that no one else could see yet.

The ability to take another shape, or enter a body and soul that are not your own, is one way to achieve a view with a larger circumference, to gain understanding outside the limitations of your own being. It is a slower way of seeing, one that threatens the neat lines we draw between ourselves and others, especially those who seem different. Yet the process is essential to democracy; in the region of the imagination, it is born from the logic of equal rights.

This moment of cordiality seems suspended in time, now hovering among many possible outcomes. Though the Cherokee had already practiced democracy through councils and consensus for generations, the delegates sought to learn more about the way democracy was instituted in the federal government. All six of his visitors were impressed by Jefferson. The president was polite and respectful. He presented his wishes as suggestions rather than commands. And the manner of the Cherokee was polite too, thanking the president for help they had been given with farming and weaving and schools that tutored their children "in the facts of English education."

Indeed, Ridge had already decided to send his children, Nancy and John, to a school run by a sect of Christian missionaries, known as Moravians, at Spring Place, not far from where they lived. Perhaps this was why, on his way to Washington, D.C., Ridge had visited another Moravian settlement in Salem, North Carolina. Like a traveler to a foreign land full of surprising customs and objects, unheard of at home, he marveled at what he saw. The community was full of activity, men and women making pottery or furniture, weaving cloth, curing tobacco. But what he liked best was the music. Played from notes transcribed on paper long ago in Germany, he found this music more complex and at the same time more beautiful than any he had known before.

Still, not all the Cherokee felt drawn to white culture. The disagreement extended into Ridge's household. When in November of 1810 he finally sent his son John to live at the Moravian school in Spring Place, his wife, Susanna, was angry. She felt her husband had forced the decision on her because he wanted his son to get a white education. But this was not her priority. The boy was only seven years old, in fragile health, and she missed him.

Had Ridge known all the ways that the Moravians would soon begin discouraging Cherokee culture, he too might have been less eager to send his son to this school. It began with the stiff and starched clothing John was required to wear. The boy was used to far fewer clothes, but the Moravians found nakedness sinful. Then the ball game the Cherokee loved to play, the sport that inspired lacrosse, was prohibited. The Moravians found it too brutal. Soon after, the Indian children were discouraged from dancing too. And this must have been hard. The stomp dance, the booger dance, were ancient forms filled with the voices of ancestors; the rhythms of these dances brought the dancers into harmony with all existence, guiding them into the tempo of the spiritual world, a world they considered part of nature. Did the Moravians sense that another cosmology was unfolding itself through these hypnotically repetitive movements? This dancing, they said, was sinful too. And they frowned on hunting as well, a judgment that proceeded from their idea of what it meant to be civil and civilized, as if to tame the land by farming would also tame the soul.

Savagery. Like a vine that winds around itself to form a knot, the concept is strangely convoluted. Even in the dictionary, the meaning is subtly tautological. The quality of being savage is defined as uncivilized, which in turn means barbarian, a term that in its earliest usage referred to those who were not part of the Roman Empire. It is as much a boundary as it is a thought, a line drawn around certain places that are defined as civilized and, by extension, the way of life practiced in these places, which is called civilized too. The logic makes no particular sense without the geography that, like an unconscious memory, lies underneath it. Hence hunting is savage (unless it is practiced by English lords or French kings), and to dance is both savage and sinful (unless it is a waltz or ballet). Ball games are uncivilized, but chess, which is, after all, based on the strategies of warfare, is not.

Along with the prejudices of their time and provenance, the Moravians made arguments against war and slavery that did not rely on circular logic. They condemned both because of the brutality and cruelty that characterizes them and thus taught their students that the warfare in which the Cherokee engaged was sinful and that to keep the Indians they had captured or the African-American men and women they purchased as slaves was also a sin, a form of savagery. But here again, the word *savagery* involves a certain circularity, since the judgments aimed at Cherokee culture were also self-reflections; the soldiers in the American army who fought in battles with British and French and Indian soldiers and white plantation owners were not called savage. Even now when this adjective is used to describe the actions of a white person, the word carries within it a hidden agenda, a form of denial, as if such evils really belong outside the ken of white civilization and thus do not reflect that civilization but rather deviate from the elevated sensibility intrinsic to it.

Whenever the mind is gripped by a shadow self, contradictions in logic appear, which to a witness from another period in history may seem obvious but remain unseen at the time, no matter how logical or brilliant the mind in question may be. I am thinking of Jefferson again. He helped to create and perpetuate the mythic figure of the noble savage in

America when, in his seminal work, *Notes on the State of Virginia,* published in 1785, he reproduced an eloquent speech made by the Native American Mingo leader Tah-gah-jute, also known as Logan. The brief speech begins with an account of the Mingo leaders' hospitality toward whites, then declares that one spring, a vigilant party of settlers had killed all of his family, and ends finally with the heartbreaking question, "Who is there to mourn for Logan?—Not one." Jefferson used a transcription of these words to argue against the naturalist Comte de Buffon, who maintained that the continent of America produced inferior beings. "Logan's Lament," as the speech was known, became very popular, reproduced everywhere, including Washington Irving's *Sketch Book* and eventually even in the McGuffey *Readers,* the textbooks read by most schoolchildren throughout the nineteenth century.

So much that Jefferson wrote reveals an appreciation of Indian cultures. In his *Notes on the State of Virginia,* he compares Logan's rhetorical skills favorably to those of Cicero and Demosthenes. He studied several Indian languages, writing of his encounter with Cherokee grammar that it provided an "addition . . . to the philosophy of language." He devoted the central hallway at Monticello to his impressive collection of Indian artifacts. Yet, alongside his admiration, he believed that Indian cultures were as static as objects in a museum and were therefore incapable of change. For this reason he argued that if Native Americans were to adapt to modern life, they would have to substitute the ways of white civilization for their own. Both for Jefferson and for American culture, the emotional contradiction between these two attitudes was resolved in a lament, the kind of *tristesse* that is often a sentimental twin to the illusion of inevitability.

SEPTEMBER

Finally the director of FEMA, Michael Brown, resigns. Some minimal justice in that. But why was such an unqualified man appointed in the first place, a man who was forced to resign as a commissioner for the International Arabian Horse Association? You don't know whether to laugh or cry.

I am thinking again of the Indian boy whose life I read about so often at breakfast each morning as a child, longing to emulate everything he did. The idea of the noble savage plays still another role in the white American psyche. In deep and unexamined layers of consciousness, this mythic figure stands for buried aspects of the soul, all the desires, insights, and states of mind that what we call civilization has excised. Now as I reflect on my wish to be like this boy, I become aware of another desire, concealed within this wish, a longing and a grief for my own body, to be again the way I was before I became my grandmother's child. I have a photograph of myself from this earlier time. I am wearing a sundress, and since my grandmother had not yet started to tell me I shouldn't soil my clothes, I am lying on my belly in a field, my elbows on the ground, supporting my chin with my hands, a playful pose, confident, with a notable lack of self-consciousness, as if I were part of the grass.

The year after he sent his son to the Moravian school, when the Cherokee council convened for a pivotal meeting, Ridge took a strong stand in favor of peace with the white settlers. Among the many Native Americans who did not welcome the influence of white culture, the Shawnee chief Tecumseh had mounted a powerful campaign for a return to traditional ways and resisting all accommodations to the whites. The room fell quiet when a speaker aligned with Tecumseh's call began to describe a powerful dream. He had seen a ghostly band of Cherokee warriors appear before him; they rode out of the sky to warn him against the incursions of whites into their land and their influence on the traditional way of life. Anyone who tried to deny the truth of his dream, the speaker declared, would be "struck dead by the Cherokee mother." But Ridge, who, like his own mother, was given to keeping his own counsel, challenged the speaker nevertheless. The dream did not come "from the Great Spirit," Ridge said. "It will lead us to war with the United States, and we shall suffer." In the customary trial by endurance through which on occasion Cherokee warriors tested the truth, Ridge was physically attacked by several men. But though he was wounded and bleeding, he stood his ground until the older chiefs ended the struggle. It was one more pivotal moment not only in his life but in the life of the Cherokee. His position once again prevailed.

Just two years later, he would take a more radical route to friendship with his white neighbors. In 1813 the man who had fought in so many battles against the settlers found himself fighting again, but this time with Creek warriors and settlers in battles against British soldiers and a different faction of Creek, who were allied with the British. All through early American history, various Native American nations or even factions within nations would align with one side or another in conflicts between whites, as part of their strategies for survival. Ridge proved such a valuable asset to the American side that soon the man who commanded all the troops, a brash young land speculator and frontier lawyer named Andrew Jackson, asked Ridge to recruit still other Cherokee to serve in his cavalry. Everyone knew the Cherokee to be superb riders. As an inducement, Jackson offered Ridge the rank of major, a title he would use for the rest of his life as a first name.

It was not just Ridge's words that would prove prophetic but the direction his life was taking. During the first three decades of the nineteenth century, as the two cultures danced on the same ground, the Cherokee people seemed to be moving closer, and even responding in harmony to steps made by their white partners. In 1821, after laboring for over ten years, a Cherokee man named Sequoya succeeded in creating a syllabary, a kind of alphabet representing syllables in the Cherokee language. Very soon the majority of Cherokee were able to read and write their own language. In 1822 the Cherokee council had established a supreme court and two years later written laws. The next year a central government was created, located at New Echota, Georgia, about four miles from where Ridge lived. And one year after Thomas Jefferson died, in 1827, Ridge helped to draft the new Cherokee constitution.

With so much change, the world must have seemed bright with possibility. Prosperity, so often the fruit of prophecy, came soon. Like others among the Cherokee who began to farm large plots of land, Ridge was soon a wealthy man. His luxurious colonial-style mansion was set on 280 acres that he had cultivated using the modern equipment introduced by Washington and Jefferson. His estate had several orchards, 1,141 peach trees, 418 apple trees, and a store and a ferry. His life was rich in other ways too. Respected for his clarity, he became an influential figure in both Cherokee and white society. He was elected as speaker of the Cherokee council in the lower house. And for many years he was the closest counselor to his good friend, principal chief John Ross.

But prophecy also has its costs. What Cassandra suffered, the anguish that comes from seeing what no one can see or will acknowledge, is just one of the consequences. There is also risk in vision itself. As with the ridge of a mountain, the footing in this terrain can be treacherous, the descent steep, even fatal. And there is this too: From a certain angle, you may see the forest clearly but not every tree. In the sweep of a larger vision, you are in danger of failing to see the smaller threads from which life is woven. Straddling two worlds and acting as a diplomat between them, Ridge knew more than either side, but he knew less too.

It would perhaps have been like a nagging doubt, the kind of recurring thought that haunts you in the middle of the night, an anxiety that, though it pales in daylight, never entirely vanishes. There was the offer, continually made, of land west of the Mississippi—an offer that was in fact a menace more than a gift, even when President Jefferson suggested it in the most cordial manner. And, despite his manner, he never really answered the request the delegation had made for citizenship. Instead he passed the question on to Congress. Year after year full citizenship was denied. And then there were the broken agreements. After the War of 1812, Jackson betrayed his promises to cede over a million acres of land to the Cherokee, claiming them for his own war reparations. Using a method that was by then tried and true, he bribed several chiefs to sign a treaty giving him the land he wanted. Ridge, who led a delegation to Washington to challenge this treaty, succeeded in getting most of the land back. But far from settling the question, attempts to wrest land from the Cherokee only accelerated, taken up now by the southern states. No wonder that the first composition Sequoya wrote in his new syllabary addressed the subject of boundaries between the states of Georgia and Tennessee and Cherokee country.

Still, even when signs of danger were visible, the weight of all his previous decisions, the convincing habits and pleasures of daily life, and his deepening connections with the white community must have encouraged Ridge to stick to the course he had chosen. He had sent his son John, who became a star pupil at the Moravian mission, to study at a special new school, called the Cornwall Boarding School, in Cornwall, Connecticut. He decided his son and his young nephew, his brother's son, called Gallegina in Cherokee, or Buck in English, ought to have a white education so that they could become leaders. He had long planned for John to become principal chief. Buck, whom Susanna and Major treated like a son and who was like a brother to John, had forged an even closer bond with white society on his way to Cornwall. When he stayed the night in New Jersey at the home of Dr. Elias Boudinot, his host, a former member of Congress, was so impressed with the boy that he offered to give him financial support. His only condition was that Buck take his name, a promise Buck fulfilled with enthusiasm.

At the new school, John and Buck read Virgil; they studied the Bible and Evangelical Protestantism; they were required to master the ever-relevant subject of surveying; and, in order that they have what today we would call a well-rounded education, they were assigned reading from Enfield's *History of Philosophy*.

Condensed from Brucker's monumental six-volume *Critical History of Philosophy* to a more manageable two, this was a classic reference work, a compendium of accepted opinion, knowledge, philosophy, history, and religious studies, chosen in 1793 by Thaddeus Mason Harris, librarian of Harvard, to be included among the "most esteemed publications" for the university's new Social Library. I imagine that while John Ridge and Elias Boudinot studied this work, Emerson, who was a student at Harvard, was studying the same volumes.

From the perspective of time, the compendium seems to capture a moment between a way of thinking that was passing and another that was arising. In this work, long passages of biblical exegesis and historical analysis are offered alongside descriptions of the latest scientific discoveries. In a letter addressed to John Adams in 1813, Jefferson cites biblical scholarship from Enfield's *History* at length, in order, as he said, to "give flesh" to his own interpretation of the Gospels. In the same period, a much younger man, Samuel Morse, was among the many students who relied on Enfield's *History;* years later he would say that a passage from these volumes on the nature of electricity had planted the seed for his invention of the telegraph.

Soon, the education Major Ridge sought for the two boys began to bear fruit. In 1821, just a few years after he began to attend the school at Cornwall, John brought home a copy of a letter he had composed in English. It was addressed to President Monroe on behalf of the whole school. Though Ridge could not read English, and thus would not have been able to see just how eloquent, clear, and powerful his son's prose was, the fact of the letter must have made him hopeful.

The word *hope* of course expresses a complexity of emotions: a wish for a good outcome but also the knowledge that such an outcome is by no means certain. "I rejoice," he writes, "that my dear nation now begins to peep into the privileges of civilization . . . and that ere long Congress will give them the hand of strong fellowship, that they will encircle them in the arms of love." Still, in the paragraph that follows this declaration, he explains that Indians east of the Mississippi are making faster progress toward civilization. It is an argument against removal.

The tug-of-war over land east of the Mississippi was to continue. When, two years later, in 1823, the state of Georgia sent delegates to the annual Cherokee council at New Echota, their goal was to remove Indians from the northwestern sector of the state. The state government of Georgia retreated when the Cherokee refused, saying they would never cede their lands. All the while, a dominant portion of the Cherokee were attempting to assimilate into settler society, trying to meet the requirements of what their white neighbors called civilization so that they could live in peace with them.

Ridge must have felt a closer bond with white society when first John and then Elias married women who were white, girls they had met while at school in Connecticut. The families on both sides, who believed in peace and friendship, eventually resolved to accept these unions. But there was a shadow side to this story too. Others in the white community responded with such hostility that both the couples decided to move back to Georgia, onto land in Cherokee territory.

Yet in another way, the young men had moved even more deeply into a white world. The missionaries offered Christianity to the family again and again, inviting Susanna and Ridge to church services. At the school, the boys were forbidden their Cherokee ways. They could not dance or drum. Every day in school they studied passages from the Bible, learning again and again, through chapter and verse, poetry and song and story, how God made the world from the word, in seven days. I can imagine that the stories of creation they had learned—how animals made the world, how raven was burned black when he tried to bring fire from the volcano and failed, and how the water spider succeeded by weaving a web in which to carry a small coal back to the forest—were not erased so much as placed into another compartment in their minds when, over time, they converted, along with, eventually, Susanna Ridge, Elias's aunt and John's mother.

Thinking of these conversions, my mind goes to the larger landscape of religion in America during the same period. When John and Elias and Susanna were becoming Christians in a conventional sense, learning to accept the host, to kneel in prayer, Emerson was beginning to question these rituals, gestures that he would eventually reject. Jefferson, who was near his death then, had already rebelled against Christian ritual. This was why he wrote his own version of the Gospels: in order to rescue the wisdom of Jesus's teaching from what he considered to be the irrational trappings of religion.

I was astonished to learn that the religion that many of the founding fathers practiced was the same one my grandfather did. That the Masons elevated reason to the level of a deity does much to explain the choice. This element was hardly evident in my grandfather's worship, nor was it present in his attitudes. Though perhaps it does explain the strangely geometric shapes traced across the floor in the rituals performed by my grandmother and her friends in the women's auxiliary to the Masons. And thinking again of Indian removal, it occurs to me now too how much this way of traversing space resembles surveying.

Did Ridge wonder about the wisdom of the course he had chosen? But this was his own family. He had come to greatly admire his sons and their learning. If there were dissonance between the world to which he had been born and the world they entered, this chasm would have made him feel his advancing age more keenly. And so too when in 1828, still riding his reputation as an Indian fighter, Andrew Jackson was elected president, as the fears of a forced removal loomed larger, it would also have comforted Ridge to know his son and his nephew were well established to represent Cherokee interests. A month after Jackson's inauguration, Buck, now calling himself Elias Boudinot, published the first issue of a newspaper called the *Cherokee Phoenix*, printed at New Echota. In his first editorial, he spoke out eloquently against the hunger that white settlers showed for Cherokee land.

Jackson must have had his doubts. Yet I sense he would have kept his fears hidden in another way, even from himself. From an early age, he would have felt that he could not afford to submit to fear. His father died just a few days before he was born, and by the age of fourteen, he was an orphan. No wonder they called him Old Hickory. As a boy, he was a courier in the Revolutionary War, and was taken prisoner by the British. He had to fight for everything he had. The family was poor, even before his father died. He was the first president to be born in a log cabin. As a child, he was well known for his temper. A school friend said that once he was in a

fight, he never gave up. Without a father and then with no parents to protect him, and with hardly any means in the world, he would not have
wanted to admit to weakness of any kind. The tide would have been too
strong. From my own childhood, I am familiar with the habit. Once I recovered from shyness, I was seized by a bravado that saw me through
many rough times, though it often separated me from what I really felt.

The anxiety Jackson must have endured as a child would have propelled his soul in two different directions, toward compassion and bel-
ligerence at the same time. In this way he embodied the mood of the
young nation. Known as a friend of working people, he fought for a ten-
hour workday and the right to unionize. And he won the vote for men
who did not own property. But I imagine his suffering had another effect
too. It would not be surprising that, driven to a dark place within himself,
his fear of his own fragility would have manifested in acts of aggression.

No doubt feeding that impulse, history gave him an enemy of mythic
dimensions, men and women with strange costumes, strange languages,
forming a menacing presence at the margins of all he did. Jackson grew
up in the borderlands of North and South Carolina, in the undefined
terrain that lay between the land cultivated by white settlers and Indian
territory; his home, the roads he walked to school, the woods where he
hunted, were all contested, threatened by a struggle for possession that
was often violent. But, of course, any mythic enemy stands for inner
monsters too. I imagine that all his buried fears would have been trig-
gered by the thought of this opponent. Along with the European culture
he had inherited, he would have associated Indians with nature and,
through this connection, with the inevitability of loss that belongs to
natural existence.

That he would have been fighting inner demons does not contradict
the fact that Jackson waged a real battle for survival. Though they may
appear to be separate, inner and outer realms are part of a continuum.
Entering a contested moment in any life you will encounter both imagined dangers and real dangers, solitary states of mind and shared
economies, at the same time. From an early age, Jackson had had to struggle to survive. For this reason he was determined to acquire land. But I
can imagine the acquisition gave him a sense of power over circumstances that would have been, in its own way, addictive. Soon Jackson became a speculator, buying up Indian land and then selling it for profit.

It is a harsh history, repeated over and over, born of democracy in a way but also undermining it. The same system that allows anyone to rise from poverty has a meaner side. When land, food, water, or any necessity is scarce, instead of calling for greater equality, those who are in need will fight one another. And those who engage in these fierce battles to survive are often willing to sacrifice justice as well as the democratic principle that freedom belongs to everyone equally. At one time, Major Ridge owned thirty black slaves, in addition to a number of Creek Indians he had captured in battle.

In the year that Jackson ascended to power, Georgia passed several laws empowering the state to annex Indian lands and divide this territory into plots to be given by lottery to settlers. Other laws were passed requiring Indians to abandon the ways of their own culture, especially the ancient tradition of owning land communally. Now the government demanded that the Cherokee abandon communal ownership and live on private property. Those who did not obey would be taken into custody and then forcibly removed to territories west of the Mississippi. They were given two years to comply. The unstated motives were clear, a need for land and the fact that gold had been discovered in Indian territory.

Then Jackson, who early in his career had called treaties with Indians "an absurdity," pushed a federal bill through Congress that authorized and mandated Indian removal. The Cherokee did not acquiesce. The ruling council hired William Wirt, attorney general under Monroe and once a neighbor of Jefferson, to challenge the law in the courts, and in 1832, they won their case. According to the Supreme Court, led by John Marshall, "the right of discovery," which the state of Georgia used as its argument, was not grounds for ownership. But the victory was moot. "Well, John Marshall has made his decision, now let him enforce it," Jackson said, announcing his resolve to do nothing to prevent the state of Georgia from acting against the federal law.

The impasse occurred in the same year that Emerson attended Ridge's lecture in Concord, one of many the Cherokee leader gave against removal. Three years later Emerson himself began to speak out. At a public meeting in April 1838, he read an angry letter he had written to Van Buren, elected president in 1836, calling Indian removal "a crime that really deprives us as well as the Cherokees of a country; for how can we call the conspiracy that would crush these poor Indians our government . . . ?"

The conspiracy Emerson described with such fury involved what he called a "sham treaty," a written contract the federal government reached with a small party of Cherokee leaders who were neither elected nor empowered as representatives. By their signatures on the document, they agreed to trade all the Cherokee land east of the Mississippi in exchange for five million dollars and 13,800,000 acres of land in the West. Yet ironically among those who signed the document were Major Ridge, his son John, and his nephew Elias Boudinot.

At the time, it appeared to be an internal battle, a struggle for power between the principal chief, John Ross, and Major Ridge. But from a distance of many years, another story appears. It is as if a lens focused on a single plant that seems to be dying of unknown causes were drawn back to reveal a desiccated landscape. So many conditions in society at large conspired to create enmity between these two men who had been best of friends for years. They had both taken the path of assimilation, both believed in peace. But as circumstances became increasingly difficult, the climate in which friendship flourishes disappeared.

And there is this too in the background: the pride you will often feel toward children who have gained skills that are foreign to you. Ridge admired his son and his nephew for the education that they had and that he lacked, schooling he had arranged for them so that they could become leaders. Now, aging, he listened closely to their counsel. Over several years, Elias had published editorial after editorial against removal in the *Cherokee Phoenix*. But both he and John had come to believe that resistance was all but hopeless. White settlers in Georgia were making violent attacks on Cherokee farms. Just as Jefferson had predicted, the hunting grounds in the eastern Alleghenies had become barren from overuse. Elias wrote an editorial for the *Phoenix* arguing in favor of an agreement to sell Cherokee land and move west. Along with Elias, John, who was by now a successful lawyer, also felt that since they were closer to the corridors of federal power than many other Cherokee, they understood the situation better.

But if they had moved closer to Washington, they had also become more distant from their own community. John Ross, the principal chief, who was more trusted by most of the Cherokee, especially those who had not received a white education, opposed their plan. When Elias, John, and Major Ridge met with the council, their proposal was voted down by a large majority. The rancor toward what they proposed was so great that Ridge was threatened with impeachment.

Democracy is embedded in a delicate ecology, a resonant field that exists between individual and shared consciousness. The man or woman who sees what others cannot see is vital to the process of self-government. Uncommon, even unpopular clarity and foresight expressed by a minority have often saved whole communities, even nations. In this light, it is easy to understand why those who are convinced that they know more than the majority may be tempted to cross the subtle line between courage and tyranny, and thus undermine democracy by violating the mutual trust on which democracy relies.

Determined that they alone understood the perilous situation, Ridge, his son, and his nephew convened another council. That only a small fraction of Cherokee attended did not deter them from drafting a proposal to bring to Washington. Chief Ross traveled to Washington too, where he made his own proposal for a sale to the federal government, but this was rejected by Congress, which considered the price as too high. For a period there was some hope for reconciliation, a concerted effort at joining the two councils. But the hostility between the two leaders prevented any truce.

When finally the members of the Ridge party signed the treaty, the ceremony took place at New Echota, the capital Ridge had helped to design for the formal democracy he had done so much to create. It did not escape him that he had placed himself above the democratic traditions of both the Cherokee and the new government he had advocated. Telling himself that at times an educated minority must wrest power from an ignorant majority, in 1835 he traveled to the Cherokee capital he loved, to sign away the rights to the land where he and his children were born, land where he had lived and worked for years, and where his mother and father and all the ancestors he could remember were buried.

In human consciousness, any awareness of the present is usually laced with relics from the past. I learned recently that the two ravens accompanying the Norse god Odin represent thought and memory. This detail explains a phrase that both my grandmother and my mother used. When either of them could not or did not want to reveal the source of something she knew, she would say, "A little bird told me." Neither of them knew the origins for the phrase. Except for my grandfather's prejudices, we had almost no knowledge of our ancestral lands in Scotland or Ireland or Wales.

Starting from the first European settlements, white Americans have been peripatetic, having relinquished the land of their ancestors, forgetting the past, always driving forward in a continual process of dislocation. And this too would have made the citizens of Georgia, so many newly arrived, callous toward those forced from ancestral lands. Was it because he knew that what he did would make him unpopular that Major Ridge decided to move his family to the land he had secured for them in Oklahoma long before the official process called "removal" began? After signing the treaty, he said he felt as if he had just signed his own death warrant. Did he also feel it as a betrayal in some buried region of his mind, a transgression even against himself, and his own earliest memories? This is the wisdom of the story of Odin: truth is inseparable from recollection. And recollection cannot in turn be had apart from the place where the events you remember happened, the feel and smell of it. Though the Ridge family finally chose to move, it must have been painful to leave behind the home they had known for so long. Records tell us that Susanna Ridge grieved over the fruit trees she had carefully planted and nurtured and that took so many years to yield.

OCTOBER

Part of the problem is that FEMA has been absorbed by the Department of Homeland Security. A metaphor for the way the war is swallowing us all.

The forced exile of seventeen thousand Cherokee would occur several months later. Preparations had already begun. To move so many people so quickly, roads had to be built. Though Jefferson had died a dozen years earlier, the mark of his hand was on these plans. As he had argued decades before, building trading stores in Indian territory would encourage Native Americans to incur debt, which in turn would make them more amenable to relinquishing their land. But as in all tragedies, the plot unraveled in a different way than he had envisioned. In order to pay off their debts, many Cherokee men and women labored to build the roads through their territory, the men digging the soil, the women cooking for the crews, routes by which soldiers and their equipment would arrive one day to force the Cherokee to move west. In the meantime, a series of garrisons was built to house soldiers.

There were many among enterprising whites who saw advantage in

the making. Not just the gold miners and settlers riveted on seizing Indian farms, but men like the Indian agent lawyer who had once represented the Cherokee, William Holland Thomas, and who was also one of
the largest slaveholders in North Carolina. Between 1822 and 1837, he
opened seven trading stores to sell supplies for the building and then the
maintenance of the garrisons. But still to the Cherokee who remained on
their land, the event these activities presaged was not inevitable. Whites
had been hungry for their land for so long. The Cherokee Nation had
won a decision in the Supreme Court. When General Winfield Scott sent
a leaflet to the families he was about to evict, warning them to prepare,
they dismissed his orders.

I understand the state of mind well. When my parents divorced or whenever I was reunited with my sister, at holidays or summer camp, though
I was informed of the eventual loss I would suffer, I did not let myself believe in this fate until it arrived. Then it seemed like a shocking blow,
sudden and terrible.

So throughout the Cherokee territories in the late spring of 1838, families continued to hunt, to care for their herds of cattle and sheep, their
crops, to mend the roofs of log cabins and farmhouses, to spin cloth,
send their children to school, while they looked as they always had for
the first signs of summer, the first fruit to ripen.

Then it began.

Along rivers and in woods, in meadows and villages, soldiers appeared
as if out of nowhere. Just after a family assembled around the table for a
meal, the glint of bayonets could be seen from the rifles of two soldiers
who stood in the open doorway. There could be no possible escape. From
the window they would have been able to see the soldiers who had quietly
surrounded their cabin, waiting to take them all at once, mother and
father, three or four children, one perhaps still an infant, along with their
aging or aged grandparents. Whenever one among them, the father or
perhaps the mother, asked for some time to assemble belongings and
supplies, the request was almost always denied. "You were warned," they
would be told.

If, as sometimes happened, a settler appeared suddenly, wanting to
purchase land and perhaps a farmhouse before they went to the lottery,

there would be no time to bargain. Though the price might reduce his family from comfort to penury in a single moment, while the owner was held at gunpoint, his wife shaken with apprehension, his children weeping in fear, he was forced to accept whatever was offered.

Once abandoned, the houses were not guarded. Settlers swarmed over farms and dwellings, taking whatever they could find—saddles and harnesses, rifles and hoes, plows, crops, geese, chickens, even money, gristmills, feather beds, blankets and quilts, dishes and spinning wheels, looms, tables, chairs, and baskets.

Or if there had been no sale, perhaps as they were marched or driven on wagons toward the stockades, one member of a family, a grandfather or his granddaughter, might look back to see flames arising from the home they had left behind; in the destructive mood that possesses those driven by unreasoned hatred, vindictive settlers would often set fire to abandoned crops and farms all across Cherokee territory.

OCTOBER

Many stories of children separated from their families in the chaos of the evacuation. A newborn, a two-year-old child. No one in the government helps the families find their children. They have been given a telephone number but when they call, it is never answered.

The tragedy did not occur in one place or all at once but was drawn across space and time so that a widening circle spread out like a deadly net cast into the sea of daily life. Women were seized in their kitchens, children grabbed as they played, men were taken from the fields where they worked, young men tracked while they hunted. When one hunter was arrested as he emerged from the forest, the deer he was bringing home to his family was seized and the venison later fed to the soldiers who had arrested him.

Among the many incidents that went unrecorded, I can imagine there must have been women who were weaving cloth when the soldiers arrived. And that more than one woman, dropping the shuttle she held when she saw her captors, was followed by tangled threads, which a soldier would have cut with his bayonet, even as she leaned back toward her loom, as if regaining the rhythm of this labor might return her to all she knew and cherished.

Stories that have been remembered illustrate patterns, appalling events repeated many times in these few days. Two children, for instance, surprised by soldiers, escaped into the woods. The mother pleaded with the soldiers to let her wait for their return, but the soldiers refused. Of the many children who were separated from their parents, then sent to different stockades, and, if they survived, eventually dispatched on different routes west, some never saw their parents again. No attempt was made by the soldiers or the government to reunite families.

Large losses were followed by smaller ones. A woman and her children being driven to the stockade by soldiers were forced to wade through a stream with their shoes on. The shoes were ruined, never to be replaced, though they would all soon be walking hundreds of miles, through terrible heat, heavy rain, and then on frozen ground. Still other injuries followed that seemed in hindsight to make what had come before just a prelude, a doorway to a world of horror. Women and girls still children raped by the soldiers. Some of mixed heritage, part white, part Indian, taken to the garrisons, passed like a bottle of whiskey from soldier to soldier.

Indignities continued all along the way: the silver pendants worn by women and girls torn from their necks as they walked, a group of riders who refused to give up their horses forced into a corral with other horses and the men, women, and children traveling with them on foot. Everywhere groups were herded like cattle, the soldiers shouting as if they were gathering livestock.

The Cherokee were being taken to a series of stockades that had been built near the military garrisons spread through Georgia, the Carolinas, Alabama, and Tennessee, designed as holding camps, temporary prisons meant to keep the Cherokee from returning home before the exodus could begin.

It is difficult to comprehend how a plan so contrary to the spirit of democracy could be carried out in the way it was. Though unintended atrocities occurred in the process, the act of removal had to be meticulously planned, designs made, buildings erected, troops moved, distances measured, routes charted, days marked on the calendar. Yet as I think of individual participants, carpenters and cartographers and accountants and soldiers, I realize that once a decision has been made, particularly by someone you have never met, who is far above you in a chain of authority, you might be able to contribute your part in the process almost without thinking, mindlessly, as you go through the habitual moves you always make, when building a fence, adding a column of figures, putting on your uniform.

Yet the way plans are carried out is never entirely neutral. The errors within the execution will betray faults in the ideas or intentions or reveal hidden emotions behind them. The policy called Indian removal required a circular line of reasoning. To make the policy legal, the government had to refuse Indians the rights given to American citizens. So by this logic, not only legally but in the imagination, they were relegated to a lesser plane of existence. The judgment could not have failed to affect the execution of the policy if only in one way. Whenever you place yourself in the scheme of things above others, your ability to feel empathy for what they suffer will be diminished.

And there would also have been this, that subliminal sense that Indians belonged to nature, while whites believed themselves to be above nature. This was a habit of mind that created no doubt an even wider gap in the imagination, so that what Indians suffered would seem outside the realm of the human and hence a natural and inevitable phenomenon.

Thus the stockades were well planned for imprisonment but not for habitation. Food and water were scarce. There was not enough clothing or any way to wash what garments the Cherokee had. No provisions for waste. Excrement was scattered everywhere. Only flimsy structures existed, which hardly protected them from the weather. Day upon day there was nothing to do but grieve the losses that had already happened and fear for the future, as rape and other brutalities continued. And with so many crowded into such small spaces, along with the feeling of being caged, the spread of disease was terrible and terrifying. Cholera, measles, smallpox, dysentery, influenza. Pain and fever were visible in every corner. As always, the youngest and oldest succumbed first. Infants born in the stockade, or just a few months old when captured, then those just learning to walk, the elderly, then anyone in frail health.

It would have been a hellish scene, even to witness. At night your sleep would be interrupted by coughing or moaning, and then, some nights, by the wails of those who had just lost children, parents, grandparents, a wife or husband. Both the white doctors and the shamans did what they could. But the manner of death was bitter, the dying deprived of the physical comforts the ailing body craves, separated from all that was familiar, safe, kindred, kind, and afterward no way to do the ceremonies properly, the burial respectfully, to complete a return into the ground of birth.

Steadily everyone, even the strongest, was weakened, already exhausted before the forced march even began.

From this history you can sense that in 1838, America was moving in two opposite directions. To the north, in New England, Emerson had launched his life's work, delivering a series of remarkable lectures that addressed a wide range of subjects from literary ethics to human life, home, duty, and genius. He had already forged his friendship with Thoreau. As he created a new American view of life, forging an empathetic connection between the human spirit and all life, over time Emerson would become known as the nation's preeminent intellectual.

It may seem strange now to realize that this revolution in consciousness would begin just as the Cherokee, a people who had connected the human spirit with the earth for generations, were being forced from their ancestral lands. But if the mind can expand, it can also be segmented, and in this way divide ideas from actions, philosophy from history. The tendency is reflected in the way the work of the Transcendentalists has often been taught, as if, despite Thoreau's "Civil Disobedience" and Margaret Fuller's feminism, the spirit evoked in the beautiful poems of Whitman and Dickinson, the haunting novels of Hawthorne and Melville, Thoreau's account of living near Walden Pond, and Emerson's ecstatic insights exists in an ethereal space entirely apart from political questions and conflicts. And doubtless what arises for me too now is the temptation toward a terrible cynicism, as if none of these fine ideas and expressions actually counted in the real world. That in his own process of thought Emerson did not create false divisions seems apparent in his journal entries during the late spring of 1838. If on one day he writes that he found God manifest in the woods, "where the thrush sang him, the robin complained him, the cat-bird mewed him . . . the wild apple bloomed him," a few days later, on June 8, he has turned his gaze toward society to see "a good deal of character in our abused age." He follows this with a list of ideas and efforts striving against abuse, including "the rights of women, the antislavery, temperance, peace, health, and money movements." Aware of the paradoxes of the times in which he lived, he notes that these are signs of "life at the heart, not fully organized at the surface."

For some Cherokee, the time spent in the stockades ended after just a few weeks. The first convoy of roughly six hundred Cherokee departed on June 6, 1838, forced at gunpoint to board a steamboat, named with a sad irony after George Guess, whose Cherokee name was Sequoya, the man who invented the Cherokee syllabary. Though it was a difficult journey, this party, taking off earlier in the month and run by a soldier named Lieutenant Deas, who had some experience with earlier emigrations, had fewer deaths than the convoys to come.

Those that followed were less prepared for the conditions they encountered. The supplies were meager, and much of that was stolen, sold by soldiers and traders along the way for a profit. The men, women, and children who set out to walk over eight hundred miles were dogged by heat and drought. The exceptionally dry weather had affected crops and rivers. There was not enough food to be found, even by foraging. Children's stomachs were distended with hunger. The parties that were to travel by a series of boats over the Tennessee to the Ohio, then the Mississippi, and finally the Arkansas rivers found the water too low to navigate. Where there were bridges across the water, each party, and sometimes each man or woman, would be charged a toll, often doubled for the occasion. Thirsty for days, some were driven to drinking brackish water that would soon make them ill. Half-starved and exhausted, many succumbed to disease, three to five a day, according to those who kept records. The fortunate few who managed to escape came back with stories of what they had suffered and witnessed. Finally General Scott ordered the cessation of convoys until September 1.

Countless witnesses who were horrified by what they saw as lines of Cherokee passed before their eyes had reported, as one person said, "They are dying like flies." But in a letter to Washington, D.C., General Scott responded with a calm dismissal; in an odd but familiar form of sophistry, he used words that were accurate and yet concealed the truth: "There is no more sickness among the Indians than might ordinarily take place amongst any other people under the same circumstances."

He must have wanted to preserve his reputation as an able commander. And perhaps there would have been another reason too: the desire to conceal from himself the terrible cost of his own commands.

I was eleven years old and living with my mother again when I first realized that on the morning after a binge, she did not remember what she had said or done the night before. The knowledge, however, cannot have been absolute. Though she never apologized on those mornings, I could sense the presence of a barrier, an invisible screen she had drawn around herself, as if she could hardly bear to have anyone look at her directly.

Though he did not acknowledge the scope of the tragedy, Scott finally proposed to President Van Buren that in the fall the command of the removal be ceded to Principal Chief John Ross. The period between the end of June and the beginning of October, when the drought broke, must have seemed endless. For four months, as the imprisonment continued, thousands of Cherokee languished in stockades, where disease was unrelenting too, and many more died—some, no doubt, of desperation.

OCTOBER

Up late last night listening to jazz from New Orleans. Louis Armstrong, Jelly Roll Morton, Preservation Hall Band, Sidney Bechet. All that music is so much a part of me, my own memories.

The westward movement. For so many in white society, the western territories had become a symbol of hope, the promise of endless opportunity and even a greater spiritual largesse. Emerson was among those who felt the possibility. In September, the same month that preparations began for the departure of new contingents of Cherokee, he made an entry in his journal that described his thoughts as he looked west, "where the sun was sinking behind clouds," as if lying "in a pit of splendour . . . in a desert of space—a deposit of *still light* . . ." At that moment, the river he could see beneath him seemed "like God's love, journeying out of the grey past into the green future."

Finally in October, under Chief Ross's command, the next parties began to depart. On one boat leaving Ross's landing, a witness reported having seen several Indian children waving good-bye to the land where they were born and raised. These groups were better supplied. Ross had gotten the government to give them more of what they needed, though still they did not have enough blankets or shoes. And many were already sick. One day a shaman trying to help a group of children, miserable and fevered with measles, led them all into the river to bathe and cool off. For a while they felt better. But all too soon they began to shiver.

The drought was followed by heavy rainfall and then bitter cold.

Groups that voyaged by water found that on reaching the Mississippi River, it was filled with treacherous blocks of ice. Over three hundred were lost in a boat that capsized into these waters. When first the Mississippi and then the Ohio were frozen, whole groups were marooned, left to sleep on the icy banks of the rivers without any fires, "like so many animals," wrote the Reverend Daniel Butrick, a missionary to the Cherokee, "on naked ground." Even when rivers were navigable, the Cherokee were made to sleep on the unshielded decks of the boats that carried them. In one of the last groups, even though she had caught a cold herself, Quatie, the wife of Chief Ross, gave her blanket to a child who was sick and chilled. The child survived, but on February 1, near what is now known as Little Rock, Arkansas, Quatie Ross died of pneumonia.

The pursuit of happiness. It seems to me now that democracy hinges on a deeper understanding of this phrase. There can be no way to understand it apart from the knowledge of the body. What it is, for instance, to be so cold for hour upon hour with no relief that your body begins to shudder and weep all on its own as pain edges all your senses until you feel thin and brittle as ice. Near breaking, your body makes its efforts beyond any will you assert, and all the while weariness hounds you, your flesh is distraught with paroxysms of alarm.

One story is strongly reminiscent of both Emerson's grief-stricken response to his first wife's death and the auguries made by the shaman at Major Ridge's birth. The tale has it that one evening on the trail, a Cherokee man sits beside his wife's grave, knowing, no doubt, that this is the last visit he will have with her. It is then in the midst of his grief that he is startled to see two figures, half raven, half human, fly to the grave. Shining with the pale blue color of fire, they set about digging up the grave, only to lift the coffin out, open it, and stare sadly into the face of the dead woman, before burying her again.

Day after day, through fatigue, illness, and sorrow, the convoys push forward. Leaving camp one morning, a wagon rolls over the head of a young boy. If anyone dies on the trail, the body must be buried quickly or even left to the elements. One afternoon a mother finally relinquishes the infant she has let grow cold in her arms. And at nine o'clock one morning, Nancy Big Bear buries her grandchild at the side of the road. As everyone continues walking, heads down, many weep. When the shamans pray for some sign to give their people strength, they notice a new white flower springing up on the path wherever tears have fallen. They name this the Cherokee rose.

When the group he led finally reached Oklahoma, the Cherokee Christian minister Reverend Bushyhead, who had lost his daughter to a river, thanked the white man's Great Spirit for sustaining his people. Others were left wondering at the meaning of what they had witnessed. Elizur Butler, a medical missionary accompanying the removal parties, put it simply: "From the 1st of June I felt I have been in the midst of death." Shocked by all he had seen and left feeling helpless, Reverend Butrick finally wrote, "It has been a year of spiritual darkness."

Many years later, one man who had lost nearly all of his family when he was a child on the long march, spoke of the sorrow. He already had reached an advanced age when he said, "I never smile, never laugh in my lifetime." In the two years over which the forced emigration took place, close to four thousand had died.

Captain W. G. Williams, who had been assigned to a team making a survey of the Cherokee Nation in North Carolina, realized that "the love of home is a paramount sentiment with the Indian." But in a military intelligence report he wrote in 1838, he declared his belief that this attachment sprang from a "limited range of ideas" and the "superstitious" reverence the Cherokee hold toward the graves of ancestors. Do spirits linger on the earth, near the places where they once lived? This experience would not be explained by the range of ideas that Williams had inherited. Yet it is undeniable that all your memories are mixed with the look and feel and even scent of the places where they occurred and that whenever you remember your parents or grandparents, you will also remember the trees and houses that surrounded them and the land or streets on which they stood. Thus, though it is ironic, it is not entirely unexpected that soon after the removal, the North Carolina legislature, which organized a new county from the Cherokee lands it had seized, should name it Cherokee County.

I can imagine that among those who survived the Trail of Tears, the urge for retribution would have been strong. It would have come as the chasm of grief kept growing larger, as it will when slowly, after a great loss, your comprehension of what has been lost grows. The quiet that descends after a violent or sudden death, an accident, a trauma of any kind, can be misleading. Your body and soul go into shock. At moments when a real-ization of what has actually happened washes over you—whether it was your mother, your sister, your child, who died; your house burned down; the land you were born to vanished—you will tremble involuntarily and perhaps weep, and yet, in your state of disbelief, it can seem as if some-one or something else that wanted to tremble and weep had taken pos-session of you temporarily. But when finally the sweet fog of shock leaves you, and you are suddenly able to see the stark facts, grief can unleash a formidable force inside you, threatening the order of your days and, if the grief is deep enough, the order even of your soul. I can imagine that if you are someone who has always been active, who could build a house with your own hands, plow and plant, hunt, ride horses, fight, you would search frantically for a remedy, for something you can do to answer the ravaging thoughts that dog all your days.

It was after a secret meeting held the night before that at dawn on June 22, 1839, three separate parties each rode to a different destination within the new Cherokee territory in Oklahoma. The first group broke into John Ridge's house. When the gun held to his head failed to fire, he was pulled from his bed and forced outside. While Sally and their son Rollins watched helplessly, each of the twenty-six men stabbed him. Then they threw him in the air, and after this each man stomped on him, as if not only to assure his death but to make their power to kill him more palpable still. Astonishingly he lived for just a few more hours, blood streaming from his mouth, his family beside his bed in a dreadful vigil.

The second party surrounded Elias Boudinot as he strolled toward the new house he was building for his family. Four men came out of the woods pretending they needed medicine. As he walked with them to-ward the mission station, one stuck a knife into his back and the other a tomahawk into his skull. On his way to visit a man whom he held in slav-ery and who had fallen ill, Major Ridge was on horseback when five shots entered his body. His death was witnessed by a boy whom he also held in bondage and who had been traveling with him that day.

Because he was warned in time to escape, one other man was spared: Stand Watie, who had been part of the Ridge party and signed the treaty agreeing to exile. But this meant the killing was not over. Watie organized revenge parties. The cycle of injury and retribution would continue for decades, driven by new conflicts, including the Civil War, in which some Cherokee men fought for the Union and some for the Confederacy.

OCTOBER

The pattern of abuse and neglect continues. People who lost everything and who need help now forced to battle with FEMA and insurance companies for the help they need. Families moved from one place to another as if they were refugees in their own country.

I cannot remember when I first heard of the Trail of Tears. I knew it referred to some kind of tragedy. But knowing little else, I never grasped the full dimensions of the atrocity. Though it is there in plain sight, still, it is hardly visible in the picture many Americans paint of ourselves. I can see now how it is a part of my story. The grim side of the movement west that eventually brought my mother's and father's parents to California.

I do not know the lineage of my own location exactly. I know that my grandmother's father's family, the Branches, came from Virginia before they settled in southern Illinois. This was where the writer James Branch Cabell, of whom my grandmother was so proud, was born. I wonder now with a curiosity I never had before, when did my great-grandfather or his father migrate west, across Kentucky to Illinois? Though I do not know all the details, it seems to me nevertheless that with my knowledge of Indian removal, a great part of the geography of my own story has been restored to me.

I can see my own family history as part of a larger story now. The land in Virginia from which Cherokee and other Native Americans had been pushed west and from which some settlers like Peter Jefferson had been able to better themselves, had all but disappeared into private ownership by the nineteenth century. Soon the territory taken from the Cherokee in Georgia and Tennessee would be gone too. By 1842, just over a hundred years before my birth, the West was already well established as a beacon of hope. And even more than that, in the American imagination, a symbol for spiritual renewal.

"Eastward I go by force; but westward I go free," Henry David Thoreau wrote. You can feel it in his tone. This was the same freedom that belonged to a certain idea of nature, of the natural, of human nature as it was meant to be. It's there in that compelling passage in the Declaration of Independence, as Jefferson writes that "Nature's God" gave all people "a separate and equal station." And it can be felt too in the mythic figures that Daniel Boone and Davy Crockett became, braving the wilds of Kentucky, wearing hats made from beaver pelts and clothes made from deerskin—the animals they hunted—as if they had become part of the woods themselves.

Following the history of westward migration, it seems possible to me now that my ancestors might have been among the many who moved to the states just west of the Mississippi River during the 1820s. It must have been my great-great-grandfather who migrated. My grandmother was born in Illinois in 1884.

Soon poverty, need, and desire would push others farther west. By 1840 most of the arable land east of the Mississippi had been settled. Then, in 1842, Kit Carson led the government explorer and surveyor John Frémont over the South Pass in the Rockies, a passage that had been recently discovered by the trapper Jedediah Smith. Now the secret of mountain men would become general knowledge. Within two years' time, settlers looking for a new life began to travel farther west to Missouri, Kansas, or north to Nebraska, in covered wagons through the South farther west to Utah, Oregon, Arizona, Colorado, and California. The whole country seemed to be leaning westward, toward opportunity, and a wilderness free of the assumptions of old Europe, a vision woven out of an unrealized element of democracy, the dream of a society without class and hierarchy.

There is, of course, more than one way to experience equality. At the beginning of the same year the existence of South Pass became public knowledge, Emerson made a sad entry in his journal. His beloved son, Waldo, then just five years old, had died two days earlier. "Sorrow makes us all children again," he wrote, "destroys all differences of intellect. The wisest knows nothing."

Later in the same year, Emerson, who was then thirty-nine years old, notes the passage of time in his own life and lists sights he has not yet seen. "For me . . . the Prairie and the Ohio and Mississippi Rivers," he writes, "are still only names." Yet his longing to travel west is balanced by an understanding of the nature of desire. Just three years later he writes in his journal that whenever you get what you wish for, you will soon see "it will be *yourself*," and then adds that "we live and die for a beauty which we wronged ourselves in thinking alien."

Over the same period, he had been taking frequent walks in the woods with Thoreau, forging a friendship that was to reverberate through the American culture far into the future. In 1845, he would give Thoreau permission to build a small cabin on his property by Walden Pond, where the younger man wrote his famous book named after the pond. "What . . . does the West stand for?" he asks in those pages before he adds, as if to answer, "It is easier to sail many thousand miles through cold and storm . . . than it is to explore the private sea, the Atlantic and Pacific ocean of one's being alone."

Standing on a mountain made of time, I am able to see another aspect of this history now. The western migration seems to be, among other things, an escape from the problems democracy was facing as well as a movement toward freedom and equality. The open spaces of the West provided a way to avoid a deeper recognition of the consequences of inequities, of the undermining force wielded by accumulated wealth and power, old hierarchies, and the attitudes of superiority, embedded in these circumstances that are contrary to democratic values.

The first major wagon train carrying nine hundred people, along with one thousand head of livestock, which reached Oregon in 1843, started an avalanche of migration. Now the fur traders, mountain men, explorers, hunting parties, missionaries, and military units who had been traveling over two thousand miles west would be joined on the trails by cattle and sheep ranchers, pioneer farmers, and even sightseeing tours.

Growing up in Southern California, I was surrounded by the mythology of the old West. Occasionally, on weekends when my father came to visit me, we would go to Knott's Berry Farm, where we could ride a stagecoach or a horse, explore pioneer bunkhouses and cabins, drink soda pop in a facsimile of an old saloon, and where in an attempt to mimic the look of the past the bar, like the ersatz general store, had signs and menus with misspelled, roughly hewn letters.

I loved these visits, but I also remember that my eager search of the place often ended in a vague sense of disappointment, as if I wanted to know something that could not be found there. Why, for instance, was the writing on the signs misspelled and so poorly executed? The version they had was actually a polished, carefully crafted simulacrum, which bore none of the signs of the actual suffering that would have driven so many west, uneducated people who never had the chance to learn to read or write properly, using a jagged board for a sign because they were pressed and overworked and had to make do with whatever was at hand.

Like many children of my generation, I was obsessed with cowboys and Indians. At one time or another, I had a pair of six-shooters and holsters on a belt, a bow and arrow, and a red cowgirl outfit. Though what I truly longed for was a pair of real chaps, made of rawhide, with silver buckles. When I asked for riding lessons, my grandmother, who always had her eye on social improvements, wanted me to learn English saddle. But I insisted on a western saddle. When my father and I rode over trails, I would go into a state of reverie, imagining myself riding through a forest in the wild, ready to rescue someone or fight for my life.

My fantasies were not unusual. Even in the midst of the twentieth century, when cars and highways defined the landscape, the dream of the West had not died. My father often took me to the movies on the weekends, and when he let me choose the film, which he almost always did, I usually chose a Western. Among the films we saw was one called *The Big Sky*. It pictured a friendship between two mountain men, a bond that was challenged by the attraction they both felt to the same woman. I thought the film supported my point of view, that romance was basically a silly distraction. This was my tomboy phase, and I remember telling my father after seeing that film that I preferred Westerns because most of the characters were men who did real things and there was not a lot of kissing to break up the action. As was characteristic of him, my father listened to what I said with full respect for my solemn expression. The memory touches me now, if only with the sweetly ironic awareness that as I confessed my prejudice against what I considered the trivial world of relationships, my father was showing the kind of sensitivity that allows for subtle intimacy and, along with this, of course, self-knowledge.

I am thinking again of that earlier day in the kitchen when I was almost six years old and he patiently tried to explain to me why I could not play with my sister. I realize now that there was another ingredient crucial to the alchemy of democracy that he was giving to me that day. In the way he spoke, he was modeling an empathetic response to my concerns. He neither dismissed nor ridiculed my wishes.

When I ask myself why it is so common for both girls and boys of the age I was then, nine years old, to dislike kissing in movies, I remember another day I spent with my father when he suggested I might try to climb up the piling of a dock at a beach we frequented in San Pedro. I told him I was not certain I could do it. But he answered that I could probably do anything I set my mind to. With his help, I climbed the piling and then told everyone what I had done for weeks. The age when children don't like kissing occurs just before they will begin doing this themselves. But in the interim between adolescence and the even more tender period of infancy, children are more focused on the heady joys of freedom and independence than relationship. There was one movie with a female heroine I did love. It was called *Calamity Jane*.

During my childhood, I saw countless Westerns in theaters and later on television. But I did not notice then how these films molded a variety of iconic tales from history, with messages that, from one film to another or even within the same movie, were at times wholly at odds with one another. The myth of the lonely hero, the embodiment of an outsized, almost transcendent independence, who saves a town practically by himself, with his courage and his fast gun, was told over and over in these films. Yet all around the hero and crucial to his story were communities of men, women, and children, dependent on one another and the land for survival. And in a sense, even the hero was depicted as dependent in a subtle way, since without a community, his heroism would have no meaning.

No wonder that *Shane* had such a powerful effect on public consciousness. The movie portrays a man who comes to town, rescues everyone, inspires and feels love, but in the end decides to ride off into the horizon alone. The ambivalence evident in Westerns mirrors an inner dilemma that has shadowed American democracy almost from the start, an unexamined conflict, yielding the confusion that comes from denial and avoidance, so that the pieces of the philosophy by which a certain way of life is explained never quite add up. There was, for instance, the predictable presence of a sidekick, the character actors accompanying the handsomely invulnerable heroes, men who were themselves flawed, usually bumbling, older, less intelligent or agile, though often more accessibly the butt of humor, and in fact, were you to admit this to yourself, more recognizable, more human.

In all these films, the West was portrayed as a wild place, where eccentric people did outrageous things, and in this sense, a place of uncommon freedom. But this was not an absolute freedom. Almost all the action was informed by a strong morality, a code that even though it was unstated, was sure in its judgments. Shane's ambivalence was displayed against the backdrop of another legendary struggle, the titanic conflicts played out between farmers and ranchers, the former portrayed as innocent families, the latter depicted as greedy, often wealthy, and ruthless men with the morality of bandits, ready to exploit every kind of weakness.

The other great conflict that was portrayed again and again, the protracted battle between white settlers and the Native Americans who hunted and lived on the land they wanted to settle, was also depicted as a battle of good against evil. But the lines of morality shifted constantly. Indians were not always bad; sometimes they were even pictured as the victims of the U.S. Army. And when they were portrayed as treacherous, threatening, or murderous, it did not seem as if they had made a choice to commit bad deeds, but instead seemed to be driven by an inchoate force, swooping down on their prey, much like a sudden storm or a grizzly bear.

Among the ubiquitous pairs of cowboys I would watch as they wandered from place to place doing good was a couple whose symbiotic relationship became strangely iconic to my generation. One had a mysterious identity, his face hidden underneath a black mask. But though his disguise was menacing, the Lone Ranger rode a white horse. By contrast, his partner, Tonto, a Native American, wore no disguise, but he had darker skin and his horse was darker too. What did it all mean? I did not ask. I was captivated by the predictable plots, nice folks threatened by bad guys. Always, in a deeply satisfying turn of events, the Lone Ranger would turn what seemed like the inevitable tragedy around. I was fascinated by Tonto, though I found something about him disquieting. I was only able to name it as I grew older and learned about the demeaning nature of racism. Yet now I detect something else too in the Lone Ranger's silent partner, a man who spoke rarely and then only monosyllabically; he seemed to know a great deal, to sense what the Lone Ranger could not; his quietness seemed to hold a deeper knowledge, denied and denigrated, yet present and still resonating the power of the greater nature to which we all belong.

October

Now everyone talks about global warming. With hurricane Rita having come so soon after Katrina, the pattern becomes clear. Not necessarily the frequency of hurricanes, though that may be so too, but the fact that so many of them are stronger has been tied to the rising temperature of the oceans.

The different version of the West brought to life in movies and on television were based on various legends of the West conceived in the nineteenth-century American imagination, when in newspaper stories, fiction, and on the stage, a version of the West was being invented, with brave men but few brave women, one that amplified both the dangers and the rewards of the westward movement and indulged in a gross and melodramatic exaggeration of the number of wagon trains and pioneers assaulted by Indians, while at the same time suppressing grim accounts of Native American communities, undefended women and children, slaughtered in their villages by the U.S. Army. The distortions and tall tales were not just the product of overzealous storytellers. Whether consciously or not, these fantasies promoted a particular philosophy, a conceptual frame that, as I consider it now, seems to mimic the philosophies of monarchies and aristocrats who once claimed that God had given the right to dominion.

Revolution alone does not ensure that ideas advocating tyranny will be entirely repudiated. It is possible to articulate a belief in democratic principles while at the same time claiming the prerogatives of a monarch. Even images of kings and knights, whose crowns and silver armor and ruby-colored capes are signs that they have been blessed with divine right, remain in memory, and though tinged with nostalgia, can exert an influence in the deepest regions of the mind, giving credence to first the wish and then the effort to have a supernatural power over circumstances.

The philosophy known as Manifest Destiny existed as a widespread belief long before it was given a name. It was there even before the United States came into being, in the philosophy that drove the Crusades, the idea that God wanted European nations to convert the world to Christianity. The revolutionaries who founded America were well aware of the dangers of claiming divine authority for the state. This is why, as he wrote the Declaration of Independence, Jefferson chose the words *Nature's God* rather than *God*. Still, the thinking was in him too, in a more subtle form, the idea that European civilization was superior and that Native Americans needed to be "civilized" before they could be given the rights of citizens. As American territories expanded and more and more white settlers moved west, so too was this point of view enlarged; the westward movement was inevitable, it was argued now. The United States ought to rule all North America, not only because of economic and political superiority and the need for more land but because it was God's will. Though the term *Manifest Destiny* was coined in 1845, in an article by John L. O'Sullivan on the annexation of Texas, the attitude that led to the slaughter of women and children in Indian villages at Sand Creek and Wounded Knee was already well established.

The doctrine was alive and well in the fifties in other more modern forms. I was not immune to its message. I have a clear memory of standing in the backyard of my grandparents' home. I was about ten years old. The sun was descending, there was a slight chill in the air, and I knew I should to go in to dinner. But as was often the case with me then at this hour, I was lost in thought, and so I lingered. An idea had come to me, a blend of the current events I discussed in class, including the dilemma of the Cold War, American technology, which I had learned was superior, my religious beliefs, and my desire to emulate my cowboy heroes and rescue those in distress. Though I did not know it, the long shadow of Manifest Destiny had brought all these strands together in a notion I came up with all by myself, a clever strategy by which Russian citizens would be aroused to throw off the yoke of tyranny. Why not, I imagined, float a blimp high enough above the clouds but low enough to broadcast a voice, pretending to be the voice of God that urged Russians to overthrow their leaders? Because I thought it an ingenuous and unique solution (I had not heard yet of the Voice of America), I was dismayed when my grandparents were not equally excited by the prospect.

The ecology of any child's mind will reveal a great deal about the culture in which she lives. Alongside my messianic zeal, like many of my friends, I was fascinated by stories of the Donner party. How they had been caught in the snow with no provisions. How slowly and agonizingly many of them died. How finally some of the living resorted to eating the bodies of those among them who had already succumbed. It thrilled me that the whole ordeal had taken place not far from our summer camp, just above us on a mountain to the east. If I ask myself what the attraction was about, I remember how much children love gruesome stories, but they also love to hear about anything that has been kept secret from them. Which makes me wonder now if much of the appeal of this tale was that it revealed a less savory but more truthful side of the glorious American West.

Yet this gory tale did not represent the whole story. I am thinking again of that image of Yosemite Valley that Albert Bierstadt painted in 1868, and the otherworldly glow that reflected from the water and the high cliffs. Romantic and overblown though it is, there is a grain of truth within it. Like the glow around Jefferson, it speaks of an inner state, an expectation, the sure belief that one can make a better life on earth—a life that seems to be promised in this painting as if by the landscape itself.

Was this what one pioneer woman, Louisiana Strentzel, meant when, in 1849, on reaching the Mission of San Diego in California, she wrote her father and mother, her brothers and sisters, "After an absence of eight long months, at last I have an opportunity of writing to let you know that we are alive and have reached in safety the border of the promised land."

She had just traveled for eighteen hundred miles, as she writes, "through wilderness," crossing "deserts and gardens," undergoing hardship, privation, and danger. If the party constantly feared attack, and at times needed the protection of soldiers, and though a band of Tonkawa Indians had stampeded some of their horses, they were never attacked themselves. In fact, they had an Indian guide to help them find water for themselves and grass for their animals along the way. Some died of disease before they reached California. Louisiana herself became very ill for a period. At the Rio Grande the wagon they rode had to be taken apart and ferried over the river in canoes. When, once in California, they were advised to go either north toward San Francisco or south to San Diego, the choice they made, to take the southern route, was fortunate. The suffering along the northern route was great, and far more died. They were lucky in other ways too. Of the deaths that occurred along the trail, many were very young. But neither of their children, not two-year-old Louie nor her younger brother Johnny had been ill even a day during their journey.

Though she told her family that the climate in San Diego was pleasant and good for the health, soon, like so many of those who came to California, the family was on the move again, this time toward a glow of another kind. As Emerson had written in his journal in the first month of 1849, "Suddenly the California soil is spangled with a little gold dust here and there." Along with thousands of others from all over the world and many cultures, a diverse group that included Chinese immigrants and free African-Americans, Rollins Ridge, who would later become famous as the author of the tales of Joaquin Murieta, and who, the grandson of Major Ridge, as a boy had witnessed his father's murder, had gone to the mining camps too. But the Strentzels did not pan for gold or stake a claim. Instead, they settled in the valley of the Tuolumne River, where they were smart enough to establish a ferry, a hotel, and a general store, all to serve the miners.

OCTOBER

The background to the disaster is coming out. Not only were so many of Louisiana's national guard in Iraq, there is this now. Needing funds for the war in Iraq, Bush cut the funds allocated for the repair of levees in 2004, repairs that were almost finished when the work had to stop.

The confluence of dates fascinated me. It was during the years of the gold rush that John Muir, then eleven years old, left Dunbar, Scotland, with his family to settle in Wisconsin. It must have been difficult to live in what was still a frontier then, and lonely. Especially since, because Muir's father, Daniel, a zealous Campbellite, regarded pleasure as corrupting, the privations at home were even more severe than frontier circumstances required. He forbade all dancing, most forms of play, and even all books except the Bible. And though, unlike the Great Plains to the west, there were trees with which to build fences and houses and barns, and water to irrigate crops, the hard and endless work of farming became even more so for John, since his father spent most of his time indoors studying Scripture and praying, while he forced his children to do the necessary labor, whipping them if they did not comply, even when they were ill.

Muir's life would be brightened and ultimately transformed one day when two neighbor boys recited a few poems to him, verses by Byron, Milton, Wordsworth, and Poe. Was "The Raven" among those he heard? In Poe's great poem, written while he was still grieving his wife, he describes the visit of a raven; the bird flies suddenly into his study and lands on top of the bust of Pallas, as if Nature herself were reminding him that no degree of reason can conquer death.

After this, Muir began to read poetry secretly by himself. He loved the Romantics and the meanings they found in nature. And at the same time, as if his own imagination had been freed by what he read, he began to invent and then build a series of ingenious tools, ways of measuring space and time and temperature, ranging from thermometers to clocks to barometers to hygrometers. Though his twin interests, science and poetry, may seem to conflict, they augured his future, the way he would combine botany and geology and other sciences with an uncommon ability to describe the dimensions of nature that science does not explain.

The turnings of a single life can seem as mysterious and unpredictable as a path through the densest forest. It was after he exhibited his inventions at a state fair and received a certain degree of recognition that Muir was encouraged to apply to the recently formed University of Wisconsin. Here he would meet Professor Ezra Carr, who had been educated in New England and had known and studied with both Emerson and the geologist Louis Agassiz. Through Carr's influence, Muir was introduced to the work of Emerson and Thoreau. He was deeply influenced by both men—inspired by Agassiz's new idea that the mountains and valleys over the earth had been formed by a period of glaciation, which he called the Ice Age.

In 1862, while Muir was still studying transcendentalism, Emerson made a sweetly sad entry in his journal. A friend who had just been to see Thoreau told him that he "Never saw a man dying with so much pleasure and peace." A few months after Thoreau died, he wrote that if Thoreau's journals were ever printed, they would inspire "a plentiful crop of naturalists." Those who read them would "fall easy prey to the charming of Pan's pipe."

By this time, inspired by Emerson himself, Muir had already begun to keep journals of his own. Soon there were other influences. Carr's wife, Jeanne, introduced him to the thinking of the Christian theologian William Ellery Channing, who, in contrast to Muir's father, believed in a loving God and indwelling divinity. Then a fellow student began to speak with him about his enthusiasm for botany. Finally, the crisis that had been rocking the whole nation since he began his studies put an end to Muir's time at the university. A conscientious objector, to avoid being conscripted into the Union army, he fled to Canada. There he earned his living as a mill hand and in his free time wandered the mountains searching for plants. It was on one of these journeys that he discovered that example of the rare plant *Calypso borealis*. Seeing it in such a secluded place, where no one else would be likely to find it, he realized that in its exquisite beauty, the plant did not exist just to please human eyes but for its own sake.

The transformation of his inner life would accelerate when, not long after returning to the United States, while working in a carriage shop, Muir suffered an accident that wounded one of his eyes. For a period, as the other eye went blind in a sympathetic reaction, he was blind. His sight returned, but his convalescence was to leave him with a more reflective nature. He felt reborn. Now he wanted to devote his life to seeing natural beauty, a capacity that he had nearly lost. First he walked a thousand miles to the Gulf of Mexico. After crossing Panama, he boarded a steamship to San Francisco and from there walked across the San Joaquin Valley and into the Sierras, which eventually he wrote were "the most divinely beautiful of mountain chains I have ever seen." Making Yosemite his home, he would wander the mountains for five years.

Three years later, Emerson met Muir in Yosemite, where the young man taught him how to tell the differences among a silver fir, a yellow pine, and a sugar pine. Muir was disappointed that his mentor would not go camping with him and sleep out in the open. But he knew that the man, whom he called "as serene as a sequoia," was growing old. As Emerson's party departed, he let his horse fall behind, and just before they disappeared over the ridge, he turned his horse, took off his hat, and waved good-bye.

Once home, Emerson wrote how he loved California: "It has better days, and more of them, than any other part of the country." A month later, he must have been thinking of his journey to the West again. He had traveled by way of the new railroad. The line had just been completed two years earlier. "In my lifetime," he wrote in June, "have been wrought five miracles,—namely, 1, the Steamboat; 2, the Railroad; 3, the Electric telegraph; 4, the application of the spectroscope to astronomy; 5, the Photograph—five miracles which have altered the relations of nations to each other." He goes on to list other miracles too: mowing machine and power presses and anesthesia, knowledge of the nature of electricity, magnetism, evolution in plants and animals, the ability to predict the weather.

All these inventions made their mark on the northern continent. Soon those who were trying to make a better life began to move to the Great Plains too, where farming had been made possible by the invention of barbed wire and a new kind of plow that could break the hard, dried sod of the plains. Like the Internet today, the telegraph made conducting investments easier and faster, as travel by train started to shrink the vast distances that just over six decades earlier, when Lewis and Clark set out, seemed almost unimaginable. In a very short time, the West had changed dramatically. The vast buffalo herds were gone. And if the West was more densely populated, it was also increasingly dominated by one culture. Two years before Louisiana Strentzel and her family reached Mission San Diego, California and Texas had been wrested from Mexico. Captain Winfield Scott, who had supervised the first disastrous attempts to enforce the removal of Cherokee from Virginia, was decorated for his distinguished service in an invasion that he led as far as Mexico City. The Civil War was over, and with its end, the U.S. Army moved west to round up Indians onto reservations.

The year that Muir met Emerson was also the year that the first of his articles about the West appeared in the *New York Tribune*. He wrote a series on the glaciers of Yosemite that captured public attention. Then, just a few years after he decided to become a professional writer, he met Louie Strentzel, the daughter of Louisiana and on April 14, 1880, he married her. By then her family had moved to Martinez in northern California, where they planted large orchards filled with orange trees. All through the next decade Muir managed the family farm. But at the end of the decade, his focus changed. He began a public campaign to create Yosemite National Park.

It was perhaps from John Muir's work that the authors who created the cards on Indian lore I found in cereal boxes got some of their material. In his account of his first summer in the Sierra, he writes about the "wonderful way of walking unseen" that Indians had. But nevertheless, he shared the prejudices of his times, marveling at Native Americans yet, at the same time, in his prose, treating the Pitt River Indians he encountered with a kind of contempt, as if they were inferior. He could not extend the reciprocity of spirit he felt with plants and stones and trees to people from a different culture.

By the time he fought to preserve Yosemite, Native Americans all over the country had been slaughtered, felled by disease, forced onto reservations, or as often happened in California, began to hide their identity out of fear.

OCTOBER

A slight shift in what seems a hopeless state of affairs. Someone has been indicted in the CIA leak case. Lewis Libby, Vice President Cheney's chief of staff, has been charged with obstruction of justice and perjury.

If, along with Crazy Horse, Sitting Bull had helped deliver a stunning defeat to the Seventh Cavalry under General George Armstrong Custer at Little Big Horn, now he was a celebrity for a different reason, a star of the Wild West show organized by William Cody in 1883.

I am wondering now if either my grandmother or my grandfather ever saw Buffalo Bill or Annie Oakley perform. My grandmother would have missed Sitting Bull. He was in the show only for a brief year, in 1885. She was born five years later, in 1890. But in one form or another, the show traveled all over the world for many more years. It is possible that as a small child, she would have been taken to Chicago to see the sharpshooters and the fancy riders. The story in our family was that my grandmother, who wanted to be an actress, was asked to join a theatrical troupe that came through town. One of the tragedies of her life was that her father would not let her do this.

Was that why she and my grandfather traveled to California? Because of her disappointments and for his dreams? I do not know the exact date. Perhaps it was 1912 or even 1913. But not later because my mother was born in Long Beach in 1914, the same year that, just a few miles north, in Los Angeles, John Muir died.

Emerson had died four decades earlier, just three years after he saw California. In one of the last entries in his journal, he wrote, "The secret of poetry is never explained—is always new. We have not got further than mere wonder at the delicacy of the touch, and the eternity it inherits."

His philosophy came to me sideways through a very long dramatic poem written by Edna St. Vincent Millay, who was still popular then. Just as Muir memorized Wordsworth and Poe, when I was eleven years old, I committed long passages of "Renascence" to memory. The poem seemed to express what I experienced when I was in the Sierra. "All I could see from where I stood / Was three long mountains and a wood," the poem begins, and moves from the palpable sky and grass to "The How and Why of all things, past, / And present, and forevermore. / The Universe, cleft to the core."

OCTOBER

It all seems connected. The psychology at least. Dominion is the word that comes to mind. The denial of our dependence on nature and the belief that we can use force to get whatever we want all over the world.

In the same year, I entered what was then called junior high school, where we had separate classes, but all that I was learning seemed to form a pattern. In my science class, I became fascinated with the cycle of reciprocity in which trees give off the oxygen human beings and other animals need and we exhale the carbon dioxide green things need. I loved to think about this quiet exchange between leaves and lungs. It resonated with the wild love I felt for trees then, to know that we were sustaining each other in this way.

At the same time, in my art class, our very stern teacher brought us all outside to look at the trees growing in the parking strip at one end of the school. She made us look for a long time before she asked us to draw what we saw. She did not want anything in a modern style. She wanted us to see and record as best we could what was actually there. I remember craning my neck to see up to the highest branches, and how the anatomy of the tree, with its roots and then wide trunk, which narrowed as it rose, and branches that split into narrower limbs and then twigs with leaves, all moved up toward the sky, the light. I had drawn trees before. But now drawing trees became my passion. And each time I traced the arc from the soil upward into the leaves, I felt within me again that sacred exchange, exhaling and inhaling, giving and receiving.

In the same year, I was undergoing another kind of religious transformation: my own private disillusionment with the church I attended. The young pastor I had so loved left for another assignment, and we were assigned an older man, prematurely shriveled in his attitude toward life, who was driven by a series of oddly impassioned opinions, among them the supposition that the King James translation of the Bible had been corrupted by Jews. It was not just the quality of his irrational fury, an overheated yet oddly dissonant racism I had also witnessed in my grandfather, that bothered me. I was offended by his attitude toward Jewish people. In that year I had gained a new friend, my first soul mate other than my sister. And she was Jewish. Since we went to the same junior high and lived just around the corner from each other, we would stand on the corner and talk before we went home. Our exchanges ranged over many topics, but the subject I remember now is theology. We talked about our different religions and came to the conclusion that the doctrine really did not matter, nor did our names for states of grace or God.

In the essence, we both felt a loving presence and sensed too that our lives had a meaning, one that could not be explained but seemed to be nevertheless within us.

NOVEMBER

Article in the Chronicle *about signs of global warming in Yosemite. It feels like a death in the family.*

Soon my friend would move from the neighborhood. I would never see her again. And after this year I would not go again to the camp in the Sierras I had loved so much either. Soon my sister would be starting college. Though I did not know it yet, this was the beginning of the end of the closeness we shared too. Though the love between us has abided, in the years to come, we were to grow further and further apart.

I moved back to my mother's house. In the last summer I spent in the Sierras, I was among the older campers, which meant I was allowed to go on an overnight trip. We hiked all day to that place above the timberline where only sugar pines grew. These trees that had been a source of inexhaustible pleasure to John Muir attracted me too, as if they held some secret they wanted to reveal. After I came home, I spent much of the rest of the summer at the beach, where I practiced bodysurfing. I loved the salty water and spray of the waves, and all the while the surf pushed me eastward onto the sand, I could feel the mountains and the sugar pines in me too, the whole topography of my birthplace in my body.

3

BLUE JEANS

He who is always at ease and has enough of the Blessings of common life is an Impotent Judge of the feelings of the unfortunate.

—A SURGEON AT VALLEY FORGE, DECEMBER 15, 1777

What Copernicus really achieved was not the discovery of a true theory but of a fertile new point of view.

—LUDWIG WITTGENSTEIN

I came to see that poverty is not ordained by heaven.

—ROSE SCHNEIDERMAN, *All for One*

NOVEMBER

A persistent thread woven through the war. Denials, misinformation, distortions, facts concealed by the government. Yes, of course, governments lie, but this seems to be the order of the day now.

OVER TIME, certain memories become maps for interior worlds. I am thinking once more of the conversation I had almost sixty years ago with my father in our family kitchen, searching for all it has to teach me, reading it the way a pilgrim might study a fresco by Giotto or Fra Angelico for the symbolic meanings shining beneath the aging colors that still give off an inner light.

NOVEMBER

When will we all pass over the thin line drawn in the mind between meaning and meaninglessness? It has happened before, whole nations, peoples enmeshed in a fog of illusions, who become indifferent to the pursuit of truth.

Now I find myself fascinated by another dimension in the response my father gave me to the question I asked him so many years ago. It contains still another lesson in democracy I learned before I even knew I was a student of the process. Freedom of speech implies an entitlement that, though it is not listed in the Bill of Rights, is equally essential to democracy. The dialogue I remember with my father was so simple, yet it provides a vital example of this prerogative. *Where is my sister? She is in the orchard.* The natural companion to, if not the consequence of, freedom of speech is the right to knowledge.

As I think of what passed between my father and me on that day, I can see an expression on his face, without disapproval or reserve, relaxed in a distinctly American way, and his posture relaxed too, approachable, a citizen, with no attitude of self-importance, I would say now, and not defined by rank. Though in that regard, I know he may have differed from men and women in different circumstances. He was a workingman.

If I have filled in certain details of my father's demeanor from later memories, I know I have borrowed them from the many times we spent together after my parents' divorce. He would pick me up on a Saturday or Sunday, and we would go someplace together. We rode horses in Griffith Park, or in Chatsworth, through the hills and fields where so many Westerns were filmed; played miniature golf, tennis, or handball on the court at the firehouse where he worked; rowed boats in San Pedro Bay; went swimming in Will Rogers State Park; attended stock car races, or conventions on various themes—the latest developments in technology or medicine; and when I got interested in the history of art, we visited public museums.

While driving here or there, we had endless conversations. Though my father was not educated, he had a curious and open mind. When we discussed political questions or films we had seen together or places and things we liked, not only did he listen carefully to whatever I had to say, he responded with the same care and respect he gave to his friends. I remember too that when we talked about our family, he spoke of these matters with a candor that I rarely encountered from other adults, acknowledging my grandmother's habit of bending the truth, for instance, or that she was a bit of a tyrant, or the way my mother became irrational, even crazy, when she drank too much.

DECEMBER

Yet perhaps we can count on the reaction I can feel even in my own body when I sense concealment or lies, like a slight nausea. Is this the threat of an unnatural sleepiness? So different from the sense of vitality I feel when at last someone reveals the truth.

But as soon as my father entered my grandparents' house, a different mood came over him. He was still receptive to me, but regarding his own sensitively calibrated intelligence, it was as if who he really was had been obscured by another attitude; in the presence of my mother's parents, he assumed the quiet obedience of a well-behaved boy. His transformation could be partly explained by the fact that he had been raised from an early age by his grandmother, my great-grandmother, whom we called Nanny, and who was more strict with him than a younger parent would have been. But, still, I had heard him raise his voice to her. As I look back now, I can see that something more than old-fashioned respect was present in the alchemy of his mood.

Though the catalytic element was never mentioned, it was present everywhere, even in the words we used. I have a vivid memory of walking with my grandmother on the cement path that led from the backyard to the front yard, feeling momentarily happy in the sunlight, as we passed by the greenery growing at the fence, when suddenly my grandmother seemed very troubled by something I had said. "No, Susie," she said to me, "don't say that again. You mustn't say 'he don't.' You must learn to say 'he doesn't.'" The tone of voice she used made me feel harshly reprimanded, as if I were somehow wrong in my very nature. And of course, on an unspoken level in her mind, it was my nature that had to be corrected, as if my father's working-class grammar were a sign of inferiority that would have to be painstakingly rooted out of me.

The fact that both of my grandparents liked my father did not prevent them from assuming that he was beneath them in countless ways. His grammar, his lack of education, the casual clothes he wore, the old Studebaker he drove, all spoke of a class not only lower than their own but far lower than the one to which they aspired. Their lifestyle was not lavish. They owned the duplex where we lived; our half of the dwelling had two bedrooms, one bathroom, a dining room that opened onto a small living room, and a kitchen with a dining nook. But despite this modesty, both my grandparents showed signs of refinement. They spoke using what was then called correct grammar. And although my grandfather preferred gory detective stories and Westerns, my grandmother, who had attended college for two years, knew more than a little about literature and the arts. Hence, she and I formed a sturdy alliance in favor of watching highbrow shows on television, performances like Thornton Wilder's *Our Town*. But my grandfather was elegant. Known to be dapper in his prime, he wore one of several cashmere cardigans daily. He had an impressive collection of silk ties and wingtip shoes too, no doubt acquired when he was an executive salesman.

There were other impressive artifacts. I remember one afternoon after I had moved back to my mother's house, during a visit with my grandparents, when my grandmother told me in a low voice that she had something to show me, and led me down the hall to the room that had once been mine, before opening the closet door to reveal a chinchilla coat. Though I have inherited my grandparents' love of sartorial splendor, I did not really know what to make of this garment. No one remotely intimate with our family ever wore such things. Los Angeles even in winter is rarely very cold. I never saw her wear it. Only now do I realize that, like the new car that my grandfather bought every year and that sat in the driveway most of the time, the coat served a symbolic purpose. Each luxurious object they owned not only provided a sign of slight elevation above various neighbors and strangers but, like a talisman or a fetish, delivered a vague sense of realization while at the same time, for the mind is full of such contradictions, helping to dull the disappointment that, I can see looking back now, pervaded the atmosphere of their household in their older years.

Though my grandmother seemed driven toward a fate that was never to be hers, she cannot be described as a social climber. In the tightly circumscribed world she inhabited, there was no avenue available by which she could rise. She had become president or a leading officer of all the women's clubs she had joined. The distinctions that eluded her were in no way precisely defined in her mind. She was far too proud to admit to the feelings of failure that Willy Loman expressed in *Death of a Salesman*. She seemed more like a member of a royal or at least an aristocratic family who had been displaced. That she was dissatisfied with her life came out in small complaints regarding the imperfections of those around her. Yet this vigilance was also directed at herself, as if, unlike any real aristocrat, the smallest misstep might make her lose her rank.

As with most children, when I was younger, class meant nothing at all to me. Still I sensed the strange, unnamed difference between my father's world and my grandparents' realm. That my father's attitude was deferential toward both of them felt in one sense normal. After all, my attitude was the same. In this way, my father and I seemed to share the same position; I knew he was not a child, but he was not an authority either. He belonged to an intermediate category. He did not insist as my grandmother did that I behave with the impeccable manners described in the book by Emily Post from which she read to me occasionally. He let me wear blue jeans when I went out with him, bought me the captain's hat of which my grandmother disapproved, and let me drink soda pop, which was strictly forbidden at home.

Yet, though I did not understand class differences when I was a younger child, I must have had some sense of the subtle prejudice that colored the air of our family gatherings. I remember, for instance, waking one night from a terrifying nightmare in which three frightening women whom I was too young to recognize as my mother, my grandmother, and my great-aunt had told me my father had died. And then there was that Christmas when the gift I had designated for my father had been given mistakenly to my grandfather. When I realized the mistake, I wept. I was heartbroken to think that my father went without a gift from me and even more distraught that he might have believed I had not thought of him. It was an understandable mistake. I called my father "Daddy," but my grandmother would sometimes call my grandfather "Daddy" too. Yet now I can see that my grief was intensified by the sense I had of the way my father was diminished in our family. This knowledge was never articulated openly, nor did I ever name it myself. It existed rather in a shadow-land of consciousness, a realm inaccessible to reason and reflection.

December

Sad to think it's come to this. In the papers today, an article about public schools in New York, desperate for funds, courting private donors.

The right to knowledge is crucial to the process of democracy, a requisite companion to freedom of speech. But as in a single life, the knowledge one needs to understand public life is not always evident, even to the most intrepid journalist. What has not been delineated or spoken can seem invisible to the mind. But contrary to the popular saying, what you don't know can hurt you, the power of a circumstance to do harm often exists in direct proportion to its invisibility.

My ignorance of class was hardly exceptional. By the time I entered junior high school, the illusion that American democracy had produced a classless society had reached its apogee. In America, the fifth decade of the twentieth century was a relatively prosperous period. With the end of the prior century, a new class in between the rich and the poor had appeared and began to grow steadily. Now many workingmen, including my father and stepfather, were able to buy houses for their families. Affordable clothes and cars were being mass-produced. Food was plentiful and cheap. In California the public school system was very good and available without charge to everyone.

This abundance coupled with America's victory in the Second World War created an ideal image of a fair and humane nation that offered equal opportunity to anyone ready to get an education and work hard. The knowledge that American planes had dropped nuclear bombs on Nagasaki and Hiroshima and that terrible poverty tied to racism was spread throughout the country existed only at the margins of the almost aggressive cheerfulness that was omnipresent.

The illusion was seductive. It was not just the saccharine simplifications of reality that Norman Rockwell's covers on the *Saturday Evening Post* or television shows like *Father Knows Best* provided but alternate worlds—worlds that, as I grew up in my troubled family, gave me no small measure of comfort. I remember peering into Rockwell's paintings with a gravely focused desire, soaking up the gentle humor, the kind smiles. (I can only imagine now how a child who was hungry on Thanksgiving would have gazed at the yearly image of a family around a table groaning with food.) Though the series was somewhat exotic to me, like stories told about a foreign land with an admirably stable and venerated culture, I loved watching *Father Knows Best*. The illusion the program cast was so perfectly encompassing that for the duration of each performance, not only did I believe this soft domesticity to exist but I felt myself to be inside it.

Yet though often I could retain a bit of an afterglow for the rest of the evening, as gradually my awareness of reality returned, the end of each show felt like an expulsion from Eden. I knew this world did not really belong to me. In my young mind, I associated the marked superiority of these shining tales over my own sordid family dramas with the elegant white colonial house where the sweetly comic action was set. There was a staircase that ascended from a front hallway; a sunny living room, accented with a few antiques that neither darkened nor overburdened the elegantly casual space; a formal dining room across the hallway. Everyone had separate bedrooms, and it was all better kept and more upscale than anywhere I had ever lived. These very pleasant surroundings seemed essential to the good life from which I had been excluded.

The last time I remember watching *Father Knows Best,* I was in my mother's small living room again. Remembering all the nights when they stayed out drinking, only to stumble home in the early morning, or even worse, when they brought me with them for their bar hops, sometimes taking me in, at other times leaving me to wait for hours in the car, I was not eager to return to them. But my grandmother had decided she could no longer manage me. After I turned eleven, since, like so many prepubescent children, I was developing a mind of my own, I began to object rather often to her rules, her ways of doing things, and even took issue with what she said. I actually objected once to the morning ritual in which she read us selections from the *Reader's Digest.* Though she was often critical of others, she was thin-skinned when it came to any criticism aimed at her. Steadily she began to warn me that if I continued to talk back, I would be sent away. "One more time," she would say, before finally she decided I had only two choices, both of which I found terrible: to live with my mother or be sent to a boarding school.

My image of the latter came from a dubious mixture of hearsay and images from a film based on *Jane Eyre* in which Elizabeth Taylor, then a child actor, was made to stand out in the cold for hours and then died. Reluctantly I chose the known evil, my mother's house.

So I was with my mother when one night, after eagerly anticipating my weekly dose of unreality, I sat down to watch *Father Knows Best* for what would be the last time. My mother had been drinking, and she had reached the stage that was characterized by a sardonic if not vicious wit. I wonder now if consciously or unconsciously the program activated her sense of guilt over her failures as a parent, which years later she confessed to me. Yet despite the delusionary quality of her alcoholism, my mother was uncommonly honest. She valued authenticity and disliked pretension (a quality that may explain in part the fact that twice she chose to marry working-class men). But whatever her reasons were, on this particular evening, she began a vituperative monologue on the foolishness of *Father Knows Best*—hence, how naive it was for anyone to watch it. I left the room angrily. I was older now and better able to defend myself. Yet the truth in what she said had burst the illusion. Her words had broken the spell of *Father Knows Best*, though, to be honest, I was already close to breaking it myself. Even before she began her comments, I had had to will myself to enter the glassy-eyed, soporific mood the show required.

I did not understand then that my desire to conjure a kinder world belonged to a larger picture. In those years, public sensibility insisted with a nearly hysterical intensity on an image of America that was without exception a very happy place. Any opinion that argued otherwise seemed threatening, if not monstrous. But nightmare creatures congregated at the borders of the shared imagination. There were those slimy, inexplicable, but terrifying phenomena, like "It" or "The Thing," staging invasions from outer space in one hugely popular movie after another, and the shadowy world of film noir, with men and women hungry for power who were masters of deceit. I remember vividly one episode in a television series directed by Hitchcock in which a seemingly sweet housewife bludgeons her husband with a frozen leg of lamb. And then there was the Red scare.

When I was younger and living with my grandparents, I was only vaguely aware of the interrogations led in the Senate by Joseph McCarthy and in the House by the Un-American Activities Committee. Occasionally I joined my grandfather while he watched the proceedings on television. But my attention wandered. I could not grasp the significance of what I was seeing. My grandfather's explanations meant nothing at all to me. I know he believed he was simplifying the matter when he told me that certain bad men wanted to do bad things to us from which the senator and his cronies with their own committee in Congress were only trying to protect us all. Yet that I never grasped the meaning of his words was partly due to the fact that there was no real meaning in them. Nor could I read the meaning in his expressions, his gestures. Indeed, I experienced my grandfather as two very different men. One who was sweet, playful, and gentle with me and the other possessed by a rage at figures the very thought of whom made him red in the face, so angry, in fact, he could not articulate his thinking, even to another adult.

It was my sister who introduced critical thinking on current events to me. She had taken it upon herself to educate me informally. I remember vividly one evening after my grandparents and I picked her up at the train station, when she brought her bags into my bedroom (the same room that would soon house my grandmother's chinchilla coat) and then told me she had something to show me. With a dramatic gesture she opened her elegant leather briefcase to reveal two thick books, one by Plato and the other by Aristotle. I sat breathless with admiration as she told me the story of Socrates's trial. The message was very clear to me: refusing to give in to the tyrants, he stood up for the truth, even though he was put to death for it.

Soon I had a chance to apply Socrates's example when, late at night, after my grandparents had gone to sleep, she revealed to me that she was going to smoke a cigarette. *Don't tell anyone,* she cautioned me. Did my grandparents ever interrogate me on the question? I rehearsed my silence so often that I'm not at all certain what actually happened. I know that they did not tie me up or threaten me with corporal punishment as I imagined myself successfully resisting. Of course, in this case, I could not have said that I was standing by or even telling the truth. Yet in my mind, I was withholding information in defiance of tyranny.

The story of Socrates showed up again after I had lived in my mother's house for over a year and was soon to graduate from junior high school. Since I was a good student and had demonstrated some talent for writing, I was called upon by a committee of teachers to give them an example of what I might deliver as a speech were I made the class valedictorian. After I pondered what my subject should be, I settled on Socrates. I had always been a great enthusiast for freedom of speech, and I thought this story, along with the scholarly aspect of it, would please the judges. My mother, who was as ignorant of current events as any adult person could be, helped me to prepare. We both thought my chances for being chosen were very good.

I could not interpret the strange silence that hung in the air after I spoke. The teacher assigned to listen to my speech seemed speechless herself. Did she thank me for my effort? Perhaps she did, but what I remember was an oddly negative look on her face, as if a shadow had passed over it. Only a year later, when I began to understand what was happening at the continuing congressional hearings, did I begin to suspect that my fierce defense of freedom of speech struck a raw nerve.

As it was to turn out, my sister's more sophisticated knowledge of the world had another and far greater consequence in my life. Since she had belonged to the debate club in her high school in Davis, that was one of the first electives I chose in my first year in my high school. On the second meeting of the club, smaller groups met in which we were invited to discuss the current events that interested us. Though I prided myself on my independent thought, many of my political opinions came from my sister. It was in fact during one of her seasonal visits and just after a Senate hearing that she discussed the question of Red China with me. It was silly, she said, to hide your head in the sand. Red China existed. We could not go on pretending it did not. So in our small meeting, I brought up this issue, proclaiming how absurd it was that we would try to act as if Red China were not there. I did not know how controversial this opinion was. The truth of it seemed self-evident, and it had the added advantage of recalling my sister to me. I was surprised at the heated debate that ensued, not just by the opposition but also by a group of enthusiastic allies—four girls, who were soon to become good friends.

It was then that new worlds began to open up for me. Earlier, my sister had introduced me to Freud and Dostoyevsky, the poetry of Hart Crane, T. S. Eliot, and W. C. Williams. But there were few other people with whom I could discuss ideas. I no longer had such long conversations with my father about the world around us as I used to have. As I was becoming more sophisticated, a subtle estrangement grew between us. And when he started seeing his new girlfriend, I saw him less often. But now, with my new friends, whom later I would recognize as "Red diaper babies," I could talk about poetry and art and ideas, and, above all, it was from them that I began to learn how to decipher a certain political language that, though I had heard it spoken for years, had meant little to me before.

Much has been written about the difference between information and knowledge. The difference is crucial to democracy. It is possible to believe fervently in the Bill of Rights and at the same time remain indifferent to the fact that a committee convened by the House of Representatives has held hearings on what it calls un-American activities. Lacking stories, frames, concepts, histories, discussions, a background through which significance can be felt, information descends easily into a free fall of nonsensical associations. In the same way, it is possible to use the word *freedom* like a rallying call for a football team, without any irony, as a rationale for depriving other citizens of their rights. In this usage, *freedom* loses its meaning entirely. I am thinking again of the significant role reason plays in democracy. But even reason cannot achieve meaning without the understanding carefully woven from knowledge.

JANUARY 2006

Stayed up very late watching a terrible tale unfold at the Sago mine. News came that the rescue crew found the men who had been trapped by the explosion still alive. The families assembled in a church nearby started to celebrate. But not long afterward, the story changed. Only one of the thirteen men was still alive, and him just barely. The disappointment terrible to see.

It was through my new friends that I came upon another narrative, hidden histories behind the congressional hearings my grandfather liked to watch on television. As I met with them after school to hang out at their houses or study together, and went with them to parties or the movies on the weekends, or to the Ash Grove to hear folk music, they began to trust me with their stories. Henry Steinberg, the father of one of my friends, had been imprisoned, a fact his daughters concealed from most of their other classmates. Henry was an organizer for the Communist Party. The family suffered in many ways when after the war the Communist Party and any ideas vaguely associated with Communism, ideas that had in the years before been popular among intellectuals and working people alike, were suddenly vilified from every direction. It was as if, after the general elation over the end of the Second World War, when the anxiety that follows any great trauma ensued, the nation needed to invent an adversary to embody the vague but persistent fears that shadowed the insistently cheerful atmosphere. The uneasy mood of the postwar years could be blamed on Communism and internal enemies, Communist Party members, and anyone with socialist or progressive views.

I can only imagine what it must have felt like to have a parent stigmatized in this way. Susie, my closest friend in the group, was my age, which meant that, like me, she would still have been in grammar school when a television show called *I Led Three Lives* became popular. The series followed the adventures of an FBI agent posing as a Communist Party member. What would it have been like at that age to hear about this program or perhaps to watch it at a friend's house? To see your father and mother portrayed as treacherous villains?

The contrast between Henry and Bea Steinberg and the cold, scheming characters on this program, who were always hatching terrible plots, would have been comical were it not so harmful. Like my mother's house, the Steinbergs' house was a simple box, a small living room, kitchen, bedrooms, part of a tract built after the war for veterans and other working-class people. Though, as with most families, I learned later there were tensions and difficulties, their home seemed far closer to what I had seen on *Father Knows Best* than either my mother's or my grandparents' houses. My grandparents did not allow me to bring home friends unannounced, nor did my mother, who said she was too shy. And when I was living with my mother, I was also afraid to bring home friends for fear that she might have been drinking. But this was a different, easier world. Bea often offered us cookies or doughnuts when we arrived after school. Frequently I was asked to stay for dinner, which was home-cooked, as opposed to the frozen food and the TV dinners my mother appropriately served in front of the television. And we would all sit around one table and speak to one another about what we had done or learned or thought during the day.

I know that my friends were grateful for the spirit in which I took the stories they confided in me and that I listened to them without judgment. But I do not know if they realized what a gift they were giving to me. Along with their trust, I was receiving a vital education. Because of what I learned from them, I was suddenly able to decipher a public world of events and political news that had once seemed wrapped in a gauze of confusion.

Before I met the Steinbergs, even the language of the Red scare was inaccessible to me. Though it was used frequently, the nomenclature of demonization seemed beyond my comprehension. Now I could understand the terms. There was the word *Reds* or *Commies* for Communist party members, those who believed in Communism, or as a generic term for all those who lived in the Soviet Union. The term *Communist sympathizer* was reserved for anyone who had not joined the party but either agreed with many of the party's views or stood up for the right of Americans to be Communists. *Pink* or the more aggressive word *pinko* was used for those whose views seemed tainted with Communist ideas, and *Communist dupes* was a double insult, suggesting that those who unknowingly associated with Communists or adopted Communist viewpoints were naive if not stupid.

When I was younger, I could not have defined those words very clearly, if at all. If on occasion I asked my grandfather what some of those words meant, he dismissed the question by telling me, "They're just all bad, that's all you have to know." In fact, I suspect he was not with-holding knowledge from me so much as covering his own ignorance. Yet the real significance of the terminology was exactly what he said: these terms were not signs of meaning but of warning. The subtext was unmistakable: *Do not go any further in this direction, not even in your imagination.*

But fortunately I did go further. I had an absorbing interest now in events that I had known about only in the vaguest way before, as if whatever scant news I had then had reached me in some secret language for which I had no translation. I was fascinated by a book about physics I had checked out of the high school library written by J. Robert Oppenheimer, and now I was to learn that he had been publicly humiliated and denied his security clearance for having espoused Marxist ideas. He was also accused of donating funds to the Lincoln Brigade to help them join the Spanish Civil War, in what was to be the first battle against fascism in the Second World War. From his story I learned still another term in my growing vocabulary that came from the critics and victims of the Red scare. In a vain attempt to save his own career, he had "named names," a phrase that meant he had given HUAC the names of other scientists he felt might be guilty of having Communist ideas and associations; the betrayal of friends and colleagues was something both HUAC and the Senate hearings required from those they interrogated, a practice that turned ordinary citizens into spies against one another. I added this term to others in the new lexicon I was learning—*Red baiter, guilt by association, witch hunt, blacklist*—each of which brought a new aspect of the history I was witnessing into a clearer focus.

In my own life, to be able to name and identify events in the external world was as crucial to the development of my soul as the ability to perceive and express my emotions. Understanding the public realm allowed me to locate my own story within a larger history. This perspective has at times been described as lending proportion to one's own small troubles. But I found that a greater knowledge of the world did not diminish the significance of my own suffering so much as enrich my capacity for understanding it so that I began to feel less helpless or isolated. I could not have articulated the feeling I had then, but it was remarkable. I had joined an infinitely larger world, not just through those I knew but through my own mind. And through my own mind, in the act of comprehension itself, instead of a passive bystander to the dramas unfolding before me, I became active, not only seeking knowledge, but shaping meaning.

I was thirteen when all this began, at the age when most children begin to enter larger worlds. I was learning a great deal almost every day about a wide variety of things: biology, American history and literature, psychology, music, philosophy, sexuality, and the subtle terrain of love. My vocabulary was expanding in many different ways too. I delighted in using the new words I learned such as *ambiguous* that seemed to express what I had sensed but had no words for before, or *aesthetic,* which suggested an approach to life to which I was drawn. And like many others, both children and adults, including the revolutionaries who founded American democracy, the knowledge I was acquiring allowed me to think independently, which in turn inspired courage.

Life in my mother's house was not easy. She was far more permissive than my grandmother, and I was no longer afraid to be in the house alone when she and my stepfather went out drinking. But when she returned home after a night visiting several bars, or when on occasion she drank at home, she almost always became abusive. Many nights when my stepfather was still out, or if he had fallen into a stupor on the couch, she would use me as a listening post. Even when I had already gone to sleep, or pretended to do so, she would come into my room to pull me out of bed so that she would have someone to talk to. As I was learning to do in the world at large, I began to employ my mind to defend myself against her verbal assaults, charting the progress of her moods until I could predict them.

She would start by laughing, making witty comments about our family, my stepfather, the television, one of our cats, but soon this laughter would dissolve into tearful self-pity. How misunderstood she was or what a mess of things she had made. If in the beginning I would be moved by her lament and I felt sorry for her, over time, whenever she would enter this phase, I learned to brace myself for the appearance of the mean side that I knew would be coming soon. She was always perceptive, but in this stage her perception would turn into a weapon aimed sometimes at her husband, her friends, and then without exception, at my grandmother and finally at me. Whether it was she who told me or my sister, by then I knew that my grandmother, the matriarch of the family, had urged her to have a second child to save her marriage. I knew her resentment had settled on my conception and birth, muddled somehow with her guilt over her abandonment of me, and I sensed that the admiration my grandmother had given me from the first day I was born, one that she withheld from my mother, angered her too.

I had already begun to stand up to these vituperative barrages, refusing to sit still for her drunken ramblings, when one afternoon after she had already had several beers, and said something objectionable, words I cannot remember now, I responded sarcastically. It was then that she came across the room and slapped me hard across the face. I was not used to this behavior. I can remember only five times that anyone in the family ever raised a hand to me, and this partly accounts for what followed. I stood up immediately from the chair where I had been sitting and hit her back. Within a few moments, we were on the ground wrestling with each other. I cannot recall who ended the physical conflict, but as soon as I was standing again, I told her that I was going to call my father to tell him I wanted to move out of her house. And that is exactly what I did.

Though I knew immediately that my response was fully justified, it took me years to integrate what happened on that day. First to be able to tell anyone outside the family what had occurred and then, almost in the same breath, to grasp the depth of the pain I felt from the fury and hatred my mother had directed at me. The pain of such a perception is often enough to prevent those who are abused from admitting the full truth of what they have suffered, even to themselves.

It is an odd connection, but it occurs to me now why a passage that has usually bored me must have felt so important in the Declaration of Independence—the long list of all the wrongs committed against the colonists by the king of England. Saying the words would have broken a trance, arresting the tendency to believe in a beneficent monarch, which would be to believe in safety itself, that the world as it is has a predictable and reliable order, and that, thus, whatever has been suffered is an anomaly and will, like all illusions, disappear by itself over time. So repeating the list, declaring it in public meetings at courthouses and meetinghouses throughout the colonies, and reading it to the new American troops would have engendered the courage that was necessary to wage a revolution.

To name injustice almost always inspires courage. Even without a long and solid tradition of democratic theory, unfairness assaults the soul, engendering an almost physical response. The difficulty is not in convincing anyone that injustice is wrong but in proving that a particular injustice has really taken place. Not only those who have witnessed injustice but even those who have suffered it are often unable to acknowledge that it happened. Over many years, I came to admire my younger self for the courage I showed when I resisted my mother's assault. Yet at this moment I am more interested in what developed before this courage. How I came to know that the way my mother treated me was wrong.

One answer that comes to me now is surprising. For many years I have known the role that my father played. He had discussed my mother's abusive behavior with me before and now he acknowledged the gravity of the situation immediately. Although he must have realized this would not be easy for him to arrange, he agreed that I should come to live with him. Since he lived in a small apartment in North Hollywood near the station house where he worked, he would have to rent or buy something larger. Tearfully I told him that I wanted to stay in the same high school. I had been moved too often already, I said, and my new friends were important to me. He must have felt some guilt over the insecurity of my childhood because finally he bought a house in a new tract at the edge of the school district.

But what surprises me now is to see that paradoxically my courage came from my mother too. Though we love to invent stories in which purely evil characters do battle with purely good heroes or heroines, most of us are far more complex. Indeed, on a deeper level, mythic conflict can be read as an internal struggle between warring tendencies within one soul. When she was sober, my mother played out a different side of herself with me. She praised me in various ways, encouraging my interests, eliciting my opinions, siding with me in difficulties. I remember clearly a day when I was seven and living with her for just a year; I came home from school saddened because the teachers would not let me play baseball any longer. The boys had let me join their team because I was such a good pitcher, a skill I had learned at the school I attended in Los Angeles, where my grandparents lived. But my teacher said I had to play jump rope with the girls. When my mother called him to complain, he said it was because girls wore skirts that they could not play. So that afternoon we walked together to the local Sears, Roebuck, where she bought me a pair of blue jeans, and the next day at school, I integrated the baseball team again. It was from my mother as much as from anyone else that I learned to fight injustice.

Perhaps it was because both my parents had usually listened to me when I expressed my thoughts that, though as a smaller child I was shy, eventually I would become articulate. The painful complexities in my family that I witnessed and suffered must have added to the natural proclivity I had for philosophy. Henry Steinberg loved philosophy too. An autodidact, he read widely and liked to discuss ideas. In fact, as I learned years later, before he was convicted under the Smith Act, he had been the educational director of the Communist Party in California.

Our discussions touched on a wide range of ideas, books, music, art. He invited me to come with his three daughters on their monthly journey to the Los Angeles Public Library, usually an hour's drive from the San Fernando Valley to the city's downtown. As we wound our way through the Hollywood Hills, Henry would ask us what we were studying. I remember we discussed Steinbeck, who was popular then, and the dust bowl that had inspired his novel *The Grapes of Wrath*. We talked about what the Depression was like. He described books to me I had never heard of, among them Edward Bellamy's *Looking Backward*, a nineteenth-century vision of a utopian society in which profits are shared and young people performed all of the manual labor as a requirement of their development. The book was revelatory to me.

Inspired by utopian dreams, I entered a romantic relationship with the Russian Revolution. I was thrilled to hear recordings of the Red Army Chorus. With my friends, I began to attend the classic Russian films that showed from time to time at art houses around L.A. When I saw Eisenstein's *Potemkin*, I was inspired by the ingenuity of the editing in the famous scene that showed imperial battleships as they turn their cannons on a crowd of civilians. After I read Maksim Gorky's account of a life of poverty under the czar in his great novel *Childhood*, my enthusiasm spread out to everything Russian: the novels of Turgenev, the poetry of Pushkin and Mayakovsky, the music of Shostakovitch, colorful scarves, dolls nested inside one another, piroshki, and blini. Along with my friends, I signed up for a class in Russian that was being taught in the method used by the army language school, in which one learned through conversation. As I mastered various guttural sounds my tongue had never made before, I felt like a traveler who has crossed into a forbidden land, where, though bit by bit the exotic becomes more familiar, nothing ever quite loses the charm that foreign places have.

In those days, I had only the vaguest sense that the campaign against dissidents in America, the destructive consequences of which I had just begun to understand, existed on the other side of the Iron Curtain too, in an even harsher form. But there was little talk of this among my friends. Just as I knew I could never discuss what I was learning about economic justice with my grandparents, I sensed that my friends were wary of any criticism of the Soviet Union. I had my first taste of this when I began to read the poetry of Pasternak. One of my friends was unnerved by this choice. She told me that Pasternak's novel *Dr. Zhivago,* which had just come out in an English translation, was being used for anti-Communist propaganda. It is difficult to capture the quality of discourse in this period. It was as if the Second World War had never really ended, only shifted ground. Warfare, even the cold variety, does not provide a climate conducive to the complexities of truth. If during the war posters cautioned ordinary citizens, "Careless talk costs lives," now even relatively innocent expressions seemed to possess the potential to arouse suspicion and fear.

This preternatural tension formed a strange counterpoint to the image of America as a cheerful place that had spread throughout popular culture. Only film noir seemed to capture the frame of mind. An illusory fear of infiltration and takeover by a stealthy foreign power on one side was matched on the other side by real fears of economic ruin, blacklists, lost reputations and jobs. Politicians, writers and artists, and businessmen alike removed books from their shelves that might identify them as "fellow travelers," excised certain words, such as *capitalism,* from their speech, avoided seeing friends who had been named or otherwise tainted. Those who did not renounce or deny their political views were careful to avoid associating with anyone who had named names or whom they suspected of being an FBI agent, only posing as a friend. Though these suspicions were not always just, this was not paranoia. As I was to confirm years later by reading the FBI files that had been kept about my own activities, the practice of planting informants in political meetings of all kinds continued through the sixties.

The fearsome atmosphere would only be heightened whenever two men in fedoras wearing characteristically plain overcoats would ring a doorbell unannounced; they would arrive at all hours to claim that they just wanted to ask questions. When I was fourteen years old, none of this daunted me. The bravado of youth combined with my passionate love of democracy and the First Amendment to make me feel invulnerable. Yet now that that bravado has been replaced by the subtle perceptions and frailty of age, I can feel, even in my body, why, in this period that came so soon after the Holocaust, so many families with left-wing views would have fled across the border to Mexico.

On our trips to the library, Henry never spoke to me about the terrors on the other side of the Iron Curtain; his silence belonged to the chill of this mood. Though the McCarthy hearings had ended, HUAC continued its public interrogations. If in the labyrinthine channels of the human heart, truth longs to reveal itself, nevertheless some realities will be denied because they seem too dangerous or too painful to behold. I can only imagine the conflict that must have raged inside him, threatened with prison, publicly villainized, and now the utopian vision for which he had given so much of his life, corrupted. The infamous purges in which so many political leaders, writers, artists, and thinkers were sent to the gulags or killed had ended when Stalin died in 1953. Just three years later, in 1956, only one year before our trips to the library began, Nikita Khrushchev openly condemned many of the terrible crimes that had been committed against human rights in the Soviet Union. But I am imagining now that Henry would have found it nearly impossible to integrate this knowledge into the way he saw the world.

JANUARY

Are we going back to McCarthyism? National Security Agency, including the FBI and the CIA, have been spying on private telephone conversations conducted by American citizens without going through the oversight procedures mandated by Congress and required by law. President Bush authorized this in 2002. The justification, once again, is that it's necessary for war on terror.

The acquisition of knowledge is not just an intellectual process; it is an emotional one too. It is for this reason that at times even the most brilliant men and women will insist on a certain theory or course of action despite clear evidence that weighs against the conclusions they have reached. Whether starting a career or even shaping a significant conversation, the idea that inspired every action you take will be associated with people and things that are vital to you: a husband or wife, a lover, children, parents, friends, memories of childhood neighborhoods, the smell of a grandmother's baking, the view of the night sky you have from your home. So that over time, as much as you love the truth, to relinquish a false picture of the world may seem as if it will tear apart your own world.

I have never forgotten the night, twenty years ago, when I attended a performance by the Traveling Jewish Theatre with Rose Chernin, for many years a leader of the Communist Party in California. Eighty years old then, she was the mother of the woman who was my partner. Since she had been born in a shtetl, we thought she would appreciate a play called *The Last Yiddish Poet*. But none of us were prepared for the experience she had when, near the end of the production, she learned that a Yiddish poet she knew when she had lived for several months in the Soviet Union had been put to death by Stalin. Though both her daughter and I had long since absorbed the dreadful picture of persecutions, Rose was stunned. For years she had clung to the illusion that the stories everyone told about those times were exaggerated. She had lived there, she argued, and everything was wonderful, people well fed and housed, culture blossoming. But now, at least momentarily, the news of this particular death, a man she had known and loved, pierced through the cloud of her unknowing.

Over the next two decades, as with many others in my generation, I pieced together a larger picture of this history, learning first, with alarm, about the Stalin-Hitler pact and then bit by bit the extent of the gulag and its horrors. But despite the eclipse of knowledge that I witnessed and experienced, what I did learn in this period of my life was astonishing. My mind was opening. There was so much more now that I understood, so many worlds revealed. I was filled with the wonder and excitement of learning—a broadening of mind that L.A.'s Central Library came to symbolize for me.

I had never been to this library before I went with the Steinbergs. I was deeply impressed with the imposing architecture that seemed to speak of vast stores of knowledge. Because Henry had introduced me to the music of Aaron Copland, I listened to *Appalachian Spring* in a large room with a high wooden ceiling filled with record players and earphones. The room no longer exists; the renovated building, glorious in its own way, looks very different than the old structure, constructed in 1926, with its mission-style architecture and broad steps leading to an impressive set of doors. Some of the old touches do remain: the serpent of knowledge; the goddesslike statue of civilization; the murals that depict California history, including the founding of Los Angeles, in the rotunda; and the fresco showing a miner during the gold rush in the Children's Room. He wears the same clothes we wore then on those weekends: this too was a part of California history. Blue jeans were invented by a tailor, Jacob Davis, struggling to survive, who responded to a complaint from a woodcutter's wife that the pants her husband wore always came apart at the seams. Davis incorporated the copper rivets he had used on blankets together with duck cloth he bought from Levi Strauss. The pants proved popular, but since for a poor tailor the price of patents was prohibitive, he encouraged Strauss to buy the patent and afterward he supervised the production of what was to become not only a commercial success but, by the 1950s, a symbol of America's egalitarian ethos. In this time when to raise the issue of class seemed like a rude disruption of the American dream, it was fashionable among the young to wear the same clothes that working people wore.

One of the great revelations that I received as part of the political education Henry gave me was that there was a working class in America. And along with that, I learned about labor unions. Before this disclosure, I had no understanding of the vital part unions had played in my own life. Both my father and my stepfather were workingmen, and at different points both of them had owned their houses; yet I did not know then that even fifty years earlier, before unions were successful in demanding better wages, this would have been an impossible feat. I was not aware that the middle-class life we enjoyed was a fairly recent phenomenon. A few decades earlier, families in which both parents worked for twelve to thirteen hours a day could still not afford to feed themselves and their children three meals a day or provide adequate clothing, let alone decent housing or medical care. That as the daughter of a workingman, I had all I needed and even what I did not need— vacations, books, movies—that I received a fine education at the public schools we attended, that I could visit a beautiful public library in our city, sit in a lovely park, or swim in public pools and hike in public parks represented a major shift not only in social policies but in an evolving American consciousness.

Since the founding days of the American Republic, the issue of class has haunted the national discourse about democracy. The class differences in Thomas Jefferson's immediate family had a profound effect on his thinking. The Randolphs on his mother's side of the family were among the most prominent families in eighteenth-century Virginia. I have seen a portrait of Isham Randolph, Jefferson's grandfather, said to have been painted in 1724. One can see from his demeanor that he is a wealthy man. After the fashion of the period, he wears a long, flowing wig, whose white curls cascade elegantly below his shoulders. Though it is not clear whether his jacket and waistcoat are made of leather or of cloth, the soft brown garments are clearly well tailored and bear that elusive yet recognizable air of a stylish and flattering cut, as if such apparel were a signature of the fine qualities of those who wear them. One hand rests in a subtle and yet authoritative manner on his hip and the other, thrust inside his waistcoat, reveals the starched and faceted cuff of his white shirt, which seems to say, *These hands have not been soiled with labor.* His aquiline nose, his left eyebrow arched imperiously, his imposing gaze, all speak of his position, an eminence that appears to be blessed by the light that fairly gleams from his high forehead. In this period, after commanding a merchant ship, he became a merchant in London. But in the next year, he would return to Virginia, where he had been born and raised and where his father, William Randolph, who had settled alongside the James River in 1650, had gained immense wealth as a land speculator, afterward holding many public offices, among them attorney general for the crown in Virginia.

But it was not only wealth and power that would have lent Isham his conceit. There was the matter of bloodlines, then more than now part of an arsenal of respect and self-assurance through which one person might acquire a sense of elevation over others. Isham knew that his father, William, had descended from squires in Northumberland and Warwickshire, that these ancestors had been allied with the famous Scottish clan the Earls of Murray, and that one among them, the poet Thomas Randolph, had even been a close friend of Ben Jonson.

Yet barely two decades after this portrait of Isham was painted, a child would be born to his daughter, a boy who would grow up to pose a forceful challenge to the significance of aristocratic lineage. At the end of the second paragraph of his autobiography, in a sentence that has become famous for its disdain of ancestral claims, Thomas Jefferson makes his attitude clear. Writing of the Randolph family, he declares, "They trace their pedigree far back in England and Scotland, to which let everyone ascribe the faith and merit he chooses."

Though Jefferson rarely revealed his personal emotions in writing, many historians have read between the lines to speculate about conflicts within his family. Between the sentence dismissing his mother's ancestry and the paragraph that follows, in which Jefferson lauds his father's accomplishments, it is easy to imagine a sea of undisclosed resentment and indignation.

The complaint that lurks behind Jefferson's description of his own family history was among those that fueled the French and American Revolutions. The idea that neither power nor honor should be conferred through bloodlines was central to them both. Though it seems a given to us now, in the eighteenth century, this was a controversial notion, and it brought about a radical transformation in the existing social order.

Yet in America the social order had already begun to change long before the American Revolution was conceived. Almost as soon as Europeans learned that a different continent had been discovered to the west, perhaps precisely because it was an unknown and unexplored realm, the New World became the repository of unrealized dreams and aspirations. In the European imagination, America came to promise freedom from every restraint, even, in the quest for the fountain of youth, the necessities of age and mortality. But soon these fantasies yielded to more realistic expectations, not only freedom from religious persecution but the injustices and privations of the Old World class system. That it was indeed possible for some to realize their hopes is made clear in the story of Peter Jefferson's life. His rise in fame and fortune has taken on the burnished quality of a legend. When, in 1812, Thomas Jefferson wrote his *Autobiography,* he must have been aware that he was telling not only his own story but the story of America. He frames his own birth with apocryphal stories of his parents that invoke two worldviews about class and social position, one from the Old World and one from the New. Just as the Randolph family's illustrious ancestry on his mother's side represented an older order that Jefferson rejected, his father's story represented the new one that he and the other founders of American democracy had helped to create. After dismissing the merit and meaning of his mother's lineage, he describes one of his father's achievements. This man who was self-educated and self-made, he tells us in a tone of glowing admiration, made the first map of Virginia.

When it is told and repeated many times, any tale takes on mythic dimensions; once given this role in consciousness, the narrative of a life becomes exemplary, a plot whose every turn is full of revelation, with details symbolic of countless meanings, some intended and some not. So Peter Jefferson's map of Virginia can be read as a metaphor for a new map of society and government, and along with this, of necessity, a new model too for charting the individual soul. Predating the Horatio Alger stories of boys who rose to fame and fortune through virtue and hard work by a century, the life of Peter Jefferson, as told by his even more successful son, stood as a solid proof that the American dream of social mobility was real. This life provided a map for the ideal American life.

I am thinking now of my father and where he fell on the scale of this measurement. He had a similar background to Peter Jefferson. Though his father made a decent living with a small business delivering ice, my father was neither educated nor wealthy. He was physically strong and could work with his hands at many trades. But in one aspect he was distinctly different from Peter. He lacked the drive and ambition that is required if one is to move upward from one class to another. Although my mother clearly preferred men without ambition, the absence of initiative in my father was a source of embarrassment for my grandparents, who would have had far more respect for him had he been more bent on success. The unstated assumption in my grandparents' household was that my father was somehow a failure.

He was, however, in no way a failure to me. In grammar school I was thrilled to be able to boast to my friends, just after the films we saw depicting firefighters as they climbed tall ladders, that my father was a fireman. In my eyes he had all the important skills—handball, tennis, miniature golf, horseback riding. He could row a boat, and hammer and saw, and he was a far better driver than my grandfather. Among the adults in our family, he was the one I could always speak with about whatever was troubling me.

As I grew older, though, I was increasingly unsettled by what I began to perceive as his passivity. Under his apparent affability, there was a mute sort of sadness in him, not resignation so much as obedience, directed not only toward my grandparents, but aimed everywhere, as if he felt he had to adapt to whatever conditions befell him.

There is more than one kind of ambition. That greatly admired progenitor on my mother's side of the family, Nathanael Greene, wanted above all to be a famous soldier, a commander of troops. Since that is what he became, this desire does not seem so strange, until one learns that his father, Nathanael Senior, was a prosperous businessman, "a man of industry," as his son later called him, a devout Quaker, and a preacher.

The religion the family practiced so strictly was opposed to war and forbade its members to bear arms. His father, who believed in the virtues of hard work, was also opposed to any education beyond certain religious texts, but Greene was eager to move past the confines of the life he had been given. Like John Muir, he found a way to read surreptitiously, fashioning toys from wood and selling them to pay for his books. It was after he read an account of the Gallic wars by Julius Caesar that he acquired a passion for the intricate strategies of battle. He is perhaps one of the few generals to have started his military life as a self-taught soldier.

When, in a letter to his friend William Wirt, Jefferson describes class in America, he does not include any category that would have described Nathanael Greene's father. He does list the class that would include the Randolphs, "certain families" who, despite the absence of European aristocracy in America, "had risen to splendour by wealth and the preservation of it from generation to generation by the law of entails." As a legislator and then a governor of Virginia, he would work to repeal the laws of entail that led to such a concentration of wealth. He also includes a class he calls "men of talent," and families who have stayed on the same piece of land forever, and solid yeomen, about whom he knew a great deal since this was the class from which his father had sprung. These were the small farmers who had made the colonial settlement in Virginia possible, among them many who came over as indentured servants, often escaping religious persecution, and who were eventually rewarded for their hard labor with land. Beneath the yeomen, he lists overseers, whom he describes as "abject, degraded and unprincipled." But he mentions neither an entrepreneurial class nor those who worked for a living in factories or businesses.

The omissions are revealing. Jefferson was not only aware of but concerned about the terrible conditions the working poor suffered in cities, the long hours of work, starvation wages, chronic unemployment, dreadful slums that Dickens would soon describe. In this way, he could see beyond the limits of his own circle. Yet when he searched for a solution, his vision seemed to fail; he did not look beyond the boundaries of the world that was familiar to him, reasoning that, if the states had not granted working men who held no property the right to vote, then every man should all be given land. With the same logic, he argued that owning land would allow all citizens to feed and house themselves and their children properly too and even give them a chance to better themselves.

In this way, he imagined the Louisiana Purchase would solve the problem of poverty.

The argument works on paper. The maps drawn of the westward territories seemed so vast, surely there would be enough for everyone. But, of course, the map is not the territory. And like maps, plans and strategies made at a distance are rarely realistic or even entirely reasonable. It is ironic thus and yet predictable in a human way that Jefferson, an ardent advocate of reason and science, should have failed to add the numbers and calculate the dimensions, and so missed the obvious conclusion that eventually there would not be enough land for everyone. If, in a certain expansive mood, the imagination has no limits, the earth is not limitless.

As much as he worked with his hands, my father had a subtle quality of groundlessness. This was not evident when he was working or driving or engaged in some purposeful activity. Nor was it apparent during the times when we talked with each other about a wide range of subjects. The quality came forward when he was at my grandparents' home, especially when he was quiet. In fact, you could only see it at moments when he was still. It is there in many of the photographs I have of him: as if, in some secret canyon of his soul, he could not entirely grasp where or who he was. And now, when I think about it, I realize he must have had a feeling of disorientation buried inside him, a feeling that most probably he could neither name nor explain. I suspect that this was the result of having been separated from his mother at a young age, and taken to a different country. But I also suspect that it would not have been the event alone that robbed him of his power to direct his life as he wished. Rather, the fact that he had been forbidden either to speak his mother's name or to discuss the causes of this change in his life would have created in him a kind of caesura, a long pause, his life suspended in a loss he suffered but never entirely knew.

Is this the reason why, except for an occasional burst of anger, he never seemed to have any intense opinions nor spoke out about injustices he experienced? In this way he formed an extreme contrast to my grandfather on my mother's side who was always very vocal if not disturbingly intense about his opinions, so much so that after I reached a certain age, like the rest of the family, I learned to ignore whatever he said. But perhaps underneath the surface the two men were alike in one way. Loud and blustery expressions are often signs of a hidden territory of silence in the soul. There were subjects about which even my grandfather rarely spoke. Though he often expressed the idea that the Catholic Irish were troublesome, inferior people, as opposed to the Protestant Irish, from whom he descended, he never said much about his father and his father's family. The story my grandmother and mother told was that when his father came to live with them for a period, the two men always argued about politics, and that at a certain point in each debate, when my great-grandfather had had his say, he would turn his hearing aid off and leave my grandfather to bluster in the void.

Was I told or did I just assume that my great-grandfather had views far more liberal than those of my grandfather? My mother's grandfather was part of the other great westward movement, one that occurred throughout the nineteenth and early twentieth centuries, and that originated outside of America, a migration propelled by the myth that American streets were paved with gold. Like countless Irish, he took his voyage across the Atlantic during the potato famine. This particular history fascinated me. For some reason, I longed to know more about it. But though the subject was not strictly forbidden in our household, I could never get my grandfather to say very much about it.

Perhaps this was because of a strange split in the American psyche, one that existed in our family too. The idea that America welcomes the cold and hungry to her shores is shadowed with a prejudice toward anyone whose parents were not born here. Even today as I write, I realize I have never thought of my grandfather as a first-generation American before now. And there would have been another reason for the absence of any desire in our family to preserve and pass on my great-grandfather's story to his progeny. Poverty itself causes shame.

The poverty suffered during the potato famine was extreme. Somewhere between five hundred thousand and a million died from either hunger or disease. The crisis began when the fungus called the "blight" destroyed potato crops throughout Ireland, where a great majority of small and tenant farmers had become entirely dependent on this crop for both food and sustenance. When landlords evicted their tenants, they often placed them on ships heading for North America with little clothing and scant provisions. Many were already ill with typhus, which, along with dysentery, spread quickly among the passengers during the voyage. The passage took three months. Ships to Canada were so crowded that some sank, one in the harbor still in sight of the families who had come to say good-bye. The American ships were less crowded and hence more expensive, due to laws designed to limit the number of Irish coming sinto the United States.

Were my great-grandfather and his brothers among the men and women who landed on the Eastern Seaboard, fevered, weary with malnutrition and exposure, wearing torn and dirty clothes? They would have seemed to themselves and others shabby and unwanted, like things crushed beyond recognition that have been abandoned at the side of the road. And this would only have added to the tangled skein of shame that surrounds poverty. That without money or housing, they became wards of the state, even if temporarily, would have been a source of shame too, and then, if they landed in the tenements, as most Irish immigrants did, the dark and soiled entrances to the buildings, the shabby, cramped apartments, often twelve or more people sleeping in two rooms or three very small rooms, some without any windows for light or air, damp from leaking roofs and cold, with no heat, no plumbing, latrines in the courtyard outside, often the only source of running water a shared pump in the hallway, the very walls that surrounded them as they slept would have driven the experience of their diminishment, their small status in the world, into their bodies, entering what dreams they had at night.

The sense of degradation would have mirrored what they endured during the long hours of work, up at dawn, not home until eleven or midnight, performing dull, repetitive tasks all day, forbidden to think independently but made instead to follow automatically the orders of others, managers who would treat them at times with disrespect and at other times with contempt. Exhausted to the point of illness, if at the end of the week they had still not earned enough to live decently, and were unable to pay their rent or their bills, they might complain; yet inwardly, they would more than likely fault themselves, as if what they suffered had merely proved their essential worthlessness.

And this inward disparagement would have had another consequence. Wrapped around the mind as tightly as a blindfold, shame obscures the knowledge that whatever is suffered—grueling work for low pay, high rent for indecent housing, prejudice and disrespect—is unjust.

Of course, there might be moments of insight, followed by flashes of anger. Forbidden curse words uttered. A drunken speech, a bragging voice promising revenge. But later, embarrassed by such behavior, or even such thoughts, a worker—perhaps my great-grandfather or one of his brothers—would be likely to weigh his temporary outrage as more evidence of waywardness, a fundamental lack of value. And then, spiraling downward into a vortex of self-disregard, an unreasonable anger might take a man over from time to time, so that he might hit another man or even a woman or a child in a moment of displaced rage. And finally, if this happened, he would have real reason to hate himself. So the cycle would continue.

Some broke it with a combination of luck, skill, and determination, by moving up the ladder to better circumstances. How did my great-grandfather get himself from the eastern coast of America to the small town in southern Illinois where my grandfather was born? And once there, how did he manage to set up his own butcher shop? This history is lost to our family too. Though it is a classic tale. The American success story. The cold, hungry, disheartened, mistreated, and above all anonymous child becomes someone estimable. My great-grandfather was not wealthy. But his home was genteel and cultivated. And I have been told he "cut a fine figure."

Though aristocratic titles were abolished by the American Revolution, many signs remain that identify those who are more favored. The cut of a suit, the feel of fine linen, how a mustache is trimmed, shoes of hand-worked leather (and not "down at the heel"). All the same signs will be read inwardly too, become part of every passing mood, stamping an impression on what is called the self, identity. I am seeing my grandfather's habit of wearing cashmere sweaters every day in a new light now. Though, of course, he had excised any knowledge of why he did so from his consciousness. Perhaps it was precisely because of this erasure that shame stayed with him, sequestered in his unconscious mind, appearing only in a disguised form, in his irrational rage at various groups of strangers he counted as enemies, Irish Catholics among them.

The cycle of disgrace does not end with poverty but instead goes underground to be passed from one generation to the next as an unspoken limit not only to memory but to perception too, if not certain dimensions of the soul. By a strange alchemy, with the acquisition of great wealth, guilt toward those who remain poor is often mixed with shame at having been poor. Does this account for the paradoxical behavior of a man like John D. Rockefeller, who, defending his own actions, declared that certain men were elevated in the economy through survival of the fittest and yet, at the same time, donated most of his wealth to helping the poor and the destitute?

At the beginning of the twentieth century, the habit of blaming working people for their poverty was widespread, not only among entrepreneurs and managers but with social pundits and politicians too. In this way, if you were born into the working class, and had thus inherited a choir of opinions that cast you as an inferior, you might, in some unspoken and inward way, begin to believe yourself that you do not deserve better treatment. And sensing that you do not count in the public world, in order to defend yourself, you might easily turn away from this world and hence be unable to understand the larger causes of the conditions you suffer. Still, miraculously there are always those who, even in the midst of such an atmosphere, are able to see past the thick barrier of shame that has been woven around them.

I am thinking now of a woman who came to America from Poland when she was eight years old. One day Rose Schneiderman would make her mark not by rising out of her class but by helping to improve the lives of everyone in it. In New York City, her family of five lived in two rooms of a tenement building. There was no plumbing inside. They had to haul water in a pail from a sink in the hallway. And the only toilet for the whole building was outside in the backyard. When their cousin Koppel arrived, he shared the same cramped quarters. Her father, a tailor, worked long hours in a sweatshop for six dollars a week. Still, the family was happy to be in America. Soon their cousin Koppel bought his own building, establishing a soda fountain on the ground floor. When Rose's mother became pregnant, so that it was too hard for her to climb five flights to their old apartment, the family moved to Koppel's building, where they had a living room as well as a kitchen. They were thrilled to have enough food, and having been subject to the pogroms that swept Central Europe regularly, they felt safer than they had in Poland.

Occasionally, in the alchemy of social change, fear or abuse leads to independent thought. Since she had lived in a nation that condoned anti-Semitism, Rose must have had the sense at an early age that those in authority are not always trustworthy. As a child, she was raised in a community that lived apart from gentile society, within a history and culture that cherished her existence. And if, within this world, she faced still another prejudice, the idea that women are not intellectual equals, though her family were Orthodox, they challenged this view. Rose's mother taught herself to read the prayer books so that she could recite prayers on the Sabbath. Even if it was not usual for a girl, Rose was sent to Hebrew school at the age of four. She loved learning and books. When she began to do well in her school in America, her father told her he hoped that someday she would be a teacher.

To give your children better opportunities than you have had is an American dream, one that many parents have been able to attain by sending their children to school. Yet Rose's life would soon follow a different trajectory. For a while it seemed within the realm of possibility that she might be able to realize her father's hopes, but that possibility began to fade on the night when he came home stricken with chills and fever. Though her mother put him to bed beneath several blankets to sweat out the illness, he did not improve. The next day he was worse, and soon he fell into a coma. One day later, he was dead.

It was over years and gradually that Rose lost any hope that she could ever become a teacher. In the beginning, all that she felt was disbelief that her father was gone. For weeks, she expected him to come home at night. Yet, for her mother, even the first shock and grief were accompanied by anxiety. She had no idea how she would manage. She was almost nine months pregnant when her husband died, and she spoke no English. Bit by bit, they limped along. For a brief period a Jewish charity provided food for the family. After her baby, whom she named Jane, was born, Rose's mother began to take in sewing, just as she had done years before in Poland, and just as Emerson's mother had done after his father died, she took in a boarder. She rented their living room to a young tailor. Some evenings she helped Koppel behind the counter of his soda fountain. But still there were many nights when she and her children went to bed hungry. Soon she had to send Harry and then Charles to the Hebrew Orphan Asylum, where she knew they would be fed. After that, the small family moved frequently, often leaving one place when they could no longer afford the rent, and so that they might have the usual concession of a few extra weeks rent free in a new place.

At first, Rose was able to go to school. But after the baby was weaned, and her mother found work, sewing linings in a fur factory, Rose had to stay home to take care of the baby. Finally, when she was ten, her mother sent her to the same orphanage where Charles and Harry were. The rules were strict, the punishments were harsh, and the surroundings, as she later wrote, were "cheerless," but she was happy nevertheless that she could attend public school again, where she had a good teacher. Though she had missed two years, she soon caught up to her grade level and was promoted at the end of the school year.

So, for a brief period, the dream that Rose might become a teacher came to life again. Even after her mother was able to bring her home, she attended the public school in the neighborhood of the tenements where they lived, and very soon, by a system in which students could accelerate in the middle of a term, she was promoted three times. But just as she reached the tenth grade, Rose was forced to quit school once more. Since fur capes were no longer as fashionable, women who made them were being dismissed. Her mother lost her job. Rose was thirteen, old enough to look for work. Her mother could take in sewing again at home.

In her first job, as an errand girl in a department store on Fourteenth Street, she earned just $2.16 for sixty-four hours a week. To save the sixteen cents that normally would have been deducted weekly from her wages for the cost of laundering the apron she was required to wear, she laundered her apron at home. She lost this job when the envelope in the account book she had carried from the cashier to a counter was missing fifty cents. But she soon started again as a check girl in a department store on Grand Street, this time earning $2.26 a week, and here, because she was favored by a group of older women working with her, who treated her, she said, as if she were their child, she was happier.

Nevertheless, it would have been easy in such a situation to sink into despair. Coming home exhausted from work to only the most meager of meals. Sometimes going hungry. Nothing left over, nothing extra for little luxuries or pleasures, not a cup of coffee in a café or the smallest of purchases, a pair of gloves, a seat at the theater. Their apartment was so small, she could never invite friends to visit, and even if they had the space, they could not offer them anything to eat or drink. In such conditions, you might feel imprisoned not only by space but by time too.

Yet Rose did not succumb. For a month, despite her continual fatigue, she attended night school. She stopped when she realized the instructor was not serious about teaching the class. But still eager to learn, she quickly found other methods. She read Bible stories to her mother in Yiddish and then turned to contemporary books. Years later she recalled reading to her mother a Yiddish translation of Émile Zola's article "J'accuse," his searing protest against injustice in the Dreyfus case, since it was a burning issue that year, Zola's essay had been serialized in the weekly journal *Abendblatt*. In the same journal, Rose read stories about Henry VIII and Thomas Becket. From the one-cent tips the saleswomen gave her when she went out to buy their lunches, she saved enough money to purchase ten-cent paperbacks, and so she began to read a series of romantic novels. And from time to time, the cashier would lend her books, among them a story that was considered risqué then, called *Camille*.

I doubt she knew that this novel was based on the life of a real woman, whose story was not unlike her own. Marie Duplessis, a lover of the author Alexandre Dumas fils and the model for his heroine, had from the age of thirteen worked long hours as a girl in the sweatshops of Paris before she became a courtesan. But *Camille,* which focuses on romance, does not include that part of the story. So as a young working girl herself, Rose did not have the great pleasure that comes from seeing an aspect of your own life in literature.

This is, of course, more than just a pleasure. When your own experience in literature is reflected back to you, you are able to understand it in a larger context. In the act of reflection itself, you will receive a crucial validation that what you have suffered, what you have felt, is not only shared by others but matters. Rose might have found stories about children forced to work very young in Dickens's great works *Oliver Twist* or *David Copperfield*. But she had not yet been introduced to the great English novels. The experience of poverty can be like the tales I have heard of hikers in the Sierras who have been lost for days, circling desperately while all along they were less a than a mile from a public road. At this time in her life, Rose did not know there were libraries she could use. The College Settlement House, where she could have found guidance in her efforts to educate herself, was just a few blocks away from where she worked, but she did not even know it existed.

In most children, the hunger for knowledge is very strong unless it is destroyed or so often frustrated that they give up their efforts to understand the world. Knowledge includes all kinds of information, but, like a living being, it is greater than the sum of its parts. To know engenders a state of being. To have knowledge will transform you. One ingredient in the ineffable mix is understanding itself or, at least, various understandings, ideas, concepts, and theories that allow you to shape data, even the information you receive directly from your own experience, into meaning. It has been almost a century since the philosopher of language Wittgenstein pointed out that those who do not have the word *sunset,* which is an idea—in this case, a way of organizing experience—do not perceive the phenomenon.

A vocabulary of concepts proves even more crucial if you are to perceive what occurs within society. Just as Rose probably passed by the College Settlement House without knowing what it was countless times during an ordinary week, she also witnessed and suffered from conditions where she worked without being able to name or even discern the terrible order beneath her own experience. The salary that did not afford her a decent standard of living; the long hours without break; that she was fired from her first job without any hearing; the expectation that from her meager salary she pay for the laundering of her uniform; the failure to pay for overtime when, during the Christmas season, she was required to stay at the store until 10:00 P.M.; the demand that each employee take two weeks off every year without pay; the absence of medical insurance, retirement pensions, unemployment insurance. Though doubtless she complained about this, when she was still a girl, struggling to survive, she did not recognize the pattern as a form of injustice.

But this would soon change. The first step Rose took was simply to improve her own circumstances. She was inspired by her best friend, Annie, who used to be a salesgirl in the same department store where Rose worked, and who had taken a job as a flower maker in which she made more than three times Rose's salary. She found an older friend, a former neighbor, who sewed linings in a cap factory and who agreed to find her a job there and teach her the trade. Even after Rose bought her own sewing machine and different colors of thread, the pay was still better.

To have increased her salary and learned new skills would have had an effect on her state of mind too. It would have been more than optimism. Something more elemental must have been fed, the sense that she could be an agent of change. Her life was expanding now in other ways too. A friend of her mother who worked in a restaurant that actors habituated began to give them the tickets that had been given to her. What was it like the first time they went to the theater? The gaslights at the edge of the stage creating a transfiguring magic, the actors gesturing, crying out, displaying a wide range of feeling, compelling narrations rising and falling, coaxing and rekindling the imagination to new heights. Over the many nights that Rose and her mother sat in the audience, as Rose thrilled to the genius before her, she must have found a form of genius within herself.

Then there were the meetings of the Manchester Ladies, a literary society that met in a settlement house, to which her friend Annie brought her one day. Years later, what she remembered learning here was parliamentary procedure. Just as *Robert's Rules of Order* had once given me the sense that my own voice had a proper place in the public world, so Rose must have felt empowered to discover a system that placed every opinion, even her own, on an equal footing.

Parliamentary procedures were developed over several centuries, from the unwritten practices of Anglo-Saxon tribes to the *Lex Parliamentaria* adopted by the House of Commons in 1689, followed in America by the compendium of congressional rules that Thomas Jefferson wrote in 1801, before they were cataloged in 1876, by the army engineer Henry M. Robert, who wrote the book called *Robert's Rules of Order,* which must be what Rose read and which years later I was to read too. Though the subject may seem dry now, a practical understanding of human psychology informs these intricate laws. The procedures are meant to ensure majority rule, while at the same time the minority voice is heard, so that debate is balanced and fair. The discussion of differences, even when those differences are extreme, makes democracy possible, not only through rational dialogue but, on a less conscious level, by creating a common language that knits the social body together.

It is perhaps for this reason above many other more obvious causes that articulation and speech, debate and argument, are so essential in a democracy. Not everyone can participate in self-government directly. But the lives of all citizens and the circumstances that affect them can be present in the public discourse symbolically, through words. This becomes most evident when the contours of your life and the problems that concern you are not part of public discourse. At such times, when what you suffer or care about is not articulated publicly, it is easy to feel irrelevant to society, if not invisible to the public eye, and at those times you may even mimic the absence of your concerns in the public realm by diminishing their significance in your own mind.

Many forms of protocol, especially those we have inherited from the aristocratic societies that preceded democracy, are designed to exclude. By elevating some and humiliating others, various manners simultaneously legitimate rank and invalidate even the most subtle or nascent forms of rebellion. At the court of Versailles, those without royal blood were not supposed to sit in the presence of the king. They had to stand for hours, and thus to be well mannered meant to recognize power. Even the discomfort that might have spurred complaint would have worked in the opposite direction, to enforce the idea that those who were exhausted from standing had inferior blood flowing through their veins.

Such protocols were still practiced long after democracy was established in America, where in the nineteenth century, for instance, in the mansions that lined Fifth Avenue, manners accentuated class and where to be polite was to display status rather than kindness. A chilling moment occurs in *The House of Mirth,* Edith Wharton's great novel portraying upper-class life in New York, as the heroine, Lily Bart, has to swerve to avoid a cleaning woman while she climbs the stairs. Wharton writes that when Lily tells her "I beg your pardon," she intends "by her politeness to convey a criticism" of the cleaning woman's behavior.

Another door to a wider world opened for Rose soon after her mother received a letter inviting her to live with her sister in Canada. Though she was reluctant to leave New York, Rose found a job in a cap factory in Montreal, while her mother set up a small business selling candy. The sojourn did not last long. Since the neighborhood was too poor to sustain her store, before the year had ended, Rose's mother decided they should both return to New York. But in the meantime, Rose had experienced a subtle change in her thinking that would have substantial consequences. She had become close with another family, the Kellerts, friends of her aunt and uncle, and from this friendship she received an education in another dimension of democracy. When she visited them, she would participate in the long discussions they were used to having, which often centered on political issues. The Kellerts were radicals, socialists, and, in the course of natural events, as they discussed various subjects, Rose was introduced to new ideas about trade unions. This is how she learned why working people go on strike.

It might seem strange that a young woman who was the daughter of two wage earners, and who, since the age of thirteen, had spent the greater part of her waking hours as a wage earner herself, would not have already understood the reasons for unions and the practice of striking for better wages and conditions. Yet the process of acquiring knowledge, and especially insight, is rarely solitary. Just as a tower in a castle has been constructed to afford a wide view, where not far beneath, a wall may obscure vision, knowledge is shaped by a social architecture, a structure that invisibility makes even more powerful. Not just the stories Rose would have read in the newspapers with a vocabulary full of implicit judgments, but a vocabulary of gestures too, of manners, clothing, and even more ephemeral, the force of the atmosphere that emanates from the exercise of power, would have occluded what otherwise might have been evident.

April

The young miner who survived is talking now about what happened. Four of the emergency oxygen packs failed. It's also come out that the Sago mine was cited 208 times last year for violating regulations and that under the current White House the safety of mines has been neglected.

Was it at a visit with the Kellerts that she first heard about the strike held by the young women who worked in the mills at Lowell, Massachusetts? Or did she learn this history after she joined the United Cloth Hat and Cap Makers Union in New York? It became a favorite tale, one she loved to hear again and again. How when the mill owners tried to lower their salaries, all on their own, the girls and young women rebelled. Just two years earlier, when five new cotton mills were being built in Lowell, girls were recruited from all over, some even from across the border in Canada, and because labor was scarce then, they were offered better wages than most factories paid. The smallest girls, between ten and fifteen years of age, who took the full bobbins of thread newly spun from the machines and replaced them with empty ones, worked a quarter of every hour, and afterward, if the manager was a kind man, he allowed them to play in the courtyard of the factory during the rest of their time. But nevertheless, along with the young women between the ages of sixteen and twenty-five, who worked steadily from five in the morning until seven at night, save for half-hour breaks for breakfast and lunch, they were expected to stay in the factory fourteen hours a day.

I can only imagine the tedium, hands and arms making the same movements hour after hour, becoming as Dreiser has written, "one mass of dull, complaining muscles"; day after day, the constant noise of the machinery in the background, and yet, despite the boredom, drifting off into reverie might be dangerous when, at certain times, the machines required an unwavering focus; not only your body but your mind would be molded to an unthinking yet relentless motion, a pace to which all your impulses and moods had to be calibrated.

Occasionally when a loom or a spindle did not need attention, a woman at the mills might fall into a state of reverie. In an essay called "A Weaver's Reverie," one of the girls who worked the looms, Harriet Farley, writes that in those moments, just as those who are starving become obsessed with images of food, "the factory girl . . . thinks not of the crowded, clattering mill . . ." but of "lovely scenes," of "nature's beauty," and of her own "yearning for the pure hallowed feelings which those beauties had been wont to call up."

The mill owners, who prided themselves on the way they treated their workers, had allowed the cultivation of potted plants in some of the rooms of the factories, in an attempt to mitigate the barren atmosphere of the workplace. They also provided access to various classes at night. Harriet Farley attended one in literature and writing. Her essay on reverie was published in a monthly periodical that published the writing of various mill women from 1840 to 1845, known as the *Lowell Offering*. Reading through a collection of these articles, I could not help thinking how in an earlier age I might well have been one of these girls. The prospect gave me that slight sensation of nausea one feels just after a car has swerved past on the road, narrowly avoiding a collision that would have severely injured you, if not taken your life. Yet the mill owners were glad that the journal was widely circulated, since they felt it advertised how well they took care of the women in their charge, toward whom they took a paternalistic interest, especially in regard to the protection of their chastity. The boardinghouses they provided for girls who did not have families nearby had very strict rules to regulate their behavior. They were rarely left unsupervised. But this must also have been why Harriet Farley, who was to become an editor of the journal, felt such a hunger for solitude; she includes the wish in her reverie to "go far away into the empty void of space beyond," before calling out in a plaintive voice, "I should love, for once, to be *alone*."

All the pieces are written with an almost feverish tone, as if just beneath constraint were an outrage never quite expressed or, if expressed, quickly suppressed with a reasoned argument. After another mill girl, Elizabeth Turner, demands, "Must I always stay here, and spend my days within these pent-up walls?" she reminds herself "to be contented with my lot, though humble, and not make myself unhappy by repining."

I am familiar with the feeling. An inner conflict, not experienced as a dialogue so much as a struggle, even a convulsion, an unruliness, that returns despite every effort at control. It belongs to the often tortured history of reason that the mill girls made many rational arguments to themselves, arguments that doubtless they had heard from others who did not share their circumstances, about how fortunate they were. They had money of their own to spend. If they were orphaned, they could be independent instead of relying on relatives. They earned a better wage, $1.85 to $3.00 a week, than many other workingwomen. They could help to support parents who were ill or, most often, put a brother or two through college. But repeatedly something in them asserted itself despite these arguments. They would have been moved by a different kind of reason, even if not articulated, as when, for instance, a girl or young woman might begin to feel the first signs of illness before she knows she is sick, a weariness, a sense of inner collapse, or sensitivity to cold, or irritability. The body, which is extremely rational, makes demands in this way for the changes you will need if you are to survive. And indeed, many of the mill women did sicken: as many as 40 percent were sent home to die of some kind of respiratory illness, what was called later brown lung, from breathing in fibers of the fabric and the fumes of whale oil lamps, in air that was stale because the windows had to be closed, and damp, from the water sprayed in the air to keep the threads from breaking.

But though the arguments the body makes will lose many of these inner debates, a kind of secular miracle occurs when suddenly a voice that has been suppressed within many women or men, boys or girls, separately, is spoken by one person who opens a corridor so that suddenly bodily reason and then outrage and then a demand for justice can emerge among the many. This is precisely what happened in Lowell, Massachusetts, in 1834, when, after the factory owners announced a reduction in wages, one young woman convinced a group of women to strike. Because she presided at several meetings the women held to discuss their grievances with one another, and then continued to persuade women at the factory to quit the mills, a manager fired her. But as she left his office, she waved her hooded scarf in the air. Hence, eight hundred women and girls, who immediately grasped the meaning of this gesture, walked out of the factories and began a march around the town.

The same day, one of the leaders of the strike stood on a stump to give an impassioned speech that coupled a defense of the rights of women with an attack on the inequities of the "monied aristocracy." She was the first woman ever to give a public speech in Lowell, Massachusetts.

It is the way democracy moves, as an irrepressible bodily passion, a lightning strike of insight, a revelation that suddenly uncovers new freedoms and new rights. All around town for the several days of their strike, the mill workers used the same language that Thomas Jefferson,

Tom Paine, Adams, and Franklin had employed to justify and ignite the American Revolution. So their petition to the manufacturers ended with this verse:

> Let oppression shrug her shoulders,
> And haughty tyrant frown,
> And little upstart Ignorance
> In mockery look down.
> Yet I value not the feeble threats
> Of Tories in disguise,
> While the flag of Independence
> O'er our noble nation flies.

No wonder Rose loved this story. It foretells her life. The tale illustrates the wondrous and unpredictable way that both consciousness and society are transformed when citizens come together to take action. And the extraordinary gifts by which organizers ignite this alchemical process are at the center of it. The outspoken young woman was well liked and trusted by her peers, enough for them to follow her to meetings and then to a strike, and this tells us she had a talent—one that may seem ephemeral, but is in fact quite palpable in its effects—for connecting to others and forming friendships. That she spoke at meetings reveals that she was good at articulating and explaining new ideas. And it shows too that she herself could see beyond propaganda and cant to uncover the basic structures of economy and power that shaped the lives of working-women. That she risked her own position to speak about these issues tells us that she had a great deal of courage and even more, the passion for justice that must have fueled her courage. Ultimately the stories we love tell us who we are. Did Rose sense that she had all of these characteristics? In a period of just a few years, she would become one of the most prominent union leaders in America.

When she returned to New York, Rose took a job again as a lining maker, but now her eyes were opened to the nature of her circumstances. She was soon to learn still more from a fellow worker, whose name, Bessie Braut, she still remembered years later. As the women worked together, Bessie began to discuss the union movement openly. "An outspoken anarchist, she made a strong impression on us," Rose wrote in her autobiography. She learned from Bessie that men in the garment trades had a union and that, because of their union, their wages and the conditions under which they worked were far better. I have some sense of the process. The way a new insight accumulates power in your mind, until finally when you make the decision to act, you will feel propelled to do so, as if by an irresistible force. Rose formed a small committee with three other women, who, in a group, "bravely . . . ventured into the office of the United Cloth Hat and Cap Makers Union" to tell the "man in charge" that they would "like to be organized." In telling her own story, Rose remembered that Maurice Mikol was an affable man, young and blond with blue eyes. He promised that, if and when Rose and her friends were able to sign up twenty-five women from various workplaces, they would be able to charter a local union for the women who were cap makers.

By standing outside a series of factories throughout the garment district, the young women were able to gather twenty-five signatures in just a few days. Was Mikol surprised at how quickly they realized this goal? Rose does not tell us. But what she does reveal is far more important. "All of a sudden," she writes, "I was not alone anymore." She meant this in a literal sense. She had begun to attend several meetings every week now, for her own shop, her local, and the executive board for the whole union. Soon, she was appointed as a delegate to the Central Labor Union of New York, which met every Sunday afternoon and where different speakers would discuss current issues. But I can imagine that her new calling would have answered a more subtle form of loneliness too. When you come to perceive any form of injustice, especially if it is one under which you yourself are suffering, the sense of the wrong will captivate you, not just in your mind but in your body too and certainly your soul. Held alone or in isolation, such knowledge can easily turn to bitterness. But when the same knowledge is shared, the mood in which it is held changes, so that speaking the truth can even engender a very particular kind of joy, a joy aligned perhaps with the audacity necessary, as Kant wrote in the eighteenth century, for enlightenment.

It is not surprising that Rose's mother, who belonged to an earlier generation, was wary of unions and hence in the beginning disapproved of her daughter's activities. In her recent understanding, Rose embodied a new consciousness, one that characterized an age. A shift was occurring. It could be registered through the dissemination of the revolutionary ideas of Fourier and Proudhon, Marx and Engels, Bakunin and Kropotkin, and the American activist and social philosopher Emma

Goldman. But the life of ideas, so often credited with leading social change, does not drive events. It is rather the reverse that is true. Changing conditions alter the ways we think, not all at once, but bit by bit and mind by mind, one mind affecting others, while experience shapes perception too, until all of a sudden, by an intricate collaboration between reality and consciousness, the intellectual climate appears to have been transformed.

APRIL

An unpredictable turn of history. John Dean has testified before Congress again. I saw him testify over thirty years ago during the Watergate hearings. As Nixon's White House counsel, he was convicted for his role in the crimes the White House committed. Clearly he's learned from the experience. Now he cautions Congress, "I hope you will not place the president above the law."

Rose's talent for mobilizing her community proved remarkable. After hearing her explain the need for unions to the ringleader of a group of strikebreakers, Mikol asked her to say the same things to a large meeting held the same evening. That she was, as she said, "scared stiff" turned out to be a sign of her ability. Perhaps it is because they are so aware of the significance of speech that so many fine orators have experience with similar fears. Partly because of this speech, and also, she tells us, because she had learned the parliamentary procedure, and knew "how to make a motion," Rose was elected to the general executive board of the United Cloth and Cap Makers. She was just twenty-two years old.

Very soon she found herself preparing for the general strike that was to be held in 1904 against the newly formulated open shop regulations, rules that used the language of freedom and patriotism to undermine the growing union movement. In response to a strike at the U.S. Government Printing Office, Teddy Roosevelt had declared that employees should not have to join any union, and that instead of union or nonunion, workplaces with this policy should be called "American shops."

The battle for the American soul often takes place through the use of particular words. On the simplest level of logic, it makes a certain kind of sense that a worker might be granted the freedom to decide whether or not to belong to a union. But this is a logic based on false grounds, built from an idealized concept of the lives of workers, as if they do not lose most of their freedom to make choices whenever they enter the places where they work. Indeed, as is also often the case with rhetoric in a democracy, regarding the word *freedom,* in this context, the truth turns out to be the reverse. With a wider range of choice, the union movement has given workers far more freedom. "The term 'American shop' was an extremely attractive slogan," Rose wrote, "for those who were opposed to unions, because it made the union shop seem un-American." It was a label that would prove to have many uses, persisting well into the McCarthy period.

A few years into the twentieth century, the members of several unions met to call a general strike demanding union shops. "The atmosphere," Rose wrote, "was electric." The determination to fight, the solidarity with one another, the unanimity of purpose, worked together to create this climate, a mood that, in itself, must have instilled another kind of knowledge, one that is not communicated with words alone but from experience, a direct knowledge of potential transformation, something that can be detected as surely as the skin can sense the coming of a powerful storm in the air.

Very soon after I graduated from high school, my own generation would experience a similar atmosphere. Whether it was Janis Joplin, Joan Baez, Ray Charles, Tina Turner, Bob Dylan, or The Beatles who performed, the mood at large concerts crackled with the charge that so frequently accompanies a major shift in consciousness. The first signs of the shift could be felt even earlier. If for a period I felt alone in my dissatisfaction with silence and the hypocrisy of the sanitized version of American life that seemed to dominate the culture, I was soon to find many friends who shared my rebellious perceptions. As if pulled by an invisible force field, along with the Steinberg sisters and Phyllis, I discovered various other like-minded friends, among them the children of actors and screenwriters, and others like me, whose parents were from the working class.

We began to gather on the weekends at the house where I lived with my father. The chief attraction of this location was the absence of any adults. Because he was a fireman, my father worked all-night shifts, and so he was usually gone on Saturday night. Even when he was not staying at the firehouse, he was likely to stay at his girlfriend's house in Los Angeles. We had the place to ourselves.

I had tacked a print of the portrait *Mother and Child* by Picasso, drawn in simple black lines on a pink and yellow background, over the used TV in the corner. I cut out a photograph of an Indian elephant from a magazine and taped it near my bed. We would sit on the ugly, dusty rose couch my father had picked up at a garage sale and read poems out loud by our favorite poets, many of whom, for some reason, had two initials in front of their surnames: W. H. Auden, T. S. Eliot, W. C. Williams. We also gravitated to Dylan Thomas, William Saroyan, John Dos Passos, and Gertrude Stein, jazz and Japanese tea, bongo drums, Mexican blouses and anthropology, Marlon Brando and Ingmar Bergman. We had learned about free love and began to practice a version of it, forming relationships we knew would not end in marriage. Because there were two bedrooms, near the end of the night, there were times when even two couples could find privacy.

We knew we were at the edge of a change in consciousness in the middle of the twentieth century. One of our group even made up a name for us. He called us "the Aware generation." We were coming of age at the end of one period and the beginning of another, and all that we longed for, everything that fascinated and excited us, pointed to a future whose dimensions we could almost feel.

During any great social transformation, certain events come to embody all the changes that are occurring. There was, for instance, the famous obscenity trial for Allen Ginsberg's poem "Howl." The proceedings ended in 1957 with a dismissal of all charges. The year before, Elvis Presley had gyrated his hips before an audience of sixty million television viewers on *The Ed Sullivan Show,* and just two years earlier a stunning moment had occurred during the army-McCarthy hearings when Joseph Welch, the special counsel for the army, defied McCarthy with the famous words, "Have you no sense of decency, sir, at long last? Have you left no sense of decency?" after which the audience burst into applause.

Much earlier in the twentieth century, a single tragic event served to awaken the public about the lives of working people. At five o'clock in the evening on Saturday, March 25, 1911, while they were finishing errands, preparing for the evening meal, or simply out walking, whoever happened to be in the vicinity of Washington Square began to see great dark billows of smoke crowding the sky.

The source was the top three floors of a ten-story building at Washington Place East and Greene Street known as the Triangle Shirtwaist Factory. It was a nonunion shop—one of the few that had managed to bring in enough strikebreakers to resist the general strike held by the

International Ladies Garment Workers Union. The strike, which had been called two years earlier, in 1909, had been announced at a large meeting held in Cooper Union, famous as the place where Lincoln had spoken in New York and for this reason revered by working people. The mood was spirited and determined. Clara Lemlich, who would be badly beaten by management goons in the course of the strike and yet still return the next day to the picket line, asked everyone present to raise their right hands and swear that "should I turn traitor to the cause ... may this hand wither from the arm I now raise." Rose had been sent by the union on a speaking tour to raise funds for the effort. She came back with ten thousand dollars, enough to allow many women to withhold their labor for weeks. Though the strikers did not get all that they demanded, the victory was significant. They had won the right to unionize, to a fifty-two-hour workweek, and to time and a half for overtime.

Rose had attempted to organize the women at the Triangle Shirtwaist Factory before but failed. Organizing in that period was not easy. Organizers would pass out leaflets, but many of the women could not read. They would try to speak with them as they left work, but many did not speak English. Still, this did not deter their efforts. Sometimes the organizers would bring translators for as many as four different languages: Italian, Polish, Russian, Yiddish. But the women who worked at the Triangle Factory presented a unique challenge. Although they would strike from time to time, they seemed predictably resistant to joining any union. Perhaps this was because the factory owners were so set against it. They took strong measures to discourage organizers, including locking the exit doors to the floors where the women worked. This was why so many women died in the fire. After they realized the building was in flames, they could not get past the locked doors.

Within the eighteen minutes that it took for the conflagration to engulf the ninth floor, where the women worked fourteen hours a day, 146 had died, some burning to death; others inhaling fatal fumes; others, in flight from the flames, jumping in terror from the windows. Among the dead, one was forty-eight years old, a sparse handful of others had reached their thirties, one was fourteen, and the rest under twenty-five years old. Lest they fall into the anonymity that so often protects history from the deeper dimensions of anguish, it seems wise to add some of their names here. The fourteen-year-old girl who died was named Kate Leone. Sarah Kupla, aged sixteen, managed to live for three days after the fire before dying at St. Vincent's Hospital. Vincenza Benanti was also just sixteen years old. Her cousin Tessa somehow survived. A young Russian girl, Rebecca Feicisch, was seventeen years old when she jumped from a ninth-floor window. She died of burns and other injuries the day after the fire at St. Vincent's Hospital. Mrs. Daisy Lopez Fitze, twenty-six years old, who also jumped from a ninth-story window, died on March 28, most probably of burns, though she had also fractured her pelvis and left arm and sustained serious head injuries. Esther Harris, who tried to escape the flames through the elevator shaft, had broken her back; she died of this injury in the early morning hours of the third day after the fire. Ida Konowitz was just eighteen years old when she perished. Her death is recorded as having occurred three days after the fire, but since no hospital is mentioned, it is likely that she died immediately, yet, as with Isabella Tortorella, seventeen, Jennie Stein, eighteen, and so many others, her identity was only discovered later, from a button on a skirt, or a patch of fabric from a blouse, a tooth, perhaps, or a familiar piece of jewelry, evidence found at the morgue where the bodies, most burned beyond recognition, were taken.

The scene must have been terrifying. In a photograph taken in the days after the fire, you can see the bodies of women lined up in caskets, which, according to the caption, were brown, crudely made, and numbered. The room, vast with the high ceiling and rough architecture of a warehouse, tends to add to the drama while at the same time dwarf the participants in a gloomy atmosphere. For hours on end, policemen held up lanterns over each casket as they accompanied the men and women who searched for members of their families, someone they had loved, who had worked at the factory and was missing. It took six days for all but seven of the bodies to be claimed. In the foreground of the same photograph, you can see three people—a young woman and man and an older woman—who stand close together while they stare down at one body. They are not weeping or crying out; rather, they seem fixed in a stunned, uncomprehending horror at what they see, as if sorrow were at that moment turning them all to stone.

But the pall that soon took over the whole city was just a prelude. The day after the tragedy, Washington Square was filled with grief-stricken crowds, not only families who had lost a daughter, a wife, a sister, but thousands of others who simply felt the anguish of the needless death that had transpired here. This is the underside of democracy, the fertile shadow-land of suffering; wherever a knowledge of the fragility of life is shared, even if momentarily, the boundaries of justice expand.

APRIL

A chilling experience. Looking again at my FBI file, I find a document with the heading "Emergency Detention Program." What does that mean? Were they planning to herd all of us with dissident or critical views into camps? The same document declares that because of various activities my name was to remain on the "Security Index."

On a rainy day in April, the International Ladies Garment Workers Union held a massive funeral for the victims of the fire who were unclaimed. From ten in the morning until four in the afternoon, 120,000 New Yorkers, including many trade union members, marched in procession through the streets. Studying a photograph of this event, I can almost detect the alchemy by which grief is being been turned into outrage.

Starting the day after the fire, the Women's Trade Union League initiated a campaign to outlaw the unsafe conditions that had caused many fires in the industry. They called a small meeting of leaders of various trade unions and from that group they immediately formed a committee to confront the issue of safety in factories. On the same day, efforts began to organize a mass meeting to protest the dangerous and unhealthy conditions that existed throughout the city. Anne Morgan, the daughter of J. P. Morgan, who was part of the league, was able to secure the Metropolitan Opera House for the occasion. On May 2, the vast auditorium was filled to capacity. There were thirty-five hundred people present that night to hear what civic leaders, clergymen, and labor leaders had to say. Jacob Schiff opened the meeting and then yielded to the district attorney, Eugene Philbin, who presided. Monsignor White, the head of Catholic Charities in the diocese of Brooklyn, told the crowd, "The workers have a right to life and it comes before our right to the ease and luxury that flow to the community from the production of wage earners." Bishop Greer, who followed him, said that the failure to protect workers in the future would be "a sin." Rabbi Wise, echoing the views of the other speakers, declared, "It is not the action of God but the inaction of man that is responsible," before calling for the legal protection of workers. E. R. Seligman, an economist from Columbia University, was met with a roar of applause when he accused Tammany Hall of "administrative impotence." But when the chairs of the meeting called for a resolution to create a Bureau of Fire Prevention and a system of workers' compensation, the crowd, furious with an endless series of resolutions that had achieved nothing, began to hiss and shout, and it seemed as if the meeting might end in violence.

In was then that Rose Schneiderman, small, just five feet two in stature, with her youthful hair still a bright red, stood to speak. Frances Perkins, who shared the stage with her, noticed how much Rose trembled as she approached the podium. She spoke in a voice hardly above a whisper. But though it was the first time she had addressed such a large audience and this must have made her somewhat nervous, by then she was an accomplished speaker. What made her voice small and her hands tremble was something else. She knew what it was to work at a young age for such long days for such small pay as the women at the Triangle Factory had done. She had been the one to lead these women out on strike in 1909. She was overcome with emotion. And the audience could hear it in her voice.

"I would be a traitor to those poor burned bodies," she began, "if I came here to talk good fellowship. We have tried you good people of the public and we have found you wanting." She described the underlying attitudes that had allowed the Triangle fire to happen. "The life of men and women is so cheap and property is so sacred," she said. What is needed, she declared, is more than charity. Workers should be free to protest. But instead, "the strong hand of the law beats us back when we rise to the conditions that make life bearable." And she ended by describing, in a few succinct words, a new and essential manifestation of democratic process. "It is up to the working people to save themselves," she said, and "the only way they can save themselves is by a strong working-class movement."

Of course, the labor movement already existed. Rose had been organizing women in the garment trades for years. But at pivotal moments in history, an authentic voice can coalesce what has been a nascent understanding in the general public into a new way of thinking. Her speech sparked a turning point. By the time she returned to her seat, the audience sat in stunned silence. A major shift in the atmosphere had occurred in the Metropolitan Opera House that night, one that would soon resonate throughout the whole Republic.

Certainly one reason that Rose's speech had had such a powerful effect was that the next day, the *New York Times* printed every word she said. In this way, her audience increased manyfold, but there was also the fact that appearing in the pages of a respected newspaper validated Rose's speech. Even events in which you participate yourself become more significant in your mind when you see them magnified in a larger mirror. Regarding stories she read in the *Times* and other papers about the general strike of 1909, Theresa Malkiel, a young shirtwaist maker, wrote, "Well, I think this strike is a more serious business than I thought. Otherwise the papers wouldn't make so much of it."

This was Rose's genius: a rare ability to teach others what she herself had learned. And that night another force too was abroad, not unlike the original spirit that fueled the founding of American democracy, a force for change that moves through crowds gathering all the available talents it can use on its way to realization. The hint of this presence can be found in the etymology of the word *genius,* which originally referred to tutelary deities. The divine in each of us is tuned to larger purposes and visions that come from, but are not limited by, our own lives.

APRIL

Apparently I was put on the security list because I was active in the student group called Slate that preceded the Free Speech Movement, wrote a few movie reviews for the People's World, *and attended a class on Marxism once or twice. They kept me on the list because, protesting the ban against travel to Cuba, I rode down Market Street in a bathing suit, before being crowned "Miss Right to Travel." I was twenty years old.*

The year before I moved into a house with my father, he began a love affair. There had been other girlfriends, whom in various ways I had liked, but, though he was seriously committed to this relationship, I took an intense dislike to this woman. She had never had children of her own, and she liked to manage everyone around her. My sister and I appreciated many of the changes she made. She got our father into a couple of good-looking suits and taught him how to silver his hair. But I found her intrusive. I thought we had little in common. In my adolescent estimation, her taste was too fussy and her values far too prissy. Yet there was one thing about her that intrigued me. She belonged to a union. And so when she invited my father and me to join her at her union's picnic, I was enthusiastic.

It was sunny and warm when the union members gathered in a large park, where they roasted hot dogs and chicken, a baseball game was in progress, and tents had been pitched where people could eat and mingle. But despite all this pleasantness, the day disappointed me. No longer religious, I had developed a passion for social justice. In my mind, I had conjured powerful speeches, rallies, or at least intense discussions about the rights of workers. Yet, despite my longing to enter this realm of meaning, I did not grasp what I was actually witnessing: workingmen and workingwomen who had long since won the right to a forty-hour workweek and who thus had their weekends free to come together with other union members and their families, who questioned neither their right to belong to a union nor to organize, whose wages kept up therefore with the cost of living so that they could afford to feed and clothe their families well.

Frances Perkins, who shared the stage with Rose that night at the Metropolitan Opera House, had been concerned about fire safety in factories years before the Triangle fire. The daughter of a businessman, who owned a small stationery store in Worcester, Massachusetts, she attended Mount Holyoke College, where one of her teachers, the estimable Anna May Soule, famous for developing several innovative courses on social justice, took her students to nearby factories so that they could observe conditions there firsthand. Frances saw for herself the slippery floors and machines without guards that could cause accidents. Workers' compensation did not yet exist then, so a single serious accident might well leave a whole family destitute. Though before this she had wanted to teach science, she was caught up now in the same forceful transformation of consciousness that was propelling Rose.

What drew her mind more than any other subject was social science, a new category of knowledge, emerging, not coincidentally, in the period when the union movement was gathering momentum. It was still an innovative method then to collect statistics about social phenomena with which to formulate judgments, instead of relying on religious or philosophical reflections alone. For her master's degree at Columbia she conducted a study of hunger, and then she went to work for the Consumers League, an organization that, as is done today, enlisted consumers in boycotts against products produced by factories whose labor practices were abusive to workers. Soon this league sent her to Albany as a lobbyist, where she pressed for laws mandating a fifty-four-hour workweek.

Perkins's early work with the league had made her aware of how few precautions most factories took to protect their employees against fire. Which is why on March 25, 1911, after looking out the window of her apartment, when she saw a commotion in the streets and followed the crowds to the Triangle Factory, she understood what lay behind the tragedy almost immediately. She saw all the signs: the flimsy fire escape crushed by the weight of women trying to flee, ladders dangling useless at the side of the building. She knew even before the report came in that the exits were not adequate, the doors probably locked. Soon after the meeting at the Metropolitan Opera House, she began talking with the legislators she knew—Al Smith, among them. And when John Dix, the governor of New York, formed a committee to take on the problem of safety, she was appointed as one of the official investigators.

Within a year, the committee suggested laws to make a fifty-four-hour workweek the maximum allowed. By the next year, Frances had piloted a bill to that effect through the legislature, along with a new industrial code of safety. Rose was deeply impressed. Now she added the powers of legislation to her approach. But the circumference of her knowledge was expanding in another way too. In her work with the Women's Trade Union League, she had begun to count many women outside the boundaries of the world she had known as her friends. As she worked with Frances Perkins, they became close allies. And if at first she distrusted Anne Morgan because of her vast wealth, she quickly came to see that Morgan's intentions were serious. Like Mary Dreier, who had independent wealth and who chaired the league, and Gertrude Barman, the daughter of a prominent judge, who volunteered as a secretary, or Mrs. Henry Morgenthau Sr., who deeded property to the Henry Street Settlement so the league could provide bail during strikes, despite their privileges, these women all braved derision from family members and others in their upper-class circles. Very soon another movement was to arise called the Red scare. J. Edgar Hoover, then a bureau chief in the Justice Department, was compiling lists filled with the names of those he called subversives, and unions were being given the label that was to become familiar to me three decades later: "un-American."

Then, in 1919, Rose who was raised in tenement housing, slums carved out of mansions that had once belonged, in their more glorious days, to the Knickerbockers, the oldest and most powerful aristocrats in New York, was to meet a descendant of one of those families by birth and, since she had wed a distant cousin, by marriage as well. Eleanor

Roosevelt's world had recently widened too when, during World War I, she volunteered in settlement houses that were assisting young wounded soldiers returning from battle. Through the women she met there, she ended up volunteering again, this time as a translator at the International Congress of Working Women held in Washington that year.

One might think that, given their histories, the gulf between Eleanor Roosevelt and Rose Schneiderman would have been too wide to bridge. Yet a certain understanding would have been there too, deep in the foundation of both memory and psyche, of injuries sustained young, yet of aspirations, not for success so much as knowledge, a leaning toward what may not have been defined but beckoned nonetheless, an unwillingness to be confined, at least in the imagination, and the strength to resist all the attempts that are constantly made to confine any woman's mind, not to speak of her life.

Soon Eleanor was joining Rose not only in committee meetings but on picket lines. They taught each other what they knew, and it was a happy exchange. Rose became a regular guest at Hyde Park and Campobello. She was amused and impressed by the fact that her regular rooms were part of a suite where the king and queen of England had stayed. But in her autobiography, *All for One,* the memory that seems to touch her most is how she would sit and listen while Eleanor read *The Education of Henry Adams* to her children. It was the first she had heard of this book, and she found it so illuminating she declared it ought to be assigned to all schoolchildren. For her part, Eleanor told Rose that all she knew about the union movement she had learned from Rose.

In the middle of the nineteenth century, while Emerson, Hawthorne and Thoreau, Louisa Alcott, and Margaret Fuller were extending the boundaries of democracy by trying to live more plainly, in harmony with nature, in New York City, a small society of highly privileged men and women, called the "Four Hundred," led by Caroline Webster Schermerhorn, or Mrs. William Astor, more widely known simply as Mrs. Astor, were busy reviving the habits of aristocracy in America. It was from this enclave that Eleanor Roosevelt rebelled.

In her own way she was continuing the movement toward equality proposed by Jefferson not only through his attempts to end primogeniture and entail, but when by one phrase he both claimed and promised that the right to pursue *happiness,* to live with meaning and pleasure, belongs to every citizen.

APRIL

Strange cloak-and-dagger efforts. Agents talked to the mail carrier, registrars, the passport office, neighbors. Much of it seems to have occurred simply to justify their salaries. One agent, who followed me from my apartment on Russian Hill to North Beach, reports ominously that I went in a door marked Ramparts. *But it was public knowledge that I worked at that magazine: I was on the masthead. After I moved to Berkeley, an agent talked to a neighbor who reported seeing cars at my address that had bumper stickers for "left-wing" causes. These were not exactly hidden either. But, as the KGB and the Stasi knew well, such strategies intimidate everyone.*

There is one more story Rose tells about her introduction to the upper classes. In her memoir, she recalls the first time she attended a reception in a fancy house. In the beginning, she was intimidated. But after a while, she found her way. And what she returned with was a stunning experience, not of architectural splendor but of a simple dish of strawberries set out on the buffet table, which were fresh and more delicious than anything she had ever tasted before.

When the wealthy, feeling dissatisfied by the confines of upper-class society, reject such sensual pleasure, it is often because beauty, and taste, and lovely scents, gardens and fine furniture, silk gowns and golden ornaments, have been displayed as symbols of power and control, as if their owners could command all that is living to serve them. Yet in that obedience, the vitality, and thus the appeal, of whatever is commanded will be lost.

In a sense, my friends and I rejected class too. Though we would not have described it as such, we did not think of ourselves as working-class or middle-class, but as belonging to another realm altogether, in between and floating, outside those systems altogether. We were artists, painters, or poets; we did not behave as we were supposed to, were not going to wear gray flannel suits or shoes dyed to match formal dresses. We were free, we told ourselves, of all that. Still, gradually, even if I did not know her name, as I became an adult, I began to realize that my desire to become a writer could be fulfilled only because men and women like Rose Schneiderman had made it possible.

Working with other labor leaders and citizens of conscience, Frances

Perkins, Eleanor Roosevelt, and Rose Schneiderman brought about a vast change in American society, introducing and instituting much that we take for granted today: the minimum wage, workers' compensation and safety laws, Social Security, unemployment insurance, Medicare. And along with these new practical solutions to suffering, a more inclusive and hence more ingenious vision of American democracy.

But still there are enclaves of the soul, secret sores, pockets of comprehension that lie outside this vision. The land itself, not the means but the manner of production, the air we breathe, the quality of light. Reseda, where I went to high school, was on the front line of urban sprawl. There were days my friends and I made forays in a borrowed car, on motorcycles, or even on horses into the remaining farmland. The landscape was charming, filled with small farms, modest orchards, fields you could take in at a glance, animals, grazing or in wooden barns.

At the far edge of the continent, this seemed like our own private pastoral dreamscape, an embodiment of Jefferson's vision of an agrarian democracy. But in a time before the manipulation of stocks and the birth of dot-coms, this region had a potential for enormous profit. We did not know that this land had once been a desert and that the water that made the land arable had been stolen, through a political power play, from the Owens Valley. Nor did we realize that the real use for which the water had been planned all along was to feed the needs of all the subdivisions rapidly covering every square foot of the valley. The same inexpensive tracts in which both my stepfather and my father had bought their home were making a handful of men very wealthy.

April

More about the torture of Iraqi men by U.S. soldiers at Abu Ghraib prison in Iraq in the news now. We're seeing more photographs of the abuse now. Horrifying images, men blindfolded, hooded, naked, and piled up on top of each other, or connected to electrodes, threatened with snarling dogs. One soldier has a swastika drawn between his eyes.

There was an Irish girl, named Dorrity, who survived the Triangle Factory fire. I wonder what happened to her. Did she grow up? Or die young of brown lung disease? Did she move from New York City. Marry? Raise a family? Was she able to enjoy for herself any of the gains the labor movement made?

As a young woman I never questioned all the gains the working class had made, nor did I believe that these could ever be lost. But I have lived to see all that was fought for threatened and diminished by one means or another. For many years Levi Strauss and Company had a reputation for employment policies shaped by a concern for social justice. Strauss plants in the South were fully integrated. When other manufacturers moved to Asia, they continued to employ American workers for awhile. But finally they too would move their operations overseas so they could pay lower wages.

APRIL

It all seems of one piece. Torture, imprisonment without charge, the government spying on its own citizens. "Crimes against liberties," as Jefferson would have put it, that characterize monarchies (or any kind of tyranny) more than democracy.

Of my high school friends, none of us hewed to any strict political philosophy. If we took "the aware generation" as a name for ourselves, it was not because we had formulated a radical new set of ideas. Rather, we sensed a change in the air, something unspoken, but still a future that we could almost taste and feel. This was such a strong sensation that it seemed as if, when we came home from school to put on our blue jeans and gather somewhere, at the park or at one of our houses, we were already living in that world.

4

JAZZ

If a man does not keep pace with his companions, perhaps it is because he hears a different drummer. Let him step to the music which he hears, however measured or far away.

—HENRY DAVID THOREAU, *Walden*

Billie Holiday. Man, it was a thrill to play for her. She had the greatest conception of beat I ever heard.

—BOBBY TUCKER, pianist and accompanist for Billie Holiday

Walking in this country you could understand the perfect gems of haikus the Oriental poets had written. . . . We made up haikus as we climbed.

—JACK KEROUAC, *The Dharma Bums*

JUNE

The art of improvisation. How to hang with the moment and see what's there.

I was very small. Too young to know that the music was coming from a record in my mother's collection or that a needle at the end of an arm over a circle turning at seventy-eight rpms was making sound rush out of the dark wooden cabinet into our living room. Generally, in the period I remember, I would have been hunkering right in front of this piece of furniture, or standing, bending my knees to the beat, as I've seen my grandson do when he was younger and heard something he liked.

JUNE

Could there be anything here in this terrible moment right now that we aren't seeing yet?

It is certainly possible that I had encountered what was also called music before I heard this particular kind. Perhaps Christmas carols, though because I was born in late January, it would more likely have been "Happy Birthday" sung to my mother, who was born in March. But nevertheless, I have the strong feeling that this sound from the phonograph was the first music I heard, and that I was listening even before I could hold up my head, maybe while my mother fed me from a bottle, while she sat in an easy chair in the living room.

The records were hers. I know that not only because they went with her after the divorce but also because these are the sounds I associate most with her, as if they came out of her body. And in any case, this was the first music I remember really loving. Jazz. Johnny Dodds, king of the New Orleans clarinet, and his Black Bottom Stompers playing with Louis Armstrong; Earl Hines; Johnny St. Cyr; Jelly Roll Morton hammering out his red-hot jazz playing the music he composed on the piano, "King Porter Stomp," "Pontchartrain," "Dead Man," and "Jelly Roll Blues"; Art Tatum playing piano too, "Sweet Lorraine" and "Tiger Rag"; the Quintet of the Hot Club of France, with Stéphane Grappelly on the violin and Django Reinhardt on the guitar. A year or two went by before I learned these names, of course, but by the time I could pronounce them, they were lodged deep in my mind, ineradicable fixtures of my inner landscape, as familiar as the palm trees on the skyline my sister and I could see out the window of our bedroom.

These records my mother loved to play were pressed early on by Decca, Victor, and Brunswick in the twenties and thirties, but I did not know that then. I did not even know the word for the kind of music I loved. I made no distinction among the styles. Nor could I name the strains of ragtime, blues, New Orleans street music, or the influence of French and Italian opera, Debussy, or Ravel that I heard, for instance, in Jelly Roll Morton's work.

But I did understand what happened to me when this music was played. Everything in the room seemed to brighten and quicken. It was not just dullness and banality that were vanquished, but anything hazy, vague, lost, disoriented, depressed, or mentally wasteful seemed to disappear too. The music did not stay in the background or hide behind my ears but instead rushed boldly right into me and, once there, seemed to wake up the most vibrant part of myself, making me want to move, not just with my body but move inside my soul and my imagination too.

From Jelly Roll Morton's account, it was like this from the beginning for him too. Though, since he would be one of the men and women who created jazz, what he heard on the streets when he was still very young was not called jazz yet but was known simply as ragtime or blues, or low-down music because it was played in places like saloons and brothels. My first memories of jazz are so vivid, it is hard for me to imagine a time when jazz was still incubating. But in 1899, the year when Jelly Roll, then Ferdinand La Menthe, was born, the word *jazz* did not exist. All the elements already existed. But the various strands were not woven together yet. Jelly Roll would be one of the musicians to do that.

JUNE

Came across an old slave song that repeats the phrase, "wrestling with the angel, wrestling with the angel." Thinking now how such vibrant music came from people who had suffered slavery.

Creole, of French and African extraction, Ferdinand La Menthe was introduced to music from the earliest age. There were, for instance, the operas he attended as a young child with his mother and, after his mother threw his father out of the house, his stepfather, Willie Mouton. At the French Opera House, a popular New Orleans venue in the late nineteenth and early twentieth centuries, he would have heard Gounod, Bizet, Debussy, Verdi and Donizetti. Then there was the liturgical music he heard at the Catholic church his family attended. And the classical music played on the piano, zither, guitar, trombone, at home. But New Orleans had another popular sound, a music different from what could be heard anywhere else. It was performed on street corners all over town or by marching bands that accompanied mourners with a dirge on the way to the cemetery and then played happier songs as they returned to the land of the living. Street vendors played this music, and so did small bands in parades led by unions. It could also be heard in minstrel shows, as well as all along Basin Street, both in front of and inside the brothels and saloons for which this part of town was famous.

Ferdinand's middle-class family looked down on these places. But he had an intimate connection to this district nevertheless. His godmother, Laura Hunter, a Vodun healer and spiritual adviser, known in her trade by the evocative name of Eulalie Echo, served many prostitutes from Storyville. Ferd, as he was called all his life, must have heard Voodoo chants from her, sounds that carried the musical traditions of African culture, the Yoruba, Dahomeans, and Bakonga into the New World.

Eulalie noticed Ferd's musical talent early. There was the time, for instance, when he was still an infant that she left him for a short while in the care of a friend. The woman, a prostitute, was arrested, and since she refused to part with Ferd, they were both put into a crowded jail cell. When the other inmates began to sing, he was calm, quiet, and attentive. But as soon as they stopped, he would start to wail.

True to her name, with its overtones of eulogy and euphony (if not euphoria), Eulalie nurtured the boy's musical talent, arranging for him to study the steel-string guitar with an older Spanish man, a friend of the family, who introduced him to the habanera rhythms he would incorporate into his own music. Then one day his musical studies took another turn. He had already been singing with one of the a cappella quartets that performed on street corners, and because they sang spirituals, this was acceptable to his family. But when he was ten years old and he began to study with a blues and ragtime piano player named Frank Richards, he brought down the wrath of his stepfather, who beat him with his belt before he told him, "Son, if you ever play that dirty stuff again, I'll throw you out on your ear." The punishment, however, had no effect except to make Ferdinand stop playing the music he loved at home. That the sound had gotten under his skin was clear. As he told the musicologist Alan Lomax years later, "Man, I could no more stop playing it than I could stop eating."

By 1895, ragtime and blues had already captivated American audiences. Those who have been marginalized by society often act as lightning rods for what the culture craves. Perhaps this is because the marginalized can more easily retrieve and make art from what has been discarded, ignored, or even demonized by the dominant culture. And then again, placed at the edge of society, you will be able to see beyond the boundaries of what is already known and has already been done.

But there is another factor specific to African-American cultures, from Missouri to Harlem to New Orleans, that would have nurtured this new music. I am thinking about the nature of the societies in both Africa and America that gave birth to this art. The music of the African diaspora, with its multiple rhythms, overlapping call and response, offbeats, and blue notes, is as much an expression of community as it is of any individual soul. In the various cultures of Africa that have been spread throughout the world, the web of connection, need, and responsibility, which shapes community, did not repress individuality but instead provided a stable ground from which flights of the imagination, innovation, and idiosyncrasy could be expressed.

You can see the balance between singularity and union played out in what is called the "second line" in New Orleans, the group that gathers and then follows behind a brass band in a parade through the streets, all dancing to the music, keeping the same beat, and yet each swaying and stepping in his or her own way; as you can hear stability and change in the syncopation of Scott Joplin's "Maple Leaf Rag," while one hand plays a steady beat and the other goes wild with unpredictable accentuations.

Traditional African music is filled with multiple, overlapping, and contrasting beats. And the dancing line is part of a long tradition in African cultures too, a procession that on some occasions marches to a funeral and at other times forms a ring or snakes through space, in communal solidarity and an ecstatic affirmation of life, all driven by the experience that every sound and each movement is ignited by divinity.

JUNE

Listened to my mother's scratchy records today. Johnny Dodds, Louis Armstrong on the cornet, Earl "Fatha" Hines on the piano. This music always leads me somewhere. Back in memory, of course, but also forward, to a place I can't yet name.

But for the most part, Ferdinand's family shunned this kind of music. They were Creoles, of mixed European and African heritage, living in a large, comfortable house, with ways that were considered cultured and respectable. Though many of them played instruments for pleasure, except for musicians who performed at the French Opera House, they considered anyone who took up music professionally "a scalawag, lazy," Morton wrote years later, someone who was "trying to duck work." And in this category, ragtime and blues musicians were the worst. Though it was popular, ragtime also inspired general disapproval. It was blamed for the loosening of morals, especially as a challenge to chastity, and in the same vein, it was associated with barbarity, wildness, and dangerous levels of sensuality.

Even during the Jazz Age, when my mother must have first heard jazz, it was regarded as a pernicious influence. In 1922 the Illinois Vigilance

Association claimed that listening to jazz had caused one thousand girls to fall from virtue. When plans were made to build a theater next door to a home for pregnant women, the Salvation Army even brought an injunction stopping the construction. They argued that if the vulnerable infants overheard the music played, treacherous "jazz emotions" would be seeded in their developing minds. Something in this quickening sound was unnerving and frightening. The *Musical Courier* even made the claim that jazz was a danger to America, with its "Bolshevistic smashing of the rules and tenets of decorous music."

Yet it was not just sexuality and disorder that the critics of this kind of music found threatening. The charge of barbarity and "unwholesome excitement" was fed from still another stream, one that has flowed through American history since the start. It is evident, for instance, in the more shadowy realms of Thomas Jefferson's way of thinking, as despite his opposition to slavery, he argued that black people were inferior. In keeping with this prejudice, when a book of poetry by Phillis Wheatley was published to wide acclaim, he declared that he found her work to be inferior and thus unworthy of all the praise it had received. The young woman, who had been seized at an early age in Africa by slave traders only to be sold in America, had been recognized as very intelligent by the Quaker family who purchased her. In a time when black people were forbidden to learn to read, this family gave her an education rare even for a white girl. She responded with an uncommon literary genius. Almost as soon as the poems she wrote were published, they caused a stir, astonishing an American public that had been happy in the opinion that Africans did not possess the same intellectual capacities as white people, a delusion that doubtless assuaged much guilt and horror over the institution of slavery. Perhaps because to hold any delusion dampens the spirit, her poems were welcomed by a large readership. Yet even otherwise intelligent men will choose delusion over truth when the truth is challenging. At the time that he read Wheatley's book, Jefferson was still dependent on slave labor to run his estate at Monticello. At one point he held 140 men, women, and children in bondage.

JULY

When I heard on the radio today that the first public places to be integrated in many parts of the country were the clubs and dance halls

where jazz was played, I felt a kind of electricity and a new awareness
I can't entirely explain to myself yet.

Though my mother told me more than once that my grandparents had a good time dancing at clubs during the Jazz Age, they retained a subtle prejudice against the form. They never talked about jazz or played this music at home. They must have heard the sound coming through the walls, in the other half of their duplex, where my mother and I were listening, but as far as I know, my grandmother did not appear to be worried about the development of my infant mind. Still, when I was older and living with her, she quietly diverted me from the fierce longing I had to learn tap dancing by insisting that I take ballet lessons instead.

Despite the severity of his father's warning, Ferdinand, who was captivated by ragtime and blues piano, kept on playing and listening. In one of her poems, Wheatley, uses slavery as a brilliantly paradoxical metaphor, to describe the compelling nature of creativity:

> Now here, now there, the roving fancy flies,
> Till some lov'd object strikes her wand'ring eyes,
> Whose silken fetters all the senses bind,
> And soft captivity involves the mind.

Driven by his new love, Ferd found other pianos to play. And he continued to roam the tenderloin district, Bourbon and Basin streets, visiting the brothels of Storyville, to stand on the sidewalks and then in the doorways and then go inside, where he could hear the repertoires of various piano men. He had an extraordinary musical ability, the capacity to hear and imitate the many different techniques and forms he encountered. So bit by bit he amassed an extensive collection of musical ideas. As he listened to various men playing in the District—Buddy Carter; Josky Adams; Game Kid; Sam Henry; and his favorite of all time, Tony Jackson—he took in the principles of the percussive explosions he heard; learned how to rag, or shift the beats in a composition; to pound the bass notes "boogie-woogie" style (called "playing the horses" then); to play broken chords and octave tremolos; to wire together elements of opera with street music.

But just as a larger and larger world of music was opening up to him, Ferd's life took a sad turn. When he was fourteen years old, his mother died. According to his mother's wishes, his uncle became his guardian. He was still part of a large family living in the comfortable house he shared with his sisters, his grandmother, his aunt, and his uncle. But like the strains of sorrow you can hear underneath the exuberance of his compositions, taken together, various comments and anecdotes indicate another story under the warm veneer. The time his grandmother came home with gifts for all the other children in the family but him, for instance. Or his disappointment over the new suit he had been promised on New Year's Day, cut down from the old and overlarge jacket and pants that had belonged to his uncle; though his aunt was a good seamstress, the clothes did not fit. And then too, times were getting hard for the whole family, with the home being mortgaged, his grandfather losing his liquor business.

No wonder that he was so happy to find a job paying two dollars a week in a cooperage. It was strenuous labor, making barrels, not only deadening but exhausting. He wanted money of his own so he could buy things for himself and be able to carry himself with pride. But very soon he was to find much more lucrative work, and miraculously, by doing what he loved. By then he was already considered one of the best young piano players in New Orleans. So that one evening while he was hanging out with his friends in the district, when one of them heard that one of the houses needed a piano player for the rest of the night, they all encouraged him to apply.

In contrast to the braggadocio he would take on later, he was polite and soft-spoken then, shy and still wary of the dangers in the district. He would not go to the house without his friends. Once there, after they were asked to leave the room, he was too frightened to play a note. But when they returned, he began to play and his talent was unmistakable.

For a golden period, he had what seemed like a blessed life. A popular professor, as piano players in brothels were called, he started making lots of money, often earning over a hundred dollars a night in tips. Knowing his grandmother would not approve of what he was doing, he told his family he was working as a night watchman at the cooperage. He gave them part of his earnings and with the rest started to buy himself fancy clothes. A Stetson hat, Saint Louis flats, silk shirts, elegant and tightly cut suits. While he was honing his music and building an audience, he was also learning the ways of the New Orleans underworld of pimps and prostitutes and gamblers and pool hustlers. And every night he could retire to the safe atmosphere of a middle-class household on Frenchmen Street.

But it did not last long. As he reported years later, his grandmother, MiMi Pechet, "could look a hole right through a door." In his later years, he told more than one story about how she found him out. But whether it was when she caught him wearing his fine clothes one Sunday, or after he beat up his uncle for borrowing and then ruining his best suit of clothes by falling drunk in the street, the eventual result was devastating. "I don't want you around your sisters," she told him. "I reckon you better move."

He was fifteen years old, and "so dumb," he said, that he "didn't know how to rent a room." He must have been desolate already and feeling like he had no place else to go as he walked into the Grand Theatre that night. When they sang a song called "Give Me Back My Dead Daughter's Child," he began to cry. He was thinking, he said, about how his mother had died, leaving him "a motherless child out in this wide world to mourn."

It is a feeling I know well, having faced abandonment more than once, taken from my mother, saying good-bye to my sister and my father, losing my father's father and his grandmother to their natural deaths, afterward leaving my mother's parents to live with my mother and stepfather, then back to my grandmother again, and then again to my mother before I moved in with my father in the new tract house he bought in Canoga Park on Bothwell Street. In some ways, I imagine my response was not unlike Ferdinand's. I was afraid at night when my father was working at the fire station or staying with his girlfriend on the other side of the hills that divided the San Fernando Valley from Los Angeles. But scared and lonely as I sometimes was, a powerful force within me called out, *Let the good times roll.* When my father was gone, which was often, the house we shared was a free zone, the place where my friends came to smoke and drink wine and make out and make love, which is why we called the house the Bothwell Brothel.

JULY

The recording was cut in 1927 when my mother was just fourteen years old. Jazz was not much older than she was then. Amazing to hear this music at its debut. As we used to say in the sixties, it had to be mind-blowing.

It was a wild time in my life, a mix of new sensations and knowledge; I had a group now with whom I could deny my despair and at the same time defy the dull suffocation of the fifties. As children who are nearly adults often do, we took pleasure in mocking stuffiness of every variety. One of our friends, who wrote satirical limericks in the style of Dorothy Parker, disobeyed her parents, who were Conservative Jews, by dating a Catholic boy, three years older than she. The shock of blond hair over his forehead and the lit Chesterfield that perpetually hung from his mouth embodied his stylishly sardonic attitude. Another friend, originally from the South and Protestant, had begun to study Hebrew. She introduced us all to Meyer Levin's collection of Hassidic tales, a book we read with great enthusiasm. One day during a high school assembly, I encouraged my friends to perform a bebop parody of genuflection, timed to the sanctimonious words of a speaker who tried to lead us all in a Christian prayer. When we were taken in to the principal's office, we invoked our right to freedom of religion. Later we laughed at the surprised look on the principal's face when I claimed I was Jewish. The fact that we were mostly well-behaved students who earned high grades must have helped to protect us from punishment. But we mocked this too. Not content to stay within the invisible boundaries that separated those measured as "high achievers" from those classed as delinquents, we treasured our connection with a brilliant girl who wore thick mascara, dyed her hair blonde, and wrote a rhyming poem that contained the menacingly hostile line "I feed neighborhood kitties ground glass."

One December night, at a late party at the home of a girl who was to become my best friend, when we ran out of beer and liquor, I climbed in a car with the group sent out to replenish supplies. One of the youngest there, I had already had a lot to drink, but when we got to the store, I grabbed a bottle of a vile concoction made of cheap wine and pink carbonated water, called Thunderbird, and slipped it under my sweater. I was not a successful thief. The next day the liquor store owner, who had written down the license number of the car, and somehow gotten the number where we all were, called as we awoke, hung over, having slept all night on the floor. Fortunately he proved a kind man who let me off after I returned the empty bottle in exchange for listening to his lecture and offering him an apology.

Yet though what I had done was foolish, my rebellion was not entirely mindless. I could not have named the source of my defiance then. The classic film *Rebel without a Cause* captures the amorphous yet aching discontent of the period. It was a time of sleepwalking, of followers in gray flannel suits or round collars and proper pumps who seemed to have traded in passion for predictability. Only years later would I begin to grasp why this collective numbness had captivated American culture after the war.

Whether or not we could name the causes, we were rejecting that frozen state of mind. True to our chosen name, "the aware generation," as we broke rules, we were also breaking through the haze that had been keeping us from life. We were set on a path full of wonders and discoveries. We wanted to learn all that had been kept secret from us and to tell our own secrets too. My Southern friend had begun to study Hebrew after working in a fabric store for a woman who had been a concert pianist in Germany. One night Frances was commanded to play for the Gestapo. Though she felt she could not refuse, she was frightened. She was married to a Jewish man who had been sent to a concentration camp. She was right to be afraid. Just after she performed for them, one of the officers cut off the fingers of her right hand. Despite the terror this image inspired, I wanted to hear the story. Somehow I knew that these horrors also offered a key to the oddly robotic silences that seemed to have imprisoned postwar America.

What I could not know then was that slowly, in countless private or isolated or as yet unnoticed corners, the golden blanket of silence that had suffocated so many of us was being torn apart, riddled with confessions. It was seven years before Sylvia Plath would publish her searing collection of poems called *Ariel,* in which one of the lines addressed to her father read, "Every woman adores a Fascist, / The boot in the face, the brute / Brute heart of a brute like you"—linked private with public horrors. In the same period, both Robert Lowell and Anne Sexton were writing poems that described the experience of mental breakdown.

These writers were at the cutting edge of a powerful wave moving through American culture. One night when my friend Kate slept over, she made a startling confession to me. Her father, she told me, had raped her when she was younger. There were photographs of her being fondled that were found by a maid. He was arrested and forbidden by the courts to ever see her again. A few months later, when my best friend, Bran, was spending the night, we drank so many vodka tonics that soon I was reeling. It was then that, weeping almost violently, I told my story: how my mother would drag me with her to bars or leave me alone for hours without food or come home at two or three in the morning only to haul me out of bed so that she could pour out her sorrows and then aim her hostility at me, slinging venomous comments in a drink-sodden, slurred but still slicing tone of voice.

But it was not self-pity we were after. Though we were flying blind, with little psychological theory to guide us, we had a sense of what we wanted. It was there in certain poems we loved. There were two by Dylan Thomas that we read again and again. It was not only the content of "The Force That through the Green Fuse Drives the Flower" we loved but the music of the words. When we read it aloud, the poem became a driving force, which married the energy of "young age" with quicksand and "shroud sail," a propelling, almost cataclysmic rush of syllables, that caught up terror and death in the same breath as life and desire. And however it was intended, the poem "Do Not Go Gentle into That Good Night," with rolling lines that rocked you into the deepest sorrow, became our anthem, a cry against complacency.

Culture preserves tradition. But art is the medium of metamorphosis too. And since democracy is a form of government responsive to the people, it is flexible, always changing, singing with innovation, ingenuity, riffing on old ideas, playing with form, the whole process of change accelerated by multiple and disparate creators. I loved the poetry of Dylan Thomas and W. H. Auden, but I was drawn to a newer, spare kind of sound. My friends and I, for instance, loved to read each other haiku, and we wrote poems more or less in this scheme too: seventeen syllables, five in the first line, seven in the second, five in the third.

It was a dramatic reversal for anyone who remembered anything of the war, as if the epitome of ugliness had suddenly become the source of beauty. I can still remember the drawings, caricatures of Japanese soldiers that decorated the surfaces of otherwise innocent objects—bookmarks or matchbooks—or that turned up in cartoons and then the drawings of my older sister's friends, bucktoothed, nasty-looking men, bent on mayhem. The word *Jap,* one syllable you would spit out with sharp aggression, made its way into our daily landscape of sounds.

But now, as we got rid of that word, so fraught with the suffering and blind rage of our elders, it felt as if we were reclaiming our own eyes and ears, our own tongues. This process seemed to be connected too with the passion we felt in our bodies, our desire for and fascination with each other, what was hidden under our clothes, as we moved our hips to Chuck Berry and Elvis Presley, or kissed with our mouths open and felt what it was like to press against each other, the sweet longing that rose inside.

The same friend who was studying Judaism began to date a soldier named George who had been in Japan as part of the American occupation. A group of us would accompany them on forays into the Japanese neighborhood of downtown Los Angeles, where he introduced us to raw fish and Japanese beer, tastes that opened our minds to the stimulating pleasure of the unfamiliar. We went to see samurai movies, and then the brilliant *Rashomon*, full of carefully composed images that reminded me of the prints of Hokusai, which I had pored over as a child in a book my great-aunt had brought back from her prewar travels. This aesthetic, with lush colors and designs marshaled into one spare, starkly dramatic composition, drew me in for reasons I could not explain even as it rearranged the very lens of my perception.

And then there was jazz, rearranging my ears. I was pulled, as I had been since the earliest age, but now more fiercely, as if this music captured the wild desire cultivating my body. Jizz, jazz. Some say the word has African roots, referring to a vital energy, the central energy of the universe, which can be found in orgasm, in jism, jizz, Jazz. I did not analyze it, I didn't need to. The action, the riffs, the beats, the raspy-voiced, then mellow tones, then laughing, soaring pitches, echoed the way I was feeling and made it part of an energy larger and deeper than myself, something palpable and mysterious all at once that entered and found a home in me, making my mind as wide as desire is.

David, my first lover, and I went back to George's place, a strange conglomeration of rooms in a warehouse, where Tammy and George and David and I made love in separate beds behind separate curtains; then George gave us tea made from roasted rice and told us tales of the beautiful Japanese woman who had walked on his back. It all came together. The sex and the images, the tastes and the new sound, the new way of writing a poem.

David had courted me with haiku. One night we broke up. He thought I had been drinking too much, and though I knew he was right, when he threatened to leave me if I did not stop, I refused to do so. I've never been able to accept an ultimatum from anyone, and in truth, I wanted to be free of him. I loved my best friend, Bran, far more than I did him. She loved me too and I knew it. But we never did more than sleep next to each other side by side occasionally.

I had learned what it meant to be gay two years earlier, when I was living with my mother. In the summers, we almost always spent our weekends at her best friend Dolly's house. Dolly had a swimming pool, the height of luxury to us, way beyond our means. Dolly's husband, Bill, had a progressive disease that had put him in a wheelchair, and with the help of a trainer, he used the pool for exercise. I loved being there. It always seemed like a party. Dolly was warm and utterly without any pretensions. She had a broad southern accent, a sense of humor to match, and she liked to cook southern food, black-eyed peas, fried chicken, barbecue, and greens. I loved her and the food she cooked. And there was this too: since nearly every weekend lots of Dolly's friends and family came over as well, even if my mother almost always got drunk when we were there, with so many other people to distract her, I could usually avoid her nastier moods. But one afternoon when Bill was asleep and Dolly was cooking, my mother, who was, as she herself would have said, three sheets to the wind, cornered me alone outside by the pool.

I sensed that in hidden ways my mother was jealous of the closeness between my sister and me, yet despite this, when she began to tell me I should be my own person and not try to model myself after my sister, I was shocked and angry. Up until this moment, my sister had been my idol. The separation between us that had made my longing for her so intense had also allowed me to construct an idealized image of who she was. An image that, since she was my sister, reflected its glory on me. I had bragged about her for years to all my friends.

My mother and I began to argue, and finally, as the hostility between us thickened, she asked me in a bitterly sarcastic tone, "Do you know what she is?"

I was silent and almost walked away from her before she answered the question she had posed. "She's a lesbian, that's who she is. Do you want to be like that?"

Ironically, though my sister had had more than one affair with other counselors at the girls' camp we attended in the Sierra, I had only learned what the word *lesbian* meant a month earlier, from a group of friends in the girls' Masonic club I belonged to, Job's Daughters. They had seen two women kissing in a public pool and described the event as a freakish phenomenon, in scandalized tones, albeit tinged with a subtle salaciousness.

Somehow the idea that my sister might kiss another girl did not really trouble me so much as the knowledge that others might see her as a pariah. And, of course, there were my own feelings for women, which I did not want to acknowledge. Even that night, when I went to bed at Dolly's house, in a room she made up for me, I wept very loudly while Dolly was in the nearby bathroom. I wanted her sympathy and attention. But perhaps since she was vomiting all she had been drinking that day, and no doubt also because she had the kind of ear that could distinguish the genuine from the exaggerated, she came into my room and told me to be quiet.

"Don't be silly," she said. "There's no good reason to be so upset."

There was, however, reason. Beyond the content of anything my mother had said, I was reeling from the nasty tone of her delivery. When I think about that scene, I realize now how much had converged to create it. My mother's alcoholism, the conventionality that had seized and constricted the public imagination in America in those years, and the many private denials with which everyone must pay for appearing to be conventional met in the words she spoke to me that day. And there is this too: if my mother's disclosure compromised the idealized image of my sister I had created, this was a shift that was bound to happen one way or another, since I was at the age when idols crumble.

August

Jazz is the quintessential American art form, everyone agrees. But why? It can't be grasped by reason alone. There's more whimsy in the story.

But though I was claiming my own identity, I had grown to love many things that my mother and sister taught me to love. Jazz and poetry were part of me now, and as I was to learn, these two went together. My sister introduced me at an early age to a poet who wrote during the Jazz Age whose work we had not read in school. When I was eleven years old, on one of our daylong forays into the bookstores that once lined Hollywood Boulevard, I found a used copy of a collection of poems by this man, published by New Directions, and he had signed it. The book was a treasure, and it cost only $1.25, marked down from $1.75. My sister encouraged me to buy it with the small cache of money I had been given at Christmas.

The poet was W. C. Williams, and the book was a collection he had written over the course of more than thirty years, from 1917 to 1949. I read them so many times that these poems began to shape my idea of language. A new music was sounding inside me. I loved "To Elsie," from *Spring and All,* for what it said:

> The pure products of America
> go crazy

I well knew what he was talking about. But I also loved these lines for the beat, which was, like the syncopation of ragtime, off rhythm, the verb *go* dropped down so that you have to take a hairbreadth of a pause and thus alter the rhythm. This creates a surprise. You jump with the realization.

The line breaks were not accidental. Williams knew just what sound he wanted, though, as with new music of every kind, there were those who could not hear it. Surprisingly, among those readers was the remarkable Harriet Monroe, editor and founder of *Poetry* magazine, who in 1916, when she published one of his poems, changed the line breaks without telling him. He was angry when he wrote her, "It will be physically impossible for anyone to guess how I intended it to be read." He was aware that the way he broke his lines constituted a radical departure from traditional form. Sarcastically he wrote that "as long as nothing is noted to disturb the gently flowing accord of the magazine from Vol 1 number 1, until the year of Grace which is to see its end, I suppose the major part of its mission is accomplished."

It makes sense, then, that the rupture from the traditions of political and social order that was called democracy would ripple out in so many different waves, transforming philosophy and religion, language, music, changing even how and what we hear. In 1929, just two years after the edgy magazine dedicated to experimental writing called *Transition* was founded, it issued a proclamation that, like the proclamation issued by the Lowell girls during their strike a century earlier, mimicked the logic and the cadences of the Declaration of Independence. "The revolution in the English language is an accomplished fact," it began, and then asserted, "The imagination in search of a fabulous world is autonomous and unconfined." Testifying to the strong influence in this period of jazz and surrealism, the proclamation describes what it calls "the rhythmic 'hallucination of the word'" as essential to the creation of this new literature, and asserts that the writer "has the right . . . to disregard existing grammatical and syntactical laws."

Among the many wondrous permutations that have marked the evolution of democracy is the fact that though Jefferson was born of the Age of Reason, his words played a significant role in an age that, in elevating the more sensual processes of the mind, challenged the narrow idea of reason put forward by the Enlightenment.

Yet even the philosophers who defined the age of reason experienced other ways of knowing. I am thinking of how every day just after he awakened, Jefferson would play his violin. The air would have been cool as, still partly wrapped in his dreams, he moved his fingers over the strings, pulling the bow across them, the melodic vibrations sounding within him until perhaps he felt himself, at this early hour, to become the music he played.

Jefferson was aware of the importance of the music in language. In his essay "Thoughts on Prosody," he describes Homer's "rhythmical composition" by which "the ear is pleased to find at regular intervals a pause where it may rest." He knew that the declaration would be read aloud to large assemblies across the colonies. And he thought about how the document ought to sound. The words he wrote capture the cadence of a particular moment in history, infused with the desire for freedom. And just as spirituals did in the history of jazz, the declaration laid the groundwork for the realization of freedom, a revolution in the music of words.

More than just a passive tool, language initiates an alchemical process that will simultaneously use and metamorphose your consciousness, your mood, even what you do. As soon as you put words on the page, or even imagine them in your head, you will be affected by what you hear. Nothing in the process is passive or safe. Even boring language will affect you, put you to sleep. Short phrases. I will. I do. A staccato of words. Stopping and starting. Will make you feel alert, driven. Mellifluous, long phrases, such as *the languid summer air murmuring over the tops of trees or a silken gown swaying through the evening,* will wash over you, bend you inward and outward at once, gently rocking you into your sensuality. And the next line you write will respond to whatever sensibility you set in motion in the line before.

The same rippling process continues from writer to writer too. Less than a century after the declaration was read out in Independence Square, Walt Whitman established a revolution in language, pushing the boundaries of form and syntax to hold a democratic spirit that had already grown beyond the confines of the eighteenth-century cadence, "Democracy! Near at hand to you a throat is now inflating itself and joyfully singing," he wrote in "Starting from Paumanok." His own language must have made him bolder and wider, taking in all he could of the soul of democracy, declaring in "Song of Myself,"

> Through me forbidden voices;
> Voices of sexes and lusts—voices veil'd, and I remove
>   the veil . . .

While Jefferson asserted the rights of every citizen, using a classical language, the style spoken in powerful institutions and in the finest homes, now Whitman would lean further toward a common language. He wanted every word to be American, urging the use of Native American instead of European names for places; embracing the slang of prostitutes, gamblers, and thieves; constantly breaking "little laws to enter truly the higher ones."

The music of words evolved rapidly. Less than seventy-five years after the first edition of *Leaves of Grass* was published, W. C. Williams would listen carefully to ordinary speech in a new way, catching the rhythms and words spoken by a wide range of people, white and black and brown, poor or well-off, speech he heard on the streets or, because he had become a doctor, heard in his examining room, letting those sounds play in his mind, then putting his radically common phrases and surprisingly true phrasing on the page.

And of course, this was the Jazz Age, and this sound too was in his ear.

A few years before the Jazz Age dawned, on the night he was forcibly separated from his family, Ferdinand La Menthe left the theater and began to walk the streets of New Orleans. At dawn he caught the first train to Biloxi, where his godmother lived. Eulalie had always understood the music he played. Now she gave him a home and taught him how to fend for himself in a rough world. At night he played piano in the brothels of Biloxi. He was not paid as much as he had been in New Orleans, but the audiences liked his hot piano. And he picked up other skills too. As he made his way to venues around the South, returning finally to where he began, to play at Frenchman's and at Hilma Burt's place in New Orleans, he learned vaudeville routines; how to hustle; to win at pool and cards; to coax favors, protection, and even money from the prostitutes, who were charmed by his manner, still somewhat vulnerable, though more and more, masked by a theatrical persona that concealed his shyness. Soon the boy who had left New Orleans saddened and dazed returned a different man. A few years into the new century, Ferdinand had renamed himself Jelly Roll Morton; he had a diamond implanted in a golden front tooth, wore only the finest suits, carried two pearl-handled revolvers, and could boast that he was one of the best piano men in town.

As early as 1905, he had begun to compose his own music, though he was not writing it down yet. Trained to read music, eventually he would be among the first to find a way to notate jazz, but in this period, like most New Orleans musicians, many of whom did not know how to read music at all, he learned the pieces he heard by ear. But all that went in his ear entered an alchemical process in which he was mixing the various elements he encountered into something new.

Many years later, in his long interviews with musicologist Alan Lomax, Jelly Roll would say that in the time when jazz was developing, the city "was inhabited with maybe every race on the face of the globe." There was French opera, and there were French music hall tunes; there was Spanish music and African music, church music, blues, and ragtime. When Jelly Roll wrote his first composition, called "New Orleans Blues," he said he gave it a Spanish tinge. "If you can't manage to put tinges of Spanish in your tunes, you will never get the right seasoning . . . for jazz," he told Lomax.

But the mixture he made went beyond all the ingredients he used. "New Orleans Blues" moves from an almost sweet Spanish sway further and further into complexity until suddenly the steady beat, and with that perhaps the idea of steadiness itself, is broken and broken again, in a cascade of surprises. The sound he created contained the essence of a new music called jazz. A few months later, after a series of improvisations, he would compose "King Porter Stomp," a piece that leaves convention behind to go toward an entirely new musical language. There were syncopations and breaks, a driving build that fused three or four tunes together. While corralling the music of a communal past into one composition, with the first emergence of what would one day be called swing, the piece looked forward too, into the future of jazz.

The process of creation in music, or any art form, is as mysterious and unaccountable as the process by which Thomas Jefferson composed the Declaration of Independence. Except one can say this, that paradoxically everything that seems wonderfully new and unique born in each human mind also expresses a larger drift, a partly invisible yet significant, even tectonic, shift shared by all society; yet to allow what is new to be reborn also requires a departure from society, a break from the traditions that nurtured it.

No wonder, then, that jazz—multicultural, improvisational, the product at once of community and singularity, a music made of breaks— would become America's greatest cultural contribution to the world. Everywhere this music was played, it seemed to open minds. The story is told that after World War I, when the American marching band the Hellfighters played in Europe, the crowds around them went wild. No wonder. Drawn from New York's African-American Fifteenth Infantry, the first unit to reach the Rhine, for which they won the Croix de Guerre, the band that was led by James Reese, included both Noble Sissle, one of the composers of the famous "Shuffle Along," and Bill Bojangles Robinson. Together they had helped to inaugurate a revolution in culture. Over the coming twenty years, the Jazz Age was to find a welcoming home in Paris.

September

Daidie called today to speak about her mother, who died recently. She loved jazz. Well into her eighties, she'd go to clubs at night and sit ringside to applaud whoever was singing or playing. A proper lady, she was famous for wearing a big hat and sporting a pair of gloves. Consequently, several musicians came to serenade her as she lay dying.

Like the current that comes from changes in a magnetic field, new movements in culture produce a powerful electricity. Earlier in the evening on the same night when I first met my friend Bran, I could feel a charge in the air as we all assembled in the dining room of Bran's house. The furniture had been removed, which allowed us all to sit on the floor in a circle, so that two young men could address us. They were slightly older, having already spent a semester at the University of California at Berkeley, from which they had returned for the holiday break. When I see them now in my mind's eye, it is almost as if they were burnished with gold or at least adorned with laurel wreaths, their eyes wide with the same apprehension as messengers who have traveled to another world and returned, eager to describe what they have seen. They had been several times to the city, they said, meaning San Francisco, across the bay from the university. They had been to coffeehouses, they said. This was

enough to startle and intrigue us. It was the end of the fifties, and though
we had heard of places that served European coffee and hosted serious
discussion, few of us had been in one of them. They had even been to
jazz clubs, they said. But what was most exciting was that in these clubs
and cafés, they had heard not only jazz, but poets who read poetry to the
accompaniment of jazz there. A man named Lawrence Ferlinghetti and
one called Jack Kerouac had read their poems to jazz, as had the poet
Kenneth Rexroth and another named David Meltzer. It was a woman
named Ruth Weiss who started the whole thing when she stood up spon-
taneously to recite while some musicians were playing at an underground club called The Cellar. Finally they told us they had brought back
books from a new group of poets, called the Beats. They had one slim
volume, and they wanted to read from it to the accompaniment of a jazz
record they put on the turntable. The book, they told us, had been
banned. It was called *Howl:*

> I saw the best minds of my generation destroyed by
>   madness,
> starving hysterical naked

the poem began. The room was suspended as if at the edge of a future
whose arrival we were all witnessing. Everyone was riveted by the words
and the rolling rhythm of the long sentences, which, as with the list of
grievances against King George in the Declaration of Independence,
outlined an angry protest, and yet with a music that broke ordinary
syntax and, like jazz, sounded blue and full of grief. Though the poem
spoke of things with which I was not familiar—drug addiction, mari-
juana, riding the subway to "holy Bronx on benzedrine"—I well understood the rage and despair at the state of affairs in fifties America. *Who
sang out of their windows in despair,* Ginsberg wrote, and I recognized the
state of mind. I saw too the suppressed spirit he invoked, "the flash of the
alchemy." I could hear it in the words he placed within the poem to describe his own poetics, so like Whitman's, with "the use of the ellipse the
catalog the meter & the vibrating plane." And in his invocation of the rejected confessions that rise "reincarnate in the ghostly clothes of jazz."

Since the year that *Howl* was published, in 1956, the music of the
poem had spread through a new generation. In some ways, we were like
any group of rebellious adolescents, testing limits. But there were other
dimensions to what we did. Although the Berlin Wall had not been built,

in a sense we were already tearing it down, along with so many other barriers that had been constructed in the past to confine our minds. Our hunger to know denied and forbidden worlds was ravenous. One afternoon my friend Bran and I went to meet with our friend Linda's lover, a man named Gino, who was a pusher and reputed to carry a revolver in his glove compartment. We sat at a kitchen table in a small tract house in Van Nuys while we studiously watched Gino roll a joint, which he lit and passed to us. It was strong stuff. I even began to hallucinate, feeling my neck grow long like the stem of a lily.

I did not smoke grass again until I was older and in college. But still I was walking a thin line, courting disaster. I went out once with a friend of Gino's who had promised to take me to hear Dave Brubeck play at the Beach House at the water. Though I was a minor, he was able to finesse my entrance. Fortunately, after he took me to his place and tried to make love to me, he passed out. I called a cab and, despite his attempts to convince me otherwise, never saw him again. I knew what had happened with him was dangerous to me in a way I could not entirely articulate. He was too old for me, too suave, and jaded in a way that had repelled me. I sensed the world he belonged to had a sinister side.

Yet the menace was inside me too. My wild ways were not just an expression of freedom. Despite the intense and brave energy I exuded, I felt unprotected and orphaned in the world. I carried a loneliness inside me that would engulf me when I was on my own at home at night. I felt afraid of intruders, spiders, shadows, memories I could not bear.

But this was to change soon. A rapid series of events would quickly take me in a new direction. The first of these was that I fell in love. Johnny was a boy from my high school who had been Bran's lover the year before. Though he still did not speak to her, secretly she encouraged the whole idea. Johnny was brilliant, and if he was not as rebellious as I was, he was hardly conventional either. He would debunk what seemed superficial or false to him with scathingly accurate comments. Though he was skeptical about ideals and causes and we argued about that, he had a bittersweet honesty, and perhaps because I had a bitterness inside me too, a feeling I did not show even to myself, this drew me closer to him.

He had been raised in a far more sophisticated world than I. Both his parents were screenwriters. As my sister had done before, he took it upon himself to educate me, for which I was often grateful. Sometimes we would spend time at a house his family owned but did not live in any longer that had been designed by the great modern architect R. M. Schindler. It was all gray concrete inside so that the walls and hallways and windows looked like one geometric sculpture. Johnny took me up to the various rooms, showing me the genius of the plan. Strong-willed and forthright, I found his aloof urbanity attractive. On the first evening we made a meal together, he disdainfully rejected the bottled dressing I tried to use before showing me how to make vinaigrette. We went to performances and lectures he chose, many extraordinary, such as the night Stravinsky conducted *The Firebird Suite* at Royce Hall, or the evening that Pablo Casals played Bach's *Unaccompanied Suites for Cello* in an auditorium in Northridge, or when Neutra addressed an audience there and showed slides of his work.

I was already writing by then. Just as Jelly Roll was drawn toward his life's work when he discovered the world of musicians in the Storyville section of New Orleans, as I entered this very palpable world of artists, the path on which I might turn my life became more clear. The process accelerated when, in the same year, I went with my friend Phyllis and the Steinberg twins to visit her father and stepmother. They lived near the park that was annexed to our high school. Morton Dimondstein was an artist. On that first day, he took us into the studio he had built from the garage of the tract house the family owned and talked with us about the portrait that he was in the midst of painting. He took out a brush and subtly darkened the edge of a sleeve as he spoke.

I went back whenever I could to visit Mort and Gerry, his wife and Phyllis's stepmother, a woman we all called Red, because of the color of her hair, and no doubt too her strong personality. A scholar and teacher in art education, she was always definite and clear about whatever she thought. My friends and I would show up in the late afternoon after school and through the summer to listen as Mort talked about the process of art to us all and Red asked us questions about what we thought and what we wanted to do with our lives. Finally at the end of the summer, before school started again, Red approached me with a proposal. She was getting her doctorate and would need someone to watch their two children, Carla and Josh, in the late afternoons, and help out with some household tasks: making beds, putting dishes she had prepared the night before in the oven. Would I like the job? I leaped at the chance.

I have often thought that this turn of fate saved my life. The whole experience was saturated with art. Mort's paintings of the family hung on every wall, canvases strongly influenced by Mexican artists. When they lived in Mexico, Mort had worked with the Taller de Gráfica Popular, an esteemed group of printmakers and artists that included the muralists Clemente Orozco, David Alfaro Siqueiros, and Diego Rivera. Mort introduced me to poems by Tom McGrath and Pablo Neruda, as well as the work of Maxim Gorky. He showed me a journal called *California Quarterly*. His woodblock prints were on many of the covers. He pointed out articles that I should read in the *New York Times* and the *Atlantic,* to which they subscribed. One Sunday morning, Red and Mort invited me to come with them to listen to the Reverend Stephen Frichtman speak at the Unitarian church in downtown L.A. and to hear someone they told me was a great folksinger, named Odetta, perform.

But my immersion in an atmosphere charged with creative ideas was just part of the story. This process of education was inextricably mixed with another development. Bit by bit I was gaining a family. Red was always asking me questions. Why was I living alone with my father? Where was my mother? What was the house where I lived now like? Where was I going to go to college? Whenever I would babysit at night, Red invited me to sleep in a spare room that led into Mort's studio. On those weekends, when I would fall asleep to the smell of oil paint, wake to the voices of the kids watching Saturday morning cartoons, and then I would have breakfast with the family, I began to feel more and more at home. Over time it seemed that I was spending more afternoons, dinners, evenings, even mornings, there than I did at my own house.

It was in the same period that I put an end to the self-destructive side of my wild behavior. I valued my new family too much to endanger the respect and trust I felt from them in any way.

Ironically it was also in this period that one night when my father came home, he found discarded condoms and other evidence that someone else had been making love in his bed. It was not me. Because Red had counseled me against moving too fast with Johnny or anyone else, I was not making love with him in the strict sense of the term. Clearly someone had used the key I placed under the mat to get in. I did not really want to know who it was, though my friends and I suspected a guy I had dated and then stopped seeing. My father was angry with me. In answer to his shouts, I quoted a book by the anthropologist Ashley Montagu about how we are all formed by our environment. Finally he relented, and we reached a rapprochement and a mutual forgiveness, for which very soon I would be grateful.

I have written about that night before, how when he kissed me good-night, my father blew into my ear. It may have been an accident. I only thought about it years later when my sister had a lover who had been sexually abused and began to ask herself if she had been abused also. She had so many symptoms of it. But finally she realized he had not done that. The way he had abandoned her was the real abuse. A repetition of what had happened to him. Telling one life, much less recording the stories of many lives to create the record that is called history, is a complicated task. Discovering the truth is a molten process. It is not truth that changes but perception, which of its nature evolves, and this too is why art must constantly change.

September

Listening to Sidney Bechet play "I'm Going Way Down Home"—the horn almost laughs as it climbs. Where? For sure, flying free.

When Jelly Roll was writing his first compositions, jazz was something new. Yet the new is shaped from what already exists. He wove together elements from long-standing traditions in European and African music. What is especially extraordinary about one of his first pieces, "Jelly Roll Blues," is that while creating a new kind of music, included the history of how this music came to be. Even the fact that he was telling a story reflected traditional African music. Throughout various African cultures, music told teaching stories. This was part of ring rituals, during which the community would assemble in a circle to dance and perform. Most African music is very close to and even at times based on speech. The slit-drum, to name one instrument, transmits messages that can only be understood by those who share the language of the drummer. The way words are spoken shapes the rhythms and notes in which they are sung. And in turn spoken language sings. Bantu languages can actually be notated.

In this way the African diaspora brought ingredients essential to democracy across the ocean. The sound of a horn, for instance, imitating the way a particular sentence is really said, the beat and melody a mirror of breath and thought and feeling, has to feed the process, if only by encouraging the impulse to speak, to join the discussion. And there is this too in the African tradition, what is called the Nommo force, an affirmative power from the all-pervasive spirit that inhabits earthly existence, according to African religions. It is this force that Ralph Ellison heard expressed in jazz when he was still a boy, the feeling from the jazz musicians he heard in Kansas City that "life could be harsh, loud and wrong if it wishes, but they lived it fully."

To stay alive, jazz would need the Nommo force. Even before it emerged, the elements that spawned it met opposition. That this new musical language should have emerged in New Orleans is not accidental. It was one of the few cities where African ritual performances were not suppressed in the brutal fashion employed in other places. But once born, jazz traveled fast. Jelly Roll took his powerfully joyous but blue, ferocious but melodic, music on the road. He went to Kansas City and Memphis; Mobile, Biloxi, and El Paso; and small towns in Arizona and New Mexico, and everywhere he went audiences would come alive to what they were hearing. Finally he had a long and successful run in Los Angeles, where he set up his own club for a while. And though he abandoned that venture to follow a woman he loved, after she left him, he found his way to Chicago, where he became a sensation with the band he formed, the Red Hot Peppers. They played in dance halls and clubs around Thirty-fifth and Calumet, the center of the action, at a cabaret called the Plantation, and a café called the Sunset. Utilizing a recent technology, the band made recordings, which made Jelly Roll famous all over town and eventually the whole country. His vital music seemed to give large audiences, both white and black, the spirit they had been craving. The same spirit never seemed to stop moving through him. As he introduced multiple improvisational solos and played with more polyrhythms and dissonance, all the while giving the music cohesion, his creativity seemed infinite.

This was a rich time in my life. As I turned fifteen and then sixteen, the possibilities grew. I was writing poems, stories, essays, on the poets I liked, reading widely, painting and drawing. With an 8-millimeter home movie camera I borrowed, I enlisted my friends to play the roles in a film I made. It was heavily influenced by François Truffaut's *Four Hundred Blows,* a work I loved. The young hero of that film had been neglected by his parents, but I did not think about how this mirrored my own life.

Then one evening, the sense of abandonment that I had pushed to the back of my mind was to take a stark turn.

One Sunday, after I had spent the night and most of the next day at the Dimondsteins' house again, Mort drove me back home. It was twilight, the sky filled with a soft early evening winter light. I was still feeling the effect of the words I had been writing that afternoon, poems filled with inexplicably ominous images of strange shadows that arose mysteriously from the hills. I could scarcely explain these poems; I had never been drawn to the gothic. But what we saw when we arrived at my house seemed perfectly integrated with this atmosphere. A stranger in a dark overcoat stood at my door, a large man, with a sad look on his face. Mort stayed in the car and watched while I approached warily. "Are you Walden Griffin's daughter?" he asked me. I nodded. "I've come with bad news," he said. Incredible as it seems to me now, I had no idea what that could be. "He's been in an accident," he said. "Your father was hit by a car." Braced with denial, I asked "Where is he?" I had not grasped what he was trying to tell me. "Which hospital?" "You don't understand," he said. "I'm sorry. He was very badly injured." I must have looked even more uncomprehending. Did he ever say the word, or did I ask him? *Is he dead? Did he die?* I don't remember either of us saying those words. But then suddenly I knew, though I could not take it in at all.

Mort must have realized there was trouble because very soon he was by my side. I was at a loss entirely. I did not know at all how to respond and could not believe what I heard. As the three of us entered the living room of the house where my father and I had lived, I fell silent. I looked around for things I associated with him to bring the reality home to me, but where realization might have been there was just a blank, and so I remained silent for the rest of the evening, nodding when Mort suggested I might return home with him and quietly going to my room to pack the few extra things I might need.

SEPTEMBER

I am thinking now about how as the members of each generation die, so too the atmosphere, and the knowledge of the particular mood and genius of their time, dies with them.

After the funeral, I went back to school, walking every weekday morning through the park from the Dimondsteins' house. Slowly my life returned to normal, though things would never really be the same. It was not just the outward conditions of my life that had changed; it was me. I knew something now I had not known before. The other deaths I had experienced—my great-grandmother and my father's father—had been in the background, each leaving an absence that was subtle, like a slow fade. But this death, the sheer fact of it, was unavoidable, slicing through every adolescent illusion of immortality that I had. My father, who had been such an intimate part of my life since my birth, was gone; it was hard to comprehend yet undeniable, no trace of him remained. I could not even begin to talk about it. I would not fully mourn until several years later, when President Kennedy was gunned down as he rode through the streets in a motorcade in Dallas.

Now I was stunned, dislocated, and temporarily speechless. The heady sense of power I had briefly experienced replaced by a ruthlessly unbending confrontation with reality. But simultaneously, if at first almost imperceptibly, something else began to grow in me. It was less with pride than with a lonely awareness that I realized I knew about life and death in a way that my friends did not. This was a sad certitude, yet it contained another kind of power, giving me instead of control over circumstances an alignment with a most basic law of existence: everything passes.

It is perhaps this knowledge you can hear in jazz. It is there in the breaks, in what Jelly Roll called "the ideas in the breaks." Listen. Listen into the pause. The knowledge is in the absence. A long open space without sound. That's death for sure. The end of a certain road. And in the quiet, a disquiet as you realize you don't know where you are going. And then. And then. Something new starts up. Perhaps teasing and small at first. And even limping in its rhythm as if it will never catch. But hang on, it will. Or maybe you will hear a loud, undeniable flood of sound, and you have no choice but to go along with it, all the time, singing,

> not the same
> not the same
> never going to be the same
> again.

When read in the way that Jefferson intended, the Declaration of Independence begins with a series of pauses that seal within them a sense of loss and yet at the same time, through the force of rhythm, transfigure mourning into a brave departure. In the rough drafts of the declaration that survive, it has been argued that Jefferson made diacritical marks to indicate where pauses in speech ought to be made. In the first printed version of the declaration, a series of odd quotation marks and later odd spaces were included, which the scholar Jay Fliegelman interprets as the printer John Dunlap's confused response to Jefferson's original marks. Using this evidence, he has constructed the preamble according to the way Jefferson wished it to be heard:

> When in the Course of human Events it becomes
>   necessary for one People
> To dissolve the Political Bands which have connected
>   them with another
> and to assume among the Powers of the Earth, the
>   separate and equal Station
> To which the Laws of Nature and Nature's God entitle
>   them,
> a decent Respect to the Opinions of Mankind requires
> that they should declare the causes which impel them
>   to the Separation.

In this pacing, you can hear a dignified sorrow at the loss of an old order, and after each break, a powerful voice rising up to claim the future.

Fliegelman points to several influences on the sound Jefferson created: the hours he spent every day playing the violin; books popular in the eighteenth century by John Rice and Thomas Sheridan about the art of rhetoric; the oratorical example of Patrick Henry, famous for the dramatic pauses in his fiery speeches. And perhaps there was another influence too. A music Jefferson and Henry, both raised in the plantation culture of Virginia, would have heard since birth: slave songs, in which, for instance, one soloist stops singing while the other voices overlap and fill in the silence with a different sound, or where the song pauses when the singer stops singing and resumes with a drumming sound, slapping thigh, chest, and thigh again, creating an interim beat, like the beat of a drum.

September

As with the great Ahmet Ertegün, founder of Atlantic Records, who established so many musicians, once the sound gets inside you, one way or another, you will find yourself celebrating at the feast.

This was the music that preceded jazz. It would link American culture forever to African cultures—cultures that for the most part express a cosmology closer to Jefferson's idea of nature's God than conventional Protestantism does, and in which, instead of being opposed, life and death, change and tradition, sadness and joy, are different phases of one cycle.

The year after my father's death was a time mixed with an intense mixture of grief and happiness, a certain frailty combined with vigor. Mort captured the feeling in a portrait he painted of me. He recorded the way I leaned forward with my head, my shoulders slumping, half my face in shadow, yet also thinking, the red stripes on the man's nightgown I loved to wear pointing upward and downward in lightning zigzags that mirror the jagged cactus, the striped cloth on the table next to me, and the diamond pattern on the floor under my feet. The process by itself was healing. As Mort worked with deep concentration, I developed a sense of viewing myself, my mood, as a canvas, a moment in time, and began to be able to accept my unruly emotions, even as material to be made into beauty.

The descent was swift. One day Jelly Roll was the talk of the town, flush with success and money. Then, and almost overnight, his high time in Chicago came to an end. His astonishing creativity never flagged. He kept turning out one new composition after another, all with innovative ideas. But the fear that jazz inspired in certain citizens had gathered force until finally a group of politicians and preachers was able to shut down the vital cabarets, clubs, and dance halls around Thirty-fifth and Calumet streets where he and the Red Hot Peppers played.

He had made dozens of records that were played across the country, and countless copies of sheet music notating his compositions had been sold. But almost none of the profits came to him. It is a story well known to artists of every kind, especially blues and jazz musicians. Soon after he arrived in Chicago, Jelly Roll hooked up with a businessman, Walter Melrose, who owned a store that sold sheet music. Business was failing. But Jelly Roll revived it by performing in the store and then offering sheet music of his own compositions. Soon Melrose's business became a great success. But Melrose wrote and controlled all the contracts and copyrights for Morton's compositions, and he included himself as the lyricist on most of them, even though his lyrics, written quickly and with little skill, were almost never used. When Jelly Roll was making lots of money in the popular clubs of Chicago, he paid no attention to royalties. But when the action was shut down and he needed money, he realized he was receiving almost none of the proceeds from his work.

September

Now Daidie's sons who are dancers have continued the lineage. They've incorporated the Lindy Hop into modern dance. They studied with one of the masters, Frankie Manning, who used to thrill audiences with his high-flying moves when he danced at the Savoy.

He must have felt the same desperation that he had experienced as a boy in New Orleans the night his grandmother threw him out of the family home. He tried every avenue he could to survive, moving to New York and then Washington, D.C. But in New York, other bands, Louis Armstrong and Duke Ellington, Count Basie, led by men who had learned from him, had a corner on the public's attention. The nation's capital proved even worse for him. With far fewer venues, he found himself part owner of a run-down restaurant in a shabby neighborhood, playing brilliant piano every night, sometimes to indifferent crowds and sometimes to the stray aficionado, but he made almost no money.

By then his health had already begun to decline. He was suffering from congestive heart failure. In some periods, he was too weak to even stand. Then he would revive, and the music, which always had a jubilance, an impossible-to-believe and yet palpable resilience, did not weaken but burned even brighter, as he went back to New York, where he could not, despite every valiant effort, survive, and then drove across the country to L.A. He had a brief bit of success there, but it never earned him what he needed to live and keep working. He could not afford any medical care now. As his breath became shorter and shorter and he knew he was dying, he still wrote a great composition called "Ganjam," something at the outer edge again, way beyond its time, that had the sounds of Asia in it and foretold the cool jazz of Miles Davis. In the last week of his life, he was finally taken to the hospital and for a few days put into a room that was so small it had been a broom closet not long before. Finally, a woman whom he loved but who had a pattern of using him and others who loved her, paid to have him moved into a better room for the seven or so days until he died. It was 1941. Just two years before I would be born in the same city, and be rocked to the beautiful music he wrote, music that is still part of me now.

OCTOBER

It's stunning sometimes, the way the past gets woven in with the present in various art forms, a kind of call and response with our ancestors, so it all makes sense. Where you've been. Where you are going.

Over time I have come to see how lucky I was to have met, at such a young age, so many men and women who led creative lives and who troubled themselves to teach me things they knew. Silvia, my boyfriend's mother, who had written the screenplay for *Ruby Gentry,* liked to hear me talk about my work. But when she read my poems, she was blunt. Much of it lacked the vibrancy I had when I spoke, she told me. What I showed her was not close enough to the bone, not true in the sense in which a pitch or a color can be true. Though it was hard for me to hear, I learned. And among the many other lessons passed on to me, I remember too the afternoon Mort looked at a later draft of a poem he had loved when I showed it to him earlier and told me I had damaged it by working it too hard, the way a watercolor can be ruined by too much brushwork.

Though I loved and admired Silvia, Mort would not speak to her. Soon I would learn the terrible and complicated history behind this decision. The reason Mort and Red had been in Mexico was to escape the atmosphere of repression called McCarthyism. Before this, Mort's work, once nationally known, had been blacklisted from many museums, galleries, and publications. Red and Mort both once members of the Communist Party, had left in 1956, in response to the Soviet invasion of Hungary. But membership was not the only accusation the witch-hunters hurled. Friends of friends, associates, even those who had been at parties or events that Communist Party members had attended, or those who signed a petition sponsored by the party or connected even casually with it, were being investigated. The most insidious aspect of the investigations was that anyone who did not give information about their friends and acquaintances would be labeled and blacklisted. And this is where Silvia came in. Her first husband, a screenwriter too, was also blacklisted. He had been called up before the HUAC and refused to give information. As retaliation, the committee pressured her to testify and give information on him and others she had met who had been in the party or held radical views. They threatened to blacklist her too if she did not cooperate. In this way, the HUAC had created an atmosphere of distrust and terror not unlike what existed in the Soviet Union, with its infamous KGB, or East Germany, with the Stasi. Silvia had been divorced for several years, and when the committee began to pressure her, she was not receiving any child-support payments. Desperate, she gave them what they wanted. I suspect this may have been another source for the bitter tone Johnny had. A knowledge of the ways of power and the shadows cast by fear.

By the time I went to college, the atmosphere was already changing. Things were jumping with promise and hope. I was part of a student group called SLATE at the University of California at Berkeley. We would meet weekly to discuss issues with such fervor it was as if we were running the affairs of the world. I went on my first picket line, joined marches against the bomb, kept on writing poems, all the while listening to jazz. I'd go into the city to North Beach with a carload of friends and sit in one of the clubs on Broadway to listen to Coltrane or Miles Davis or Big Mama Willie Mae Thornton or Dixieland or the Preservation Hall Jazz Band.

OCTOBER

Looking at reproductions of paintings by the Colombian artist Fernando Botero that were just published. The work was inspired by the abuse and torture of Iraqis who were imprisoned at Abu Ghraib.

One summer, thinking I would go back to Berkeley in the fall, I moved to North Beach. I met Shig, who worked behind the counter at City Lights Books and had been prosecuted for selling *Howl*. And after a while, I learned to recognize and then know the wonderfully beatific poet Ferlinghetti, who had been one of the first to read poetry to jazz and had been prosecuted for publishing Ginsberg's long poem. I would meet with the poet Bob Kaufman, who had also read his poetry to jazz, when I hung out at a pool hall where we all went to get a great hamburger with onions on a French roll. In the afternoons, I'd go to the Trieste to eat Italian pastries, drink espresso, and listen to opera on the jukebox. I met an artist there, a habitué of the place, who specialized in sumi brush painting, a "Japanese visual," the great jazz pianist Bill Evans wrote, "in which the artist is forced to be spontaneous." Then there was The Committee, the theater started by the brother of one of my friends in the student movement. I studied improvisation there. And late at night my friends and I went to hear jazz. Until I got a fake ID, I would often have to stand outside the clubs that had no section for minors. This was the way I first heard Ornette Coleman. At the end of the summer, I decided not to go back to my studies at Berkeley. I was not going to take a safe and conventional path. I was going to be a writer.

OCTOBER

So many of these images recall paintings by the old masters that depict the stations of the cross, even down to the crown of thorns.

When my roommate met and then fell in love with Charlie Haden, who played with Ornette Coleman, we got front-row seats for the whole run. Charlie was fun and sweet to spend time with, especially in the mornings when we all met in the kitchen. A bit shy, struggling hard to break the drug habit that he had picked up from his older brothers so young, he had a baby face, and despite his great talent, you could tell the fact that he had no formal education embarrassed him. But when he played, he became a different man. Bent over his bass, deep into himself, and at the same time letting the whole world in, he produced a sound you had never heard before, though it seemed that this was how the instrument had been longing to be played. The sorrowful sensuality he brought out of the strings, the dark bass notes, seemed to touch the deepest recesses of the soul, describing an America no rhetoric could ever conjure. Just like Jelly Roll had done before, he was carving out a new territory, giving anyone who cared to listen the courage to follow liberty where it wants to go. Setting the tone and the beat one more time for that dance we do together, called democracy.

5

SONG OF MYSELF

I celebrate myself;
And what I assume you shall assume;
For every atom belonging to me, as good belongs to you.

—WALT WHITMAN, "Song of Myself," LEAVES OF GRASS

We, the black and the white, deeply need each other here if we are to become a nation—if we are really, that is, to achieve our identity, our maturity as men and women.

—JAMES BALDWIN, The Fire Next Time

We are all bound up together in one great bundle of humanity, and society cannot trample on the weakest and feeblest of its members without receiving the curse in its own soul.

—FRANCIS ELLEN WATKINS HARPER, IN A SPEECH DELIVERED AT THE ELEVENTH WOMEN'S RIGHTS CONVENTION, 1866

JANUARY 2007

Who would I have been had I not been born at the time that I was?

MY SISTER AND I were not the first women in our family to attend college and enter the public world. My grandmother's sister, my aunt Nelle, who raised my sister after our parents' divorce, had gotten a degree from the University of Illinois. Eventually she became a librarian. We were all impressed with the fact that she had set up the library at the University of California at Davis, a largely agricultural school in those days. She told us a story about having to persuade the dean that the purchase of screens to keep the cow flies out of the reading room was a necessary expense. But the family pride about her accomplishments was laced with another attitude. She was, after all, an old maid, and for this she was pitied.

My mother and grandmother lived more conventional lives. Both of them were born before 1920, the year women got the vote. If for a period after my parents' divorce, my mother worked behind a lunch counter, it was not for long. She thought of herself as a housewife, and that's the way my grandmother thought of herself too.

As a homemaker, my grandmother was a force to contend with. She was raised on a farm and, as much as was possible in a city like Los Angeles, kept her farm ways. She canned—or as she said, *put up*—fruit in the spring and summer, baked at least one cake and a batch of cookies every week, ground her own meat, always used fresh vegetables, made candy for the family and to give away to friends on holidays, sewed all my clothes. Yet, even so, she had other aspirations. When she was still a girl in Champagne–Urbana, Illinois, she wanted to be an actress. She had been invited to join a traveling theater company that passed through town, but her father would not let her. She spoke of her disappointment more than once. It was a central chapter in our family history.

She did study drama for two years at the University of Illinois. But something else interrupted that effort. She never told the story directly to me. I heard it first from my sister and then my mother. She and my grandfather, a handsome man who always dressed impeccably, were lovers before they married. And when she became pregnant, my grandfather abandoned her to this condition. So, to avoid scandal, she was sent to relatives in Virginia, where after a while she delivered a stillborn child.

This must have taken the wind out of her sails. I remember a sad moment I spent with her, when I was six, and we were visiting the farm where she grew up. She showed me the grave of twins who had died. She was taken up with the sorrow of it, these early deaths. Somehow even today I associate the stillbirth of her own first child with those small gravestones.

JANUARY

In just two weeks I turn sixty-four. It's just as everyone says, "How did this happen so quickly?" Yet I'm also aware of how much change I have witnessed.

Sometime after she came back home to Illinois, she and my grandfather reconciled, married, and moved together to California. How soon after that my mother was born I do not know, but the year was 1914. She would soon experience other disappointments in her life, among them my grandfather's alcoholism and his womanizing. The story I was told was that when he would come home after a bender, having been off in hotels with women and bars with his friends for several days, he would be repentant. More than once he got down on his knees and begged my grandmother to take him back. She always did. What else could she do? But each time her attitude stiffened.

By the time she was raising me, my grandfather was retired and thoroughly faithful. Yet my grandmother often seemed unhappy with her role. She did not express this openly but rather through a series of sighs, uttered especially when she did not get her way, that made it seem as if she were martyred by all she did for us. Despite my grandmother's intense domesticity, she was not a doting parent. My mother, who was an only child, complained that she felt lonely when she was growing up. During the Roaring Twenties, my grandparents often went out on the town. My grandmother was also good-looking and more than a little vain. My mother, who was shy, regarded her parents as glamorous people, and she said she longed to be closer to them.

Perhaps the nature of my grandmother's unspoken rebellion turned my mother away from domestic life. Though she performed all the necessary tasks, she was not enthusiastic about keeping house and cooking. She embraced all the shortcuts, modern conveniences that ironically, in the period after the war, when women were urged to return to traditional roles, were designed to save housewives from drudgery. She loved frozen vegetables before she took to serving the entirely frozen meals called TV dinners.

She had tried earlier to break free of the confines of the home. When my parents were still married and I was just four years old, I remember seeing her spread out a cardboard replica of a house on the floor. I wanted to play with her. But she told me I could not, that she was working. She had been taking a course in home decorating, the one aspect of domesticity she truly liked. For a while she had the dream of becoming an interior decorator. But these plans were nipped in the bud. As my sister told me years later, together my father and my grandparents talked her out of her ambitions.

She knew somewhere within herself in a way not fully articulated that the life she had lived was not right for her. When she was sober, she used to tell me that I should follow my dreams. That I could do or be anything or anyone that I wanted. She was fascinated with the lost generation, the American writers and artists who lived in Paris in the twenties and thirties. Looking back now, I can see that it must have given her pleasure to imagine being among them, living in a small apartment, going out to cafés, a woman on her own, free to breathe the air of city life.

In the realm of the imagination, she was not departing from my grandmother but continuing an inclination. My grandmother loved rebellious women too, especially Dorothy Parker. In my first year of junior high school, when I was asked to do a recitation, she helped me memorize and perform one of Parker's monologues. I remember too that later, in the solemn discussions my father and my grandparents held about what I should do after I graduated from high school, though my father and grandfather argued for secretarial school, my grandmother took my side in favor of college.

Had I been a boy, no one in the family would have opposed my wish to go to college. But the prejudice I faced was so woven into daily life, so normal, I neither named it nor thought much about it. I knew about the suffragists. But what they had won for women was also so much a part of the background of my life, what I learned about them did not inspire me. There was, however, one form of prejudice that had caught my attention.

JANUARY

How are these times affecting my grandchildren now? My granddaughter was six years old when the war started, my grandson just a year. So much violence, so much fear.

In the late fifties, as America slowly emerged from the repressive silence of McCarthyism, the issue that captured public awareness more than any other was racism. Segregation and prejudice existed throughout the United States, but it was most visible in the South and parts of the Midwest. Now this injustice was being challenged. I was still in junior high school when Thurgood Marshall argued before the Supreme Court in favor of school integration in a landmark case known as *Brown v. Board of Education* of Topeka, Kansas. The earlier Supreme Court ruling that schools could be "separate but equal," a decision made in 1896 known as *Plessy v. Ferguson,* was overturned. On May 17, 1954, the Court ruled that segregation is unconstitutional.

The new ruling could not change the course of history by itself. That summer the newspapers would be filled with a grim story that revealed the virulent brutality of racism, when a fourteen-year-old boy from Chicago named Emmett Till, while visiting his family in Mississippi, was kidnapped, beaten nearly to death, and shot before his body was dumped in the Tallahatchie River. The boy was attacked because he had whistled at a white woman. And as if the murder itself were not enough, in an all-too-familiar pattern of injustice, the two white men who were arrested for his murder were acquitted by an all-white jury.

Movements grow from many diverse events and causes. Looking at what led to the American Revolution, one finds a mixture of atrocities, grievances, articulations, defiances, and victories. In the worst of cases, atrocity generates a fear that can undermine the desire for justice. But whether from a success in fact or a triumph in consciousness, the light cast by even the smallest victory can transform the way an atrocity is received, making the suffering more visible, the injustice more clear, the causes intolerable.

In December of the following year, 1955, as the public began to awaken bit by bit to the dimensions of racism in America, another event occurred that, though it may on the surface seem small, took on a profound and catalytic significance in public consciousness. In Montgomery, Alabama, on her way home and tired out from a long day at work as a seamstress in a department store, Rosa Parks took a seat in the middle of a section reserved only for whites. Because just one white man wanted to sit down in that area, the bus driver asked her to move. But Mrs. Parks did not.

Despite the simple dignity of her response, it was a brave act of defiance. African-Americans had been arrested and even killed for refusing to obey bus drivers. What is it that gave her the courage to resist at that moment? Though it is crucial to the survival of democracy, this question has no easy answers except to say that it was part of a larger motion that had begun in fits and starts since the end of the Second World War, a motion greater than any one person could see, and formidable in its power, though, like the shifting of a tectonic plate, not always immediate in its effects.

But the effects arose nevertheless and, through the tumult and danger of the times, commanded the attention of a rapt public with what I can only describe as the stunning beauty that all struggles for justice possess. Two years after Rosa Parks set off the Montgomery bus boycott, in 1957, the year that I began to attend high school, nine black students enrolled in classes at Central High School in Little Rock, Arkansas. Photographs of one eventful day in this struggle, published in newspapers and broadcast on television all over the world, had a powerful effect on everyone who saw them. The images are indelible: students carrying books, quiet, yet determined, walking toward the wide steps of the high school, navigating a jeering, near-hysterical crowd of white men and women, girls and boys, who, in their violent gestures, seem like archetypal monsters of unconsciousness, possessed by what appears to be a shared and dangerous form of madness, made frighteningly manifest.

These images took up a permanent place in my mind, marking an unbreachable divide between my sensibility and the way the older generation in my family thought. If I remember with such vividness one discussion we had at my grandparents' home around the time of the confrontation at Little Rock, it is not because this was the first time I became aware of racism within my own family. I had heard my grandfather make many racist remarks. But what was extraordinary now was that instead of indulging my grandfather's rants, we were all discussing the issue openly. And this argument was remarkable for me for another reason too. It is the first time I remember entering any discussion of events in the world as an equal participant, expressing a different point of view and holding my own.

Because it was Sunday dinner, the table was covered with a white linen cloth. As usual, my grandfather sat at the head and carved the meat. My sister was there, visiting over what we called then the Easter holiday, and my father was at the table too. If my mother and stepfather were there, they were both quiet when somehow the subject of integration came up and a full-scale argument began. And since my grandmother did not like politics to be discussed at the table, the real debate ensued between my sister and me on one side and my father and grandfather on the other.

The injustice of segregation and prejudice seemed self-evident to my sister and me. We talked at length and with some passion about justice and equality as promised in the Declaration of Independence and guaranteed in the Constitution. But these arguments crashed like waves on a seemingly impenetrable wall, having no effect at all. It is not that my father and grandfather failed to listen. If they did not answer our arguments about democracy, it was rather that what we said on that subject was irrelevant to the cast of mind that had determined their opinions.

JANUARY

Bush seems as impervious to reasoning as my grandfather was so many years ago. Even when the great majority want the troops home, he comes on the television last night to declare that 20,000 more troops will be deployed to Iraq.

Though my grandfather was the more active racist, full of epithets and bluster and a strange bilious anger that would come out, when he had had a whiskey, in the form of diatribes he directed into the air, my father's words did more to reveal the shadowy substratum of both their arguments. He explained, with an uncharacteristic indignation, that if the fire department in Los Angeles were to be integrated, he would have to eat with black people and, what's more, even sleep in the same dormitory with them. When he described that possibility, my grandfather shook his head, as if the end of the world were coming.

In light of the fact that the woman who had been cleaning my grandparents' house every week for years, and who ironed all my grandfather's shirts and the sheets he slept on, was a black woman, the aversion he expressed was an odd contradiction. Yet, in my own understanding of racism, it would prove to be a valuable piece of the puzzle. Over and over again in the ensuing years, as my consciousness grew, I would go back to my grandfather, trying to probe beneath the surface of his attitude. I could sense that in some strange, as yet unexplained, way, racism both provided a structure for his psyche and yet had also distorted his soul.

During my college years, I discovered how deeply racism was embedded in American society. In the fifties and all through the early sixties, the white world remained astonishingly ignorant about what black people suffered, and I was no exception to this rule. Now I was learning. Along with many others in my generation, I read poems and novels by black writers, Gwendolyn Brooks, James Baldwin, and Ralph Ellison among them. The things they said and the stories they told brought me inside the experience of racism from the other side. I could see how when it is directed at you, no matter how irrational it is, hatred works its way into you and can wound your soul.

Baldwin's famous book *The Fire Next Time,* in which, among other things, he delineated the psychology of racism, riveted me. "The white man's unadmitted—and apparently unspeakable—private fears and longings are projected onto the Negro," he wrote, words that seemed to explain the inexplicable irrationality I observed in my grandfather. One other book that offered an analysis of racism fascinated me too. It seemed to point to a new way of thinking, an intellectual territory I had not yet encountered, though I sensed it would be vitally significant to me in the future. The book, called *The Mind of the South,* had been written in the year America entered World War II by a white southerner named W. J. Cash. In its pages he traced the energy of racism to white fantasies about black male sexuality, which was conceived as a threat to the equally fictitious notion of white racial purity.

Without being fully aware of the process, I was absorbing ideas that were to become crucial to the work I would do one day and even help to shape who I would become. Both the concept of projection and the understanding that those who are abused internalize hatred were soon to throw light on my own life. The practice of turning the mirror around to scrutinize those filled with harmful prejudices was one I would use in the future myself.

But what I was learning did not only come from books. As I came of age, one of the most significant movements in American history was taking place. On February 1, 1960, five months before I graduated from high school, four black students from North Carolina Agricultural and Technical College, most of them not much older than me, employed a new tactic in the movement for equality. They would sit all day at Woolworth's segregated lunch counter in Greensboro, North Carolina, waiting to be served. Quickly *sit-ins* became part of the vocabulary of our times. The Greensboro lunch counter was integrated six months later, but because not all the stores changed their policies of segregation, Woolworth's stores all over the country were picketed in solidarity. And in the meantime, the strategy of sitting in spread; it was used to integrate parks, swimming pools, even movie theaters. Influenced by Gandhi, the students chose to remain nonviolent in the face of the continual assaults they endured. White segregationist men and women swore at them; spilled drinks, ketchup, and sugar on them; spit on them; and tried to put out lit cigarettes on a student's arms or shoulders. And yet instead of being stopped, these young men and women kept protesting and were soon joined by other black students until all the available seats had been filled by protesters.

These events made an indelible impression on me. Along with many others in my generation, besides horror and revulsion, as I witnessed these extraordinary moments of courage, I was also being brought to the realization that the way things are can be changed. And I realized then that even when things do not change immediately, taking action eases a pain that is scarcely ever spoken of, the sorrow we all bury when we live with and tolerate any form of injustice.

Perhaps this is why political action is known to have such an electric effect on your mood. Paradoxically, while what Gandhi called standing by the truth and Thoreau called civil disobedience can place you in the path of danger, it is also known to produce an uncommonly intense feeling of joy. Years after he took part in the original sit-in at Woolworth's in Greensboro on February 1, 1960, Franklin McCain described his memory of that day to the British journalist Gary Younge: "I had the most tremendous feeling of elation and celebration," he recalled. "I felt that in this life nothing else mattered. I felt like one of those wise men who sits cross-legged and cross-armed and has reached a natural high." Nothing else in his life after that, he said, "Has ever come close."

I was just seventeen years old when I joined my first picket line. It was 1960, after I became active in the student organization at the university, called SLATE. We found someone with a car and then went together to San Francisco to picket the branch of Woolworth's there in sympathy with the sit-ins that had spread now throughout the South. We went on marches, sponsored speakers, attended rallies, and held meetings to address civil rights. One night James Baldwin came to speak with us at a meeting at a private home. He was not easy on us. He let us know how much we did not know. As harsh as his attitude was, it was hard to ignore the authority of his words. The knowing in him ran deep, and it was incandescent.

During the summer after my first year at the university, students all over the country were going down south to participate in what were called Freedom Rides. The plan was to challenge segregation on buses that ran between states, a practice that was against federal law. Several of my friends decided to go. I wanted to join them. But the summer before, the Dimondsteins had left the country to live in Italy, and as a result, my grandparents had become my legal guardians again. Because of this, I thought I could not join my friends. I knew my grandparents would oppose it. They were only in their late sixties then, but they seemed so old to me, I was afraid it might kill them. And I was equally afraid that in order to stop or punish me, they might force me to leave Berkeley and live with them. Still, I went to meetings where we organized support for the students who did go. And when they came back, we all heard their stories. How they had been jailed; their mattresses taken away; the heat turned high in the midst of a hot summer; deprived of water; served food they could not eat—pieces of pork, for instance, with the hair still on it. Yet hearing these stories put us in high spirits. We were not as terrified as we had been about the story of Emmett Till. These were stories of resistance, after all, and they liberated the imagination.

Later, as the civil rights movement gained more and more victories, the opposition would get even more violent. A few years later, in 1964, three civil rights activists—James Chaney, a twenty-one-year-old black man from Meridian, Mississippi; Andrew Goodman, a twenty-year-old Jewish anthropology student from New York; and Michael Schwerner, a twenty-four-year-old Jewish social worker also from New York—would be murdered in a small southern town. And countless others were beaten terribly, including one of our friends who came close to dying. Yet even then there was no going back. Something had already changed. The act of resistance had produced the feeling of equality, and just as with a chemical solution that has been altered by the introduction of just a few drops of another element, the process could not be reversed.

FEBRUARY

The House of Representatives has finally summoned the courage to pass a resolution opposing the escalation of the war. What's at stake here is not just the war, but the right of Congress to legislate. The president seems to want to rule all by himself.

In the same summer, I participated in my first sit-in. It was in the first spring after I had moved to San Francisco that I got a telephone call from one of my friends in the student movement at Berkeley. He was among the organizers of a protest against the discriminatory hiring practices of the city's largest and finest hotels. After some deliberation, they decided to focus on the Sheraton Palace, an elegant, old-fashioned institution that occupied one of the few buildings that had survived the earthquake. It was famous for its brunches, held in a garden room under a beautiful old glass dome. I had been taken there once with my sister by our great-aunt. A string quartet played Mozart as we passed by a smorgasbord filled with eggs Benedict and bacon, oysters and caviar, and the inevitable fruit salad. All the tables were dressed in white linen.

It felt to me as if we had somehow slipped back into the nineteenth century. Caught up in the romance and luxury of it, I had failed to notice how utterly white the people who filled the room were, both the staff and the clientele. Though in the segregated world of America in the early sixties, this was not unusual.

My friend invited me to join a demonstration at the Sheraton that night. A few days before, it had started as a picket line to protest discriminatory hiring practices. Negotiations were proceeding. The day before, the hotel had hired one African-American waitress. But the negotiators were seeking more than a token gesture. Demonstrators showed up from all over the Bay Area, and I was among them. At one point, there must have been nearly three thousand of us in front of the hotel. Slowly the numbers diminished, but around ten at night, as it got colder, those of us who were still present, about fifteen hundred, violated the court injunction against entering the hotel and went inside. Jammed up against one another, we formed an ocean of bodies that covered the spacious entry and hallway.

The whole night was to give me a profound lesson, one that was doubtless being taught all over America, as demonstrators challenged Jim Crow in different cities, not just in the South but now in the North too. We were learning how much racism had become part of the structure of daily life in the North as well. And at the same time, we were also coming to understand something else in a particularly vivid way. We could see that democracy cannot be confined to government alone but must be extended to every aspect of public life, including privately owned businesses. And we were also learning that every business relies on the goodwill and the silent permission of ordinary people, citizens. On this night, because we understood the hotel to be violating the principles of democracy, we decided to withdraw our permission. And so we saw that even this impressive and elegant hotel was ultimately subject to the will of the people.

For several hours, we left a pathway for hotel patrons and officials to come and go. But near three in the morning, when negotiations broke down, the organizers asked those among us who were willing to be arrested to lock arms and block the doors. The great majority of us were college and university students or recently graduated, young and hardy enough to withstand sitting on the floor for the long hours ahead. Though I had turned twenty-one years old a few months earlier, this was my real coming of age. I decided to join those blocking the Market Street entrance. We were quickly schooled by the organizers, who told us not to resist arrest but to go limp as we were carried to the paddy wagons. At first it seemed that the police were going to arrest us first. But at the last minute, they changed their strategy and began arresting those who blocked the side entrance. It was a long procedure that took several hours. To sustain ourselves and broadcast our cause we sang "We Shall Overcome" and African-American spirituals, like "Follow the Drinking Gourd," which in the days of slavery had contained hidden references to the Underground Railroad. Every so often, we would get a report about what was happening at the other door; at one point we heard that a woman's arm might have been injured as a policeman pulled her to the wagon. By that time the side-street doorway was cleared, and 167 men and women had been arrested. Since the police never came to our door, we were free to stand up. I wandered the littered hallways with a friend, then washed up a bit before returning to the street. The sun had come up and it was a beautiful day as I made my way home, elated at how, for a few hours at least, we had faced down formidable powers.

As I emerged from the hotel and stepped onto Market Street, the morning light seemed to sparkle off every surface. I felt as if I were filled with the same light. But though I had somehow voyaged to the essence of my own existence, I knew this light did not belong to me exclusively. It belonged to the world. And for a few hours I had just had the good fortune to see it.

If this sounds like a description of a religious experience, it is because in one sense perhaps it was. Certainly starting from the founding days of the American Republic, the passion and struggle for justice have had a nearly spiritual resonance. And Gandhi, whose words and actions inspired so many leaders of the civil rights movement, developed the stance of resistance to injustice called *satyagraha,* or "standing by the truth," the means that India used to win independence from Britain, from a profound religious practice that reflected the Hindu notion of *Ahimsa,* or the unity of all life.

The philosophy expressed in Gandhi's thought also had an American influence. He had read Thoreau's essay "Resistance to Civil Government" (more commonly known as "Civil Disobedience") and been deeply inspired. The American writer and philosopher wrote this famous work after his own act of civil disobedience. In 1846 he spent one night in jail after refusing to pay a poll tax in protest against the institution of slavery and the Mexican-American War. In this essay, he asks the same question that many religious thinkers have: "Why has every man a conscience then?" The remedy he counsels is consistent with a belief in the unity of life. Arguing that slavery is a form of imprisonment, he says, "Under a government which imprisons any unjustly, the true place for a just man is also a prison."

There is an implicit sense of connection to wider worlds in all struggles for justice. This is made clear whenever any single form of injustice acts as a metaphor for other kinds of oppression. The founders of the American Revolution often borrowed language from early movements to abolish slavery. They used the words *slavery* and *bondage* to describe the injustice the colonies suffered under the governance of Great Britain. In this way, the word *freedom* has been forged in the American mind with the image of a man or a woman breaking the bonds of slavery.

The alchemy through which empathy with the suffering of others leads you to recognize and then protest against your own can be seen in the story of the abolitionist leader and feminist Angelina Grimké. At the dawn of the nineteenth century, she was born to an elite southern family that held many slaves. As a small child, what she witnessed in her own household disturbed her: women forced to sew and mend late at night by lamps that were so dim that they had to stand to see what they were doing, the men and women who served the family sleeping right on the floor without mattresses or bedding.

Angelina's mother was a hard taskmaster. In her home, with both children and servants, obedience was bought through punishment. "Mother," Angelina wrote in her journal, "rules slaves and children with a rod of fear." After her father died and her brother became the head of the household, the atmosphere became even harsher. He beat one house servant so severely and hit him so often on the head that the man developed epilepsy.

It was not only at home that she witnessed such cruelty but throughout her community. One of her young friends lived close to a building where slaves were taken for punishment, and often when she visited her, she could hear "the screams of the slaves under their torture." On one memorable occasion, in the upper-class school she attended, she watched a young black boy who had been so "dreadfully whipped that he could hardly walk" cross the room to open a window. The state of his soul worried her as much as the condition of his body, evident in what she described as his "heart broken countenance."

In such circumstances, where suffering and injustice are clear, why do some respond sympathetically and others with increased brutality? It is a question that bears on democracy, a form of government that rests on reciprocity, and some degree of empathy. I am thinking now of the screams Angelina heard. Somehow it seems crucial that the knowledge of injustice she received did not come to her as a reported fact or a number but as sights and sounds. The sound, for instance, that someone being beaten makes would have been inarguable. The sounds that come from a body in extreme pain are always recognizable. Even a man's voice goes to higher registers, in which terror can be heard, and for this reason, the sound itself is terrifying. Whoever hears it can hardly stop from starting or shuddering. And just as Angelina's body would have reacted without forethought, so too would she know that this sound would not have been uttered voluntarily but instead burst out in response to the extremity of violence, pushing past the barrier masters and overseers placed against complaint from anyone held in bondage. Yet there is this too: these very screams would have let her know at once that the man or the woman who made these sounds shared an inner nature with her, and at the same time she would have been able to see the depths of what was suffered on a daily basis from the threat of violence and with it, at every moment, an unutterable debasement and powerlessness.

Still another response was certainly possible: an inner deafness, one that would have to be, along with hatred, taught. What did Angelina's brother, for instance, say to himself each time he struck the man who served him for some minor or imagined infraction of his rules? Did he repeat his mother's philosophy? She must have had words to accompany her regime of terror by the rod. Some of the logic echoes Jefferson's ideas about race, his notion that blacks do not share the same nature as whites but are inferior, closer to animals, with fewer feelings, less intelligence; that the only reason they know is force; that unless you keep them in line, as Jefferson did as he walked through the grounds of his plantation, with the crack of his whip, they will turn on you with violence. It was a common logic yet strangely confining, an argument that, to work, required one to diminish one's own capacity for direct perception. And thus applying this logic, day after day, month after month, over years, would have sealed away something else too: the capacity to respond and feel the suffering of others altogether.

Angelina went in another direction. Devoutly religious, in 1827, when she was still in her twenties, she established a "colored Sunday school."

And along with organizing prayer meetings, she also did charity work among the poor. Even early in her life, she went far beyond the usual pieties. I can imagine that while her brother would have had to harden himself to others and come thus to live in increasing isolation, while the walls of his fortification grew steadily more impenetrable, through entering the lives of others Angelina would have found larger worlds within and without herself.

Eventually, her spiritual journey led her to join her sister, Sarah, in Rhode Island, where soon after she became a Quaker. It must have been a relief to her to leave the world where she had had to witness the cruelty of slavery every day. Doubtless she was also pleased that the church she joined condemned slavery as a sin. Once you have felt the awful dimensions of any injustice, you will be drawn to others who share your response. Yet in this regard the new church did not satisfy her enough. She had joined the sect to which her sister belonged, the Orthodox Quakers, a group committed to avoiding controversy. "We mingle almost entirely with a Society that appears to know little of what is going on outside of its own immediate precincts," she wrote home. For several years, from 1829 to 1835, in a silence that was uncharacteristic, she hardly spoke at all in meeting. But in this silence she did not forget what she had witnessed, the terrible images and sounds that she still carried inside her.

In the following year, she articulated her experience more plainly: "My spirit is oppressed and heavy laden and shut up in prison," she wrote. By that time she had already embarked on another course. Gradually she was drawn into the antislavery campaign led by William Garrison. After she went to hear the famous British abolitionist George Thompson speak in Philadelphia, she began to attend meetings of the Philadelphia Female Anti-Slavery Society. She read Garrison's publication the *Liberator* regularly, including accounts of abolitionists threatened by angry mobs. When mobs in Charleston burned Garrison in effigy, she wrote to him that she considered abolition a cause worth dying for. "O! How earnestly I have desired," she wrote, "not that we may escape suffering, but that we may be able to endure to the end."

The image invokes the crucifixion. Grimké constantly conveys an almost visceral sense of fusion with men and women held in bondage. This made her an effective speaker. When in 1836 at the request of an abolitionist leader she began to lecture to small groups of women, word spread swiftly that she was exceptionally moving. So began an extraordinary campaign against slavery, during which Angelina, and eventually

her sister Sarah, would speak before countless citizens in New York and
New England, in one six-month period alone reaching forty thousand
people. In 1838, near the end of her brief career, Angelina spoke to an
audience of twenty-eight hundred; and a month earlier she addressed
the Massachusetts state legislature, becoming the first woman to do so.

During their travels through New England, the Grimké sisters visited
Concord, where over a week's time, they dined and took tea with Lydian
Emerson. Lydian was impressed by what they taught her; she resolved
to find something to do "and bear to forward it." The Grimké sisters influenced Emerson too through Lydian. The connection is evocative.
Though Emerson had abandoned Christian dogma and refused to give
the sacrament any longer, he understood the meaning of the image. Like
Gandhi and Thoreau, he believed that ultimately no single life can be
separated from any other.

The various effects we have on one another do not stop at the boundary
of what is called the self but migrate inward, shaping thought and emotion, the soul, and even individual character. Angelina's story provides a
dramatic illustration of the way that democracy intensifies the process.
Who she became was shaped by her attention to the fate of others. In a
letter she sent to the abolitionist Theodore Weld, the man she eventually
married, she describes how the strong passion she had about the cruelty
and injustice of slavery had transformed her. "The tremendous pressure
of" these feelings, she said, burst "with volcanic violence from the bottom of my soul." It was this violence that propelled her to end the silence
imposed on her by the Orthodox Quaker sect to which she had belonged. Her fervent opposition to slavery gave her, she wrote, "the first
long breath of liberty which my imprisoned spirit dared to respire whilst
it pined in hopeless bondage, panting after the freedom to *think aloud.*"

Though the metaphor she uses makes it clear, she did not begin with
the understanding that as a woman her own life was confined or that,
also like African-Americans, she was subject to abuse because of an unjust inequality. But very soon she began to be aware of the parallels between the two conditions. "Since I was engaged in the investigation of
the rights of the slave," she wrote, "I have necessarily been led to a better
understanding of my own; for I have found the Anti-Slavery cause to be
the high school of morals in our land, the school in which human rights
are more fully investigated, and better understood and taught, than in
any other benevolent enterprise."

Finally Angelina would be forced to address the issue of women's rights publicly. Though the elected leaders of the movement were all men, women were vitally important to the abolition movement, providing much of its membership, gathering signatures on the petitions sent to legislators, writing letters, playing crucially supportive roles in the Underground Railroad. But until Angelina Grimké arose as a formidable speaker, women did not speak at any meetings attended by men.

This practice was maintained in deference to the conventional Christian doctrine that women should never lecture to men. Various ministers cited the teachings of Saint Paul in this regard: "Let your women keep silent in the churches for it is not permitted unto them to speak." In the beginning Angelina did not intend to defy the convention. But when her speeches became so popular among women, men began to find their way into the crowds. Because they were so persistent, they could not be kept out, and over time she found herself speaking to mixed audiences.

The prohibition against what she was doing had strange sexual overtones. Mixed audiences were commonly called *promiscuous*. The same suggestive implications can be heard in the pastoral letter issued by the Council of Congregational Ministers of Massachusetts at the height of the controversy Grimké ignited by speaking to mixed audiences. Using symbolic language, the document warned that the vine ought to lean on the trellis. If the vine assumes the "independence and overshadowing nature of the elm," the letter warned, "it will not only cease to bear fruit, but fall in shame and dishonor into the dust."

The meaning here is implicit if not coy. What would the dishonor and shame be? Would speaking to an audience in which men were present inhibit a woman's ability to bear children? Or would addressing a promiscuous audience lead to sexual promiscuity? As is most often true with discourse that is guided by unconscious fears, the logic is contradictory. Though the church fathers had invoked an underworld of scandalous sexuality, they were shocked at what the Grimké sisters were saying themselves on this subject, when the sisters revealed the fact that southern men who owned slaves would sexually exploit and rape the women and girls they held in bondage. Angelina and Sarah said that such practices shamed and dishonored the wives and daughters of these men, but, as if the real sin lay in women's talking about the subject, the church leaders tried to shift the shame to the Grimkés.

There is a buried species of reason here. According to the murky logic of projection, if white women, who, as W. J. Cash writes, stand for the purity of the white race, know and speak about these violations, they threaten the mental boundaries that have been carefully drawn between white and black and men and women. It is what I read between the lines of so much I had learned about racism, the intricate way the prejudice against African Americans and the diminishment of women are tangled together. I could also sense a thinly disguised layer of panic in my grand-father's diatribes. But so well concealed is the meaning of this fearful rea-soning that several years would pass before I understood that in the supremacist mind, women and black people alike are vessels for his dis-owned earthliness, his fragility and mortality, and it is because of this he imagines that the boundaries he has erected are crucial to his survival.

Of course, it was common knowledge among white plantation owners that many of them exploited and raped the women they held in bondage. But since customarily that knowledge was not aired in public, it could also remain compartmentalized. For many years Jefferson maintained a sexual relationship with Sally Hemings, but he kept this private. And thus he did not have to face the implications of his attraction. Perhaps she re-minded him of his wife, who had died so young. And since Sally was the half sister of Martha, fathered in the same way Sally's children were, by a plantation owner who had his way with her mother, the resemblance would not be surprising. Yet what, then, did he do with this breach of the divide that had been drawn in his mind?

What does it mean, for instance, that a man who insists that African-Americans are inferior is so drawn to a black woman that he risks his entire political career to be intimate with her? Where in his conscious-ness does he place his desire? What does he do with the undeniable incli-nation of his own flesh toward hers, his longing to lie with her, to feel her skin against his, his body rise to her touch?

Angelina Grimké took on the challenge that the ministers posed directly. "What can a woman do for the slave when she herself is under the feet of man and shamed into silence . . . ?" she argued. Determined to remove "the stumbling block" of discrimination against women from the road to abolition, in the autumn of 1837 Angelina, joined by her sister, who had finally become fed up with the silence imposed on her by Orthodox Quakers, holed up at a friend's house in Brookline, Massachusetts, for the month of October to write answers to the doctrines against women's speaking out. Using spiritual language but turning her thought in another direction, Sarah Grimké wrote a series of articles for the *New England Spectator,* and Angelina wrote a series of letters that were soon distributed widely as pamphlets.

For a decade, until the Declaration of Sentiments and Resolutions was drafted at Seneca Falls, these small books provided the best-known written arguments for the equality of women. In one famous letter, Sarah succinctly outlined what she called the legal disabilities of women: that a married woman was under the law subsumed by her husband, that all her property became his, that she did not even have the right to her own inheritance or what she earned, that she was not allowed to spend any money beyond bare necessities for the household, that she could bring no legal action against her husband, that he had the right to "restrain her" by chastisement even physically for disobeying him, that she could make no contracts. And she pointed out that these laws "are not very unlike the slave laws of Louisiana. 'All that a slave possesses belongs to his master; he possesses nothing of his own, except what his master chooses he should possess.'"

All the arguments the sisters made circled around one concept: the idea that, as moral beings, women are the equals of men. In contemporary thought, it is easy to reduce the idea of moral being to the collection of social prohibitions and rules that Freud called the superego. But this was not what the sisters had in mind. Many times both of them stood up against conventional morality in the name of a deeper morality, what they felt was right beyond any proscription.

MARCH

The Senate has passed a bill that, while authorizing spending for the war, requires that American soldiers leave Iraq by the end of March 2008. One hopes that at least some of these votes come from conscience and not just a response to the polls—though the latter is not all bad, since it means at least the will of the people is being heard.

In his map of human psychology, Freud did not account for the urge to serve the common good. It is a desire unto itself, and perhaps it reflects the connectedness to other human beings and to nature that is part of who we all are. The Grimké sisters argued that to isolate a woman from society and deprive her of the right to take political action was to violate her soul.

Grimké gave her last speech on May 16, 1838, to a large and enthusiastic audience at Philadelphia's Pennsylvania Hall. Some of what she said was recorded, and those words coupled with descriptions of the atmosphere give us a sense of what it might have been like to be in that audience. While she spoke, an angry mob outside attacked the building. As bottles hurled against stone and glass, she said to the congregation that during her childhood, "every southern breeze wafted to me the discordant tones of weeping and wailing, shrieks and groans, mingled with prayers and blasphemous curses." As the noise outside grew louder, she told her audience, "I thought there was no hope. . . . My heat sunk within me at the abominations in the midst of which I had been born and educated." But then, as the attacks increased, she turned the mood of her speech: "But how different do I feel now," she said, "animated with hope. Nay with the assurance of the triumph of liberty and good will to man. I will lift up my voice like a trumpet." She went on, unshaken by what was transpiring around the hall: "There is nothing to be feared from those who would stop our mouths but they themselves should fear and tremble. The current is even now setting fast against them."

Angelina's speech that day went on for over an hour. She was interrupted several times by shouts from the angry mob or by the rocks they hurled that broke windows. She responded to one loud round of yelling by asking her audience to feel sympathy with the mob. "They know not what they do," she said, turning scripture into a lesson on the reciprocity at the heart of democracy. "They know not that they are undermining their own rights and their own happiness, temporal and eternal."

More than once, members of the audience got up to leave. But Grimké persuaded them to stay. She addressed their fear and despair directly, telling the women in the audience that since they could not vote, "It is your duty to petition." Speaking to their hopelessness, she asked, "Do you say, 'It does no good?'" before answering, "The South already turns pale at the number [of petitions] sent." She then declared, "There is, therefore, no cause for doubting or despair, but rather for rejoicing."

These words would be needed to weather what was to follow. Since the Anti-Slavery Convention of American Women did not obey the mayor's demand to restrict the meeting to white women, all of their next scheduled meetings were canceled. But the mob returned anyway. And Pennsylvania Hall, which had been built with contributions from citizens and donated labor so that abolitionists would have a place to meet and speak, and which had opened just four days earlier, was burned to the ground.

Nonetheless, Grimké knew her work had had a profound effect. She wrote to her good friend the African-American abolitionist Sarah Douglass, "The world has turned upside down." It had. Two years later, when Elizabeth Cady Stanton and Lucretia Mott were sent as American delegates to the World Anti-Slavery Convention, the convention ruled that only male delegates could be seated. Yet as the two women walked through the streets of London together, a friendship formed over this grievance, and eight years later they organized another convention, this time for women and men to address the question of women's rights. Held at Seneca Falls, in upstate New York, a few blocks from where Stanton lived, the convention adopted the Declaration of Sentiments and Resolutions. The document was to provide the basic arguments for the movement for women's suffrage and equal rights over many decades. The first paragraph recalls an earlier declaration. It begins:

> When, in the course of human events, it becomes necessary for one portion of the family of man to assume among the people of the earth a position different from that which they have hitherto occupied, but one to which the laws of nature and of nature's God entitle them, a decent respect to the opinions of mankind requires that they should declare the causes that impel them to such a course.

The second paragraph echoes the Declaration of Independence too, but this version expands the scope of democracy: "We hold these truths to be self-evident: that all men and women are created equal."

Women would not achieve the vote until 1920. It is a sad part of the story that along the way, significant factions in the suffrage movement would make an appeal to racism by arguing that women, being educated, would make a better electorate than African-Americans or immigrants.

In 1964, the year I participated in the demonstration at the Sheraton Palace and just over a century since the Emancipation Proclamation ended slavery in the United States, the civil rights movement was gaining momentum. Yet I had not thought very much about women's rights. I had never heard of the Grimké sisters. I did not know very much about the history of how women got the vote. Nor, though I considered myself equal to men, did I turn my attention to the ways I was not treated as an equal. When I had been part of the student movement at Berkeley, women were rarely elected to positions of leadership, and this angered me but I did very little about it. I did not fully grasp the effect of the omission of books written from a woman's point of view from my college classes on my own development. As a writer without my own experience and my own point of view, I was left with no real subject matter.

Other issues seemed as if they were just part of the atmosphere, less man-made than natural. Though I had never been raped, I had been taught from a young age to be careful, to pull down the blinds, look behind me as I walked down the street, avoid being alone with a man I did not know or trust. When the woman who lived next door to the apartment I shared with friends in North Beach was assaulted, we were all frightened, but after a period the fear subsided. It was something we were all accustomed to feeling, not just whenever we read about rape or rape-murders in the newspaper but every time we walked down a dark street. Sexual harassment seemed almost ordinary. It had been a daily fact of my life since I was an adolescent. The inevitable phone calls, men breathing heavily or asking provocative questions. I had been groped when I went for a job interview, followed home from parties, pestered by men on the street. But I looked at all this as a necessary evil and not as a political issue.

Then there was the issue of abortion. Until 1973, when the Supreme Court decided *Roe v. Wade,* abortion was illegal. But this did not stop anyone I knew from seeking one. The term *back-alley abortion* was very real then. One friend of mine was blindfolded and then taken to some out-of-the-way place—she thought it might have been a warehouse or a garage—only to be placed on a dirty table and operated on by a man who seemed to have little medical knowledge. Wealthy women often flew to Europe to have safe surgery. Those of us who could not afford this relied on informal networks. You would call a friend who knew someone who had gone to a doctor who operated illegally here or just across the border, in Mexico, and hope for the best. Sometimes a woman, a former nurse, a healer or midwife, would do it; though she was breaking the law, she was usually protected by her patients, who were grateful to her and who had their own secret to hide.

Usually women who had abortions told only their closest friends about it. A woman would rely on a friend, most often a woman too, to drive her where she needed to go and then take care of her afterward. Still, someone you knew quite well might tell you she was ill from the stomach flu or menstrual cramps when, as you would find out years later, she had had an abortion.

In 1965, when I was twenty-two years old, I realized I had skipped a period, and soon I began to wake in the mornings with nausea. It was during perhaps the wildest period of my life. Over the previous two months, I was between lovers and could not say exactly who the father was. Though it wasn't the Summer of Love yet, serial monogamy was already common among women of my generation then.

I had read *The Second Sex* by Simone de Beauvoir and admired the free union she described with Jean-Paul Sartre. (I did not know its complexities then.) But like everything else in my life that pertained to womanhood, I never reflected with any depth or clarity on what kind of union I wanted, allowing conflicting desires to coexist without any critical examination. I knew I wanted children. I liked men and making love with them, yet though I found it hard to admit this to myself, I was drawn to women. I worried that I would grow bored being with just one man all my life. And yet I also assumed I would be married one day and, in a part of myself I did not often reveal, hoped this might give me the security I never had as a child.

I cannot say this was the happiest time in my life. Yet it was intense and memorable. Something valuable was happening to me. Though my behavior was tame compared to what occurred in the hippie years, in contrast to the restrictive fifties, this seemed like a period of liberation. I was well aware that the sexual revolution was lopsided. Women were still judged for having more than one lover in a way that men were not. But the virgin bride had lost her appeal.

Accordingly, my friends and I behaved as men have traditionally done for centuries. My explorations gave me a confidence that was by no means confined to sexual pleasure, though I doubt I could have achieved it by any other route. In the past, men had been allowed a time in life to sow their wild oats, and this gave them a psychological edge. They knew the ways of the world while women remained childlike and ignorant.

And there is this too: to know yourself, you must follow your desire. I was in the first generation of women allowed this freedom.

But now I was facing another order of experience. I was not ready to raise or support a child alone. So I entered the underground network, asking all my women friends who they might know who would be able to help me find an abortion. Finally a woman where I worked as a cocktail hostess gave me a contact. She knew someone who had been to see an African-American pediatrician in downtown L.A. There was a certain code word I would have to use when I made an appointment. The procedure would be done in the office. I would have to bring someone with me because I could not stay there even for a quarter of an hour to recover. To protect both the doctor and me, I had to leave as soon as possible. And there could be no anesthetic.

I was reassured that I would be operated on by a doctor and I would be in his office. And it appealed to me that somehow what I paid him would help him to treat children from families who could not afford medical care. One of my lovers, the married man, gave me a check that paid for part of the costs. And a friend who lived in the building next door chipped in too. That the other man did not contribute in any way angered but did not surprise me. This was the shadow side of "free love," something women talked about with one another but rarely saw in a political light.

I would not allow myself to be afraid before the abortion, as my sister and I took a flight to L.A. and then a series of buses downtown. But I was relieved when I met the doctor, who though not overly kind was nevertheless the sort of man who inspires trust. Everything in his office was in good order. As he worked with a stern, attentive look on his face, he told me I could not scream when I began to feel intense contractions. Finally, overwhelmed with the pain, I decided to sing. I imitated a diva expressing emotions of tragic dimensions, and this served me well. Impressed with how I handled the pain, he told me, "You've become a woman now." At the time, I took his words as a compliment. Only later did I question the many levels of meaning in what he said.

He sent me to a pharmacy across the street for codeine and antibiotics. Only then did I feel the danger of the situation. Not just from hemorrhage or infection, but from the possibility of arrest. What if the druggist figured out what had happened? It seemed to take forever to fill the prescription. Finally the little bottles arrived, just in time for my sister and me to climb into the car that would take us to the San Fernando

Valley. Since my adoptive family was in Italy and I did not want to tell either my grandmother or my mother about the pregnancy or the abortion, I had asked Silvia, my high school boyfriend's mother, if I could stay with her for a couple of nights before flying home.

Silvia was just as I remembered her, kind in a very sophisticated, casual way. I rested during the day, and when we got together in the late afternoon, we spoke about everything else but why I was there. Film. The civil rights movement, in which Silvia was active. When her second husband, the screenwriter Buzz Bezzerides, joined us for lunch, we never spoke about why I was there. He may not even have known why we had come. This was the kind of thing women kept among themselves in those days, along with menstruation and menopause.

Only later would I learn that my mother would have understood my experience very well. Though the story she told me did not come as a complete surprise. She had spoken to me openly about sexuality when I was a teenager. Sexual pleasure, she said, was something good, not bad. And she wanted to make certain I knew that. The subject of abortion came up just after my daughter had been born, while my mother was visiting. This birth had been planned. Yet because my experience with abortion five years earlier remained with me, I was doing a series of interviews with friends and friends of friends who had all had illegal procedures.

"I have a story to tell you," my mother said, when I was explaining this work to her. "You probably don't know it. But I had an illegal abortion." Hers had also been without anesthetic, done by a doctor who practiced in Los Angeles. She was young when it happened, not yet twenty. And she told me that her mother, with whom she had fought bitterly for most of her adult life, went with her and was very kind. Despite her constant worries about what the neighbors might think, my grandmother knew from her own experience what it was to face a pregnancy as an unmarried woman, and she stood by my mother.

By that time, I had already begun to regard the experiences women share, especially those described until then as private, with a new political scrutiny. The process began when, three years after my abortion, I went to work for a new radical magazine called *Ramparts*. It was exciting to be working there during this astonishing time in American history. *Ramparts* was among the first muckraking magazines to have a popular format with glossy photos. We broke one story after another. There was, for instance, the piece about the thirteen eerily mysterious deaths of journalists and other witnesses who perhaps knew too much about

President Kennedy's assassination. By then I was doing research too and rewriting articles the editors submitted. The magazine became famous after publishing several stories about the Vietnam War, which was becoming increasingly unpopular, as scores of American soldiers returned home in body bags.

Ramparts was the first American magazine to publish photographs of Vietnamese people, including children, who had been wounded by napalm bombs. Because we were worried about numbing our audience to the horrors with sensationalism, we ran the photos in small size. We were all young, passionate about social justice, and willing to work, especially near deadline, through the night, with little pay.

MARCH

Finally news that Libby has been found guilty on several counts, including the obstruction of justice, perjury, and lying to the FBI. The future seems a bit brighter now.

In one sense, dramatic events at the magazine served to diminish the effect of events in my own life. The year before I graduated, I had become involved with another woman. I met her when we worked together in the theater. I felt I had never truly been in love or loved before. Although the relationship was not perfect, it was transformative in this way. But I did not want to be a social pariah. I could not transfer the courage I had summoned so many times in response to issues that were more widely seen as political then. The relationship could not survive my fears. It all happened at the same time: I left the woman I loved, fell in love with the man I would soon marry, and took a job at *Ramparts*. Still, in their own way, these events too were auguries of a future I had not predicted.

Behind all the social change the magazine advocated, another revolution was quietly taking place. The women who worked at the magazine began to notice a clear pattern of discrimination. The editorial board never considered making any of us who worked as copy editors or secretaries into staff writers. When Jann Wenner was made the editor of the *Sunday Ramparts,* a weekly we put out during the 1967 *Chronicle* strike, I became a staff writer for the temporary newspaper, but I was never made a writer for the magazine. In general, the work that women contributed was rarely acknowledged. But this was just one aspect of the story. When, near the monthly deadline, we would work around the clock, sometimes for two or three nights running, the whole staff would usually take a break at dinner and go up the street to eat at one of two Italian restaurants in the neighborhood, either Vanessi's or Enrico's. No one was being paid overtime. But the salaries the men earned were higher. And when we went out to eat, the women were expected to pay for our own dinners, while the men's meals went on credit cards that were billed to the magazine.

Finally, the women rebelled. The insurrection seemed to arise naturally out of the complaints we aired over coffee breaks. We were not able to achieve anything near equity, but after a few meetings with the editors, we finally got our meals paid for, though soon the meals we got when we worked all night were downgraded to sandwiches. But the significance was not in the immediate consequences. We did not know then that our rebellion was just one of countless events that were taking place all over the country, in radical political organizations such as SDS and alternative newspapers like *Rat* in New York City.

As young women of my generation left college, married, and took jobs, we discovered that despite the changes the suffragists accomplished, we faced a pervasive atmosphere of discrimination. As with so many other women, my entrance into the world led to a rude awakening. I had not anticipated the degree of prejudice I faced.

What happened next has happened at the start of countless movements for social change. Bit by bit, seemingly isolated incidents and complaints began to coalesce, forming a new, political force to be reckoned with. At first the phenomenon was barely visible. Yet disparate groups across the country began to communicate. Cyberspace did not exist then. And photocopiers were uncommon. But even with mimeograph machines and typewritten letters, a network evolved almost overnight. A friend who had visited one of her friends from college in New York returned with a petition demanding rights for women that had been presented to an alternative newspaper there. Soon it was being passed around and read everywhere. A woman with family in Florida found out about a women's group in Gainesville that was publishing a series of mimeographed articles about the circumstances of contemporary women's lives. Known as the pink papers (for the simple reason that they were printed on pink paper), these articles had an explosive effect on many women's lives, mine among them.

At home, I was suffering the same sea change I experienced at work. Though I was supporting us both while my husband went to school, I was also doing all the housework and cooking. On the night before our wedding, I was shocked when he handed me a large bundle of his socks and asked me to wash them. I washed them but not before telling him, "I'll never do this again." Yet I took an almost proprietary attitude toward running the household. It was as if the idea of marriage had transformed us both into conventional stereotypes.

As much as I was dissatisfied, I did not want to acknowledge it. Yet I could not escape my doubts. And soon my awareness would be accelerated by what other women were doing and saying. Though our efforts to end discrimination at *Ramparts* did not get very far, I was surprised to discover new allies, a group of women I knew casually, some the wives and lovers of progressive leaders, others of writers and editors at the magazine, were meeting to talk about a cause that had just been given a new name: *women's liberation.*

Before the first meeting I attended was over, a radical transformation of how I perceived myself and other women had already begun. I had met most of these women before, some at parties given by the magazine. But though I had always had good women friends, since I met these women as adjuncts to the men with whom I worked, I had assumed they were uninteresting.

The mind has a powerful capacity to maintain an opinion that flies in the face of evidence to the contrary. I also assumed that women who were not working but instead staying home with infants or small children must be intrinsically boring. The contradictions implicit in this particular prejudice become even more apparent in light of the fact that I myself soon became pregnant and fully intended to stay home with my child for at least two years.

Yet when the timing is right, prejudices easily evaporate into thin air. As I listened to each of the women talk about the issues we had come together to address, not only was I impressed by the intelligence I was witnessing, but I was presented with the implications of my own misjudgment. That night, a whole new world had been made visible to me, a world that I had inhabited every day without really seeing it.

At times the transformation of public consciousness seems to occur in pockets, as if offstage, and almost inaudibly, until one day discourse has altered radically. Ideas that once seemed to be permanent fixtures of the mind, unassailable assumptions, will collapse suddenly, like buildings whose foundations have gradually rotted. In my own life, the change was rapid, if uneven. For a while I clung to the safe world I shared with my husband. And yet evidence accumulated, trivial and large, forcing my feelings past every wall of denial I had built. There was that item in the pink papers, for instance, that asked who got to read the front pages first, *you or your husband*. Though I was already a writer and seriously involved with political issues, it was my husband who always got those pages first. It seems like such a trivial complaint now, but it sparked a process of deconstruction in which, among other things, I began to notice my own complicity with my young husband's sense of entitlement. We began to wrangle over who would do the dishes, whether or not I would make his lunch; above all, I wanted him to be able to meet me on an emotional level that he had not yet developed. Over time, as my demands for change continued, his resistance also grew stronger.

Even a bloodless revolution alters the soul in profound ways. And when the combatants are intimate, the effect can trouble the deepest waters of the psyche. As women changed the way we thought, many relationships ended. Most of us were young and did not have the maturity that would be needed to handle what felt to be, in the terrain of the soul, like a tsunami or an earthquake, upending or leveling every habit and cherished illusion in its path. Though it was exciting to wrestle free of the bonds that had been confining my life, it was also frightening. I decided to leave my husband almost overnight. Had I planned to leave more carefully, I might not have done it. But the suddenness was hard on everyone, including my daughter, who was just twenty-two months old then.

It was only years later that I could think about the effect of my decisions on my husband, who, when confronted by the mix of rage and sorrow and joy and ferocious determination that women were expressing, like other men in this period, must have felt that his life had suddenly spun out of control. We were demanding that men participate more in domestic life and in caring for their children. But since by itself the struggle to free ourselves seemed so monumental, few of us had the spaciousness of mind to understand the ways that gender is a system in which everyone suffers. The masculine analogue, for instance, to domestic servitude is the terrible pressure that men endure as the sole breadwinners of the family. I had seen the effects on my husband, who periodically suffered debilitating bouts of anxiety, fearing that he would be fired.

And in this period, another aspect of my emotional life returned with force. One night I attended a poetry reading held at an empty house that would soon become a women's center. The poet who performed, Judy Grahn, was extraordinary. As I listened to her read from a series called *The Common Woman*, I experienced something like what Jelly Roll must have felt when he listened to piano men play blues in the district. My ears opened to a new music, one that was inside me too. The sound of her words was syncopated with the fact that Judy was a lesbian. It was not that this sound was gay. Rather what I heard in her voice was the sound of courage. She was not hiding who she really was. I realized then I could not run away from my own love for women any longer.

As I explored every area of my life, a new territory of consciousness was being forged within me. I knew there was no way I could turn back. Yet this was also a terrifying time. Too many ghosts in my psyche were being resurrected. If, in an effort to order consciousness, we give various memories, desires, histories, and inclinations different names, in the unconscious mind they are all connected. So the loss of my marriage pierced through another form of denial I had carefully built for years. It was as if I were revisiting the abandonment I had suffered as a child. I was more in touch with myself than ever before, but the process of inner change was so rapid that at times I felt almost as if the center would not hold. I had never felt so sane or empowered before, yet the force of my feelings, held back for so many years, was almost too strong to bear. Now my conscious and repressed thoughts and desires were reversed. If in the daylight I felt the courage of my choices, at night I would cry with fear and loneliness. Over and over again, I dreamed that I had gotten back with my husband. I felt comforted by the dream for a period and then would wake with alarm, relieved to find that I had not gone back to my former life.

My fear took on many different shapes. How would I support my daughter and myself? I would have a small salary as a teaching assistant, child support, and a temporary grant of spousal support, but still, as again and again I added the figures in my head, the ends did not meet. I did not have the option of going into debt. Before the women's movement challenged the policy, single and divorced women were rarely issued credit cards. There was no one with whom to share my worries. Though gradually I pieced together a way for my daughter and me to survive, it seemed to me as if society were organized to defeat us. Finally,

I found a good day-care program for my daughter, though all of my child support went to pay for it. And I rented out two rooms in my house. But when I went to apply for food stamps, I encountered still another fear. The requirements were impossible: to fall into the absurdly narrow category of eligibility, you had to pretend to have either less or more income and expenses than you really did. Before and during my interviews, I felt as if I were a criminal evading apprehension instead of a mother simply trying to feed her child.

Yet through all this, I came to a visceral understanding of the way women have been robbed of power. Even as I found myself longing to be supported, I also felt angry, and this anger was clarifying. I began to see the notion that men were supposed to protect women in a new light. Plainly speaking, I experienced that the motive—at least of society, if not of all men—was less to care than to control. That the protection society offered to women contained a barely concealed threat became even more clear when I began to think seriously about another fear I had as a single woman: rape.

Like all women, I had learned at a young age to be careful at night, to look over my shoulder as I walked, avoid empty streets or garages, and lock all my windows and doors. In this way, I learned to live with a siege mentality, knowing that whenever I was alone, I might be subjected to an unpredictable, random, and vicious attack. The notion was not abstract to me. I had endured one attempt to break into my house and another to wrestle me to the ground. The prevailing idea in that period was that rape was part of masculine nature. Along those lines, it was argued in both popular and academic discourse that men who raped were frustrated by the attempt to find a mate, and therefore they acted out of urgent and overwhelming sexual need. The corollary notion to this idea was that women did not rape because our sexual needs were not as great. Now I began to question these assumptions.

Every revolution is nurtured by a resonant field of new ideas. These insights arise one by one at the edge of public discourse and may seem random or irrelevant, like the counterrhythms of a side player in a band, entertaining but not central, until gradually, as they begin to connect, they change the course of the whole composition. Just as Benjamin Franklin's experiments with electricity would add force to the American Revolution, Kinsey's studies of sexuality, which had recently revealed that women had sexual feelings as strong as those of men, had a similar effect. Something was moving within us all, both women and men—a shift larger than could be detected from any single perspective. Suddenly, the studies that the sociologist Menachem Amir had done on men who had been convicted of rape seemed to dovetail with the way I was beginning to see this crime, not as a natural event but as a socially constructed behavior, one that functioned to support the dominance of men over women.

In a culture that values individuality and self-reliance, we forget that as unique as it is, the self is also built from received ideas, conventions, historical influences, social habits, and common designs. We are always with one another; made from one another; entering others we do not know, even with our fantasies of who they are; receiving elements from strangers we will never meet or who are long gone from this earth. For better or worse, we cannot avoid the union.

Much of the process by which we barter elements of identity is unconscious. I am thinking now of the shadow side of the exchange, the troubled projections that lie at the heart of misogyny and racism. Both women and minorities have been called "other" and consigned to the margins of society, both described as more emotional and sensual than white men, both called intellectually inferior, both described as having a more animal nature and as being closer to nature. By this complex process of denial and displacement, even Thomas Jefferson, who in his declaration cited "Nature and Nature's God" as the final authority, could sever himself from nature and place himself above it by projecting the vulnerabilities of his own natural existence onto the African-Americans whom he held in bondage and who made it possible for him to live with a relatively gracious ease.

While tyranny is enforced with fear, democracy is more grounded in trust. But this does not mean that democracy erases fear. I am thinking of Little Rock again. You can see terror in the faces of the mob surrounding Central High that September day in 1957 as the school was being integrated. Barely beneath the surface of the rage they expressed, an elemental fear is evident; loss of control no doubt blended in their minds with thoughts of their own mortality, transformed to mythical monsters that grow more strong and pervasive the more they are evaded.

That day this terror found an especially clear expression in Margaret

Jackson, who broke down in hysterical sobs when she heard that the children had entered the school, wailing, "My daughter's in there with those niggers. Oh, my God! Oh, God." Of course, the only "nigger," as James Baldwin has written of the word, was inside her own mind. Her fear of her own knowledge had been transformed into a bogeyman, the specter of what was called miscegenation, a process by which, if a black man and white woman came together, the "purity" of the white race would be assaulted, and hence dragged to the earth, forced to face the exigencies of life on earth.

Such terror rarely remains in the imagination. You can almost predict the chain of events. A man feeling powerless regains his sense of mastery by overpowering a woman, making her bend to his desire. Above all, it is his violation of her will that excites and satisfies him. Or, knowing that in a racist climate they have impunity, a group of white men, afraid of what is inside them, will ride out at night, setting fire to houses, or shooting into windows, beating up young men for minor offenses that are nonexistent (except perhaps that of being out alone at night), in a display of momentary and stolen power.

But because we are not separate from one another, the chain of terror never ends but only stretches further and further. It will grow inside each of us, enclosing every thought and inclination in fear. So a woman who wants to go out at night but who has no one to accompany her stays home. She does not go to the dance or the library, the lecture or the meeting, because she is afraid of having to walk a few blocks alone. She may not tell herself she is afraid. But she wastes her time, never quite gets ready to go, telling herself instead that she really just wants to stay home anyway. So her connection to the public world gradually diminishes. An older man, African-American, asked by a young civil rights worker to sign up to vote, registers but, on the day of the election, cannot get past a fear, engendered for years by all the reprisals he has witnessed. He may not tell himself he is afraid to vote. He simply never gets around to it in time.

I was fortunate to be born in a time when women began to brave the threats and cross the boundaries, real and imagined, that had been confining our lives. I can so easily imagine that had this not been the case, my life would have been very different, that I might have ended up like my grandmother or my mother, whose dreams were frustrated, forced into lives they did not really choose. The calamity of such an experience is often underestimated. Their bitterness flooded through the whole family, depriving us all of joy. My life has not been perfect. I have made mistakes, suffered failures, done things I regret, but it has been my own life that I lived.

Yet another element belongs to the equation too. Through the alchemy of influence, a process that is almost the reverse of denial and projection, we are led to ourselves by the example of others. As I came of age, in the second half of the twentieth century, I was given an astonishing example of courage by the small group of children, a group which included a bright young athlete named Jefferson Thomas, who became the first African-American students to attend Central High in Little Rock, Arkansas. Among them was a girl named Melba Patillo, now Melba Patillo Beals. I remember that just as the feminist movement was beginning, I used to watch her deliver brilliant analyses of the news on our local PBS station. I knew nothing then of her history, though what she did as a child had already begun to liberate my mind.

Despite the fear of white people she had had since she was very young, Melba volunteered to be among the first black students to register at Central High. "By the time I was three years old," she writes, in her memoir *Warriors Don't Cry*, "I was already so afraid of white people that when my red-haired, white-skinned cousin, Brenda, came to baby sit I hid beneath Mother's bed." No one told her to be afraid in so many words. But she had read fear in what she observed in her family, in a tone of voice or an expression, a posture, a quickened pace whenever white people were spoken of or encountered.

Her courage is even more remarkable in light of what had happened to her three years earlier, on the day that the Supreme Court decision known as *Brown v. Board of Education* was announced, ruling against the doctrine of separate but equal and mandating the integration of public schools. On that day, Melba Patillo, then just twelve years old, left school early, cautioned as all the other black children were, to go directly home and to walk with a group for protection. Wisely, her teacher had anticipated that there would be reprisals in response to this turn of events. Yet Melba, usually an obedient child, longed to take the shortcut she usually took alone, across a field on the way; this would give her the solitude she craved. She liked to dream about her future. Every time she crossed this field, she knew she was taking a risk. Sometimes her reveries would be interrupted by another girl, Marissa, a big child and a bully, who would often force Melba to give up food or pocket change. But this time when she felt a hand cross over her shoulder pulling her down, it was not a child's hand but a man's. As he slapped her to the ground and prepared to rape her, he muttered, "I'll show you niggers the Supreme Court can't run my life." Fortunately, just in time to save Melba from rape, Marissa came from behind him, struck him with her book bag, and then kicked him where she knew it would cause the most pain, so that the girls were able to escape.

Yet though the atmosphere of the segregated South was thick not just with fear but with danger, the idea of liberty played a pivotal role in Melba's mind. In the diary she had kept since she was six years old, after her grandmother counseled her to keep some thoughts private and write them down, she used the word *freedom* often. She longed to be able to go wherever she wanted, to the places, for instance, in Little Rock where African-Americans were forbidden to go. The merry-go-round, so enticing with its beautiful painted horses; the town's main auditorium, where big entertainers like Elvis performed. To drink from the new, cleaner, and more conveniently located water fountains, marked *For Whites Only*.

Although, as a strategy of survival, they obeyed various trivial injunctions, her grandmother, India, and her mother, Lois, both had a strong sense of what was right. They had defied racism in their own ways. Her mother, who was a high school English teacher, had been one of the first African-Americans to attend the University of Arkansas, where she earned a doctorate. Her grandmother had an almost unwavering sense of her intrinsic value, a state of mind that was given to her, she believed, as to every human being equally, by God, and she passed her deep sense of dignity on to her daughter and her grandchildren.

By some inner mandate that has never been fully explained, democracy evolves within each of us. Just as light will find every possible way to illuminate space, this mandate is insistent, compelling us beyond the most formidable boundaries. Melba had plans for her life. She wanted to go to college, and then perhaps to be an actress or a journalist. And there was this too: along with all the other forbidden places, she wanted to be able to go inside the impressively grand Central High School building. Two blocks long and standing seven stories high, beautifully landscaped with a pond in front, it looked like an Eastern Seaboard college. It was reputed to be one of the best schools in the country, with the latest laboratory equipment used in its science classes, projectors for showing movies, no fewer than three kitchens for home economics. Melba had had fine teachers at the segregated school she attended, but the textbooks she was issued were old editions that had been used and discarded by white students; and the furniture and equipment were secondhand from Central too, three-legged tables and other damaged goods.

Her family was shocked by the news that she had been chosen to be one of the nine students to integrate Central High School, especially since, fearing perhaps that they would not want her to take this risk, Melba did not tell her family that she had volunteered. She was selected, along with eight others, because she lived near the school, had good grades and a solid churchgoing family to sustain her. And after their initial dismay, her mother and grandmother did rally in what would become a grueling and dangerous battle.

At first, they hoped that the angry statements of segregationists in the press and the belligerent calls they received, including a threat to bomb the house, would be the worst of it. But on the first day that Melba tried to enter Central, they saw signs of what was to come. As soon as her mother parked the car, as close to the school as she could, they heard the noise of the crowd, a mob filled with a few who had just come to witness history but many others who were angry and shouting, determined to prevent integration. As they walked closer, they could hear what was being called out. "Niggers go home" the crowd was chanting, in a frenzied chorus, "Niggers go back where you belong." Realizing that, for their safety, they would have to find the other students who had come in a group with an escort, Melba's mother pushed through the crowd to get as close to the high school as she could. But when they got close enough to see the focus of the crowd's rage, they watched in horror as one of the students, Elizabeth Eckford, stood alone, a long line of soldiers from the Arkansas National Guard on one side, keeping her from entering the school, and the jeering crowd on the other. It was a terrifying moment.

As someone in the crowd that followed close behind her called out "Hang her black ass," the soldiers did nothing to protect Elizabeth. Neither Melba nor her mother could do anything at all to help her, and in a moment Lois could see that they were almost trapped too. With a group of men chasing them, one who had a rope in his hands, they ran toward their car. Before she could open the car door, another man swung the branch of a tree at Melba. Fortunately he missed her, but as they drove away, still another man hurled a brick at the windshield.

APRIL

The violence and fear are coming home. So many soldiers trauma-tized, untreated, even sent back to combat. One man who was blind and disabled set fire to the trailer where his sister-in-law lived with his niece.

For a period, because of this violence, integration of Central High re-mained at a standstill while legal arguments continued in the courts. Though President Eisenhower had demanded that the integration pro-ceed, the governor of Arkansas, Orville Faubus, was resisting his orders. Still, there would be no turning back. No matter how it had occurred, a space had opened up in the public mind. The whole nation was engaged. As alone as Elizabeth Eckford had been on that first day, now the wit-nesses were legion.

But this did not mean that, during the year to come, the violence would stop. After the first day at Central, a group of men shot into Melba's home, shattering her grandmother's favorite green vase and, along with it, what was left of Melba's sense of safety. This kind of assault was business as usual at the home of Daisy Bates, the chair of the NAACP, who was coordinating the challenge to segregation. When Melba at-tended her first meeting there, she was chilled to see guards armed with rifles marching in front of the living room windows. But the danger made it especially crucial to meet. The students and their families needed to shore up their resolve together, remind themselves how much what they were doing meant for all African-American people, and embrace the danger in a larger spirit.

In these meetings, they also learned the rudiments of nonviolence, how to respond to violent behavior without violence. And so that the ef-fort might garner a wide circle of public support, journalists were often invited to the meetings, not just from other cities in the South but from the *New York Times* and foreign countries too.

Yet though these reporters were friendly to the cause, rarely was the depth of what the children endured reported. In the beginning, so that integration could be achieved, the students were cautious about describing the violence. And there is this too: it would not have been easy to do justice to the experience in a few words. It is as if the language itself were still inaccessible, as if to describe the way the nine children were being terrorized every day would be to look too directly into this disturbing mirror of American racism. What Melba liked best about the meetings was that she could spend time with the others who were integrating Central. She had known them all since she was a small child, from church and school and other places in the community, but now they shared a geography that few others had encountered let alone understood.

After Faubus was forced to obey Eisenhower's orders and remove the Arkansas National Guard from in front of the campus, the children could go up the steps to the school. But as the angry mob started to breach the barriers, the nine students had to flee out a side entrance into a car that waited for them and then gun the engine through the crowds. A few days later, Eisenhower ordered in federal troops, the 101st Airborne Division, famous for their role in World War II at the Battle of the Bulge. These soldiers kept the mob away and guarded the hallways in the school. One soldier was assigned to escort each of the nine from class to class. Melba was grateful for Danny, the soldier assigned to her. Not only did he walk behind her everywhere but he taught her how to defend herself. To be a warrior, he said, she must not let the students who constantly harassed her see her cry.

Every day she went to school was full of terrors. And among the many dangers, some threatened her soul. All the people in your life, including those you know only casually, contribute to your sense of yourself in good and bad ways. The various responses you encounter even in a single hour will all meet in you, if not influencing who you will become, at the very least shaping your mood. So it is easy to understand why Melba dreaded the hours before and after lunch when she was separated from her friends. In an act of singular maliciousness, the school administrators decided to make each of the nine children be the only African-Americans in all of their classes. Even when they did not throw pencils and other objects at her, the white students made continual comments, sometimes sly, sometimes angry, sometimes threatening, always ugly, about her.

However you reason with yourself in such a circumstance, mean-spirited remarks will invade your mind and start to break you down.

Had someone who cared for Melba been there to share and witness the verbal assaults, these comments would have been much easier to take. But she was alone, surrounded by white faces. Not all of the white children were malicious. But none of them did anything to help her. Silence in the face of injustice is never neutral. The failure to respond with outrage gets folded into the force of any crime. Mute approval—however unwilling—quietly lays the ground for justifying brutality.

The students who acted directly against Melba were being tutored in the arts of malice at night and on the weekends by their parents and the White Citizens' Council. The council had even asked psychologists to teach them techniques that might undermine the black students. One day Melba was met with a sheer wall of hostility, as students turned to stare at her all day. There is no way to avoid such an assault. Even if you avert your eyes, you will feel the effect of a menacing gaze. On other days the white students would chant in unison in the style of a football rally, simple rhymes like *Two, four, six, eight, we ain't gonna integrate*. But as painful as this must have been, the campaign did not stop at dirty looks and nasty words.

The threats of death that all the students received on the telephone or whispered in hallways and classrooms were reinforced with physical attacks. In the beginning, these were less frightening. A girl would walk so close behind Melba that she abraded her heel with every step. Another student spat in her face. During gym, one girl aimed a volleyball and threw it hard at her head. She learned to dart through pencils and other objects thrown down the stairwells at her. Her locker would be broken into, everything in it shredded, thrown on the floor, or covered in ink. Sometimes someone in the hall would come close to her and spray the clothes she was wearing too with ink. But occasionally, even in the beginning, the attacks were more dangerous. In one class before the teacher came in, a white girl poked Melba and punctured her back with the sharp tip of a small metal pole holding a miniature Confederate flag.

Though after the attack she was bleeding, Melba decided not to report this event to the principal's office. What the best strategy might be was never clear. Most often when one of the nine reported an attack, the school officials would belittle the offense, or dismiss the report for lack of evidence, claiming there would have to be a witness for any disciplinary action to be taken. And then again, there would be the fear, one all children who are bullied share, that if they tell on the bully, the attacks will only grow worse. So Melba went alone to the bathroom to wash her wound.

But the bathroom was a dangerous place too. Though for the first months, the soldiers from the 101st accompanied each of the nine children as they walked through the halls, they did not enter the classrooms where a teacher would be in attendance. If usually the teachers did not prevent hostility, they could not allow outright violence. But the soldiers could not go into the bathrooms either, a place where there was no supervision at all. So on one occasion, when Melba was sitting in a stall, she suddenly smelled smoke and realized that the girls outside were setting fire to paper towels and throwing them down at her. When she tried to get out, she found she was trapped. Some of the girls were holding the door shut. Dodging flames and coughing from the smoke, she reached frantically for her books, and began to throw them on their heads. This sent her attackers running, but afterward Melba tried to avoid the bathroom.

When, after just two months, right before Thanksgiving break, the federal troops were removed from the school, the violence increased. As soon as the guards left, the segregationist students began to pass out cards reading "Open Season on Coons." The idea that things were likely to get worse than they already were must have been chilling. One day as she approached her homeroom, Melba found a doll fashioned to look like her hanging from the doorframe. Where before one boy or girl would walk on her heels, now whole groups followed Melba this way, until her ankles were bleeding. The segregationist students became so brazen they even began to hurl rotten eggs near the principal's office.

In this period, Melba wrote in her journal that one of her goals was simply to stay alive until the end of the semester. This was not a metaphor. In the locker room one day, some of the girls forced her to stand under scalding water in the shower. On another day, as she stood in the hallway in front of her locker, she heard a noise. Turning, she put her hand up to her face to ward off an object flying toward her. It was one of several firecrackers wired together. Her hand was burned, but she was glad it was not her face.

Another day when Melba was tripped in the hall and fell to her knees, a group of boys set about hitting and kicking her with such force that later she coughed up blood. On still another occasion, while she was walking from one class to another, a student sprayed acid in her face.

Had she not flooded her eyes with water immediately, she might have lost her sight, and as it was, it took her several weeks to fully recover.

When you are subjected to danger over a longer period of time, fear starts to pervade every moment. You will never be able to relax completely. You will always be looking for signs of danger or trying to plan what you should do to survive. Dreams, casual desires, reflections or ideas, insights into others and even into your own feelings, all diminish, cede their place in consciousness immediately and without question to thoughts about the danger you face. You will go over what has been done to you and what might be done in the future almost compulsively and with an equal compulsion repeat various plans you have made, all hinging on how to escape unharmed and sustain yourself through a series of disasters that seems to have no end.

You may know or at least expect that it will all be over someday, but this seems like such a faraway prospect, so abstract and pale compared to how you are living, on the edge, like a runner perpetually at the start of a race, your adrenaline always high, ready. And at the same time, you will have forgotten what it was like to be free of fear. Though you will be able to remember days when you were not afraid, you will not be able to remember how it felt, that sense of calm and comfort. Somewhere inside, though you do not admit it to yourself, you are convinced you will never feel safe again in your life.

And there is this too: rage is the constant companion of fear. In the spring, as the violence began to accelerate, Melba came close to breaking down. "I'm so angry, I'm afraid it's going to well up and explode," Melba told her grandmother. "Not likely," said her grandmother, who remained calm herself in the face of what must have been her own considerable fear. It was then that she told her granddaughter to read Gandhi. What Melba learned from him would save her more than once.

Courage takes many different forms. At the frayed end of her resolve not to fight back, as she was sitting alone and feeling vulnerable in the large, unsupervised cafeteria at the end of a lunch period, when a boy from a group of hecklers approached her, Melba bent her head into her book, which happened to be Gandhi's prison diaries. "Niggers are stupid, they gotta study real hard, don't they?" he said to her. To which she responded, "Thank you," keeping a pleasant expression on her face. It was a powerful paradox she posed to the boy; she had stepped outside the parameters of the game he was playing and by this move won back her dignity. When her tormentor answered with a threat—"You got to leave this place sometime, and then we got you"—she answered by saying thank you again, and smiled. Confounded, the boy walked away.

Among the many corrosive effects of abuse is a hardened anger that can turn to hatred. It is another hazard to your soul, a way you can lose yourself, be taken prisoner and invaded by your abuser, even in your deepest thoughts and emotions. Thus those who are oppressed often develop an extraordinary skill. They learn how to walk the thin line that is drawn between denial and soul-crushing obedience on the one hand and devouring rage on the other.

This was not a skill the white segregationist children had developed. They failed to realize that by what they did, they were imprisoning themselves too. The hatred that they expressed did not belong to them. Heirs to the contorted psychology of racism, they had been schooled in a practice of unknowing, a studied ignorance, by which elements of the self are projected onto others. "The nigger" they feared and excoriated so much was not only an aspect of the racist imagination but an image of themselves, secret and reviled, the product of a veiled but deeply entrenched self-hatred that they had learned along with their hatred of others.

MAY

Recalcitrant to the last, Bush has vetoed the bill sent by both houses mandating that the withdrawal of troops begin by October.

Over half a century later, it is astonishing to think that their parents would not only condone what these children did but also teach them to do it. Even if they had little concern for the welfare of the African-American children, they seemed unaware of the consequences that proceed from committing any violent act. What happened inside each of these boys and girls, as they hit and spit at, burned, and heckled and threatened? I can easily imagine an inner conflict, a battle waged at times between the desire to conform to the wishes of parents and friends, and another impulse welling up toward this other in whom they might find a mirror of themselves unexpectedly, feeling kindness or even recognition. In denying the impulse, they would have silenced the subtle intelligence inside themselves with the same brutal terror that they aimed outward.

What is lost in any such bargain is self-knowledge. When you are hiding from yourself, reflection can be dangerous. Melba, who was acutely aware of the changes she suffered in herself, could write in her journal, "Only the warrior exists in me now. Melba went away to hide. She was too frightened to stay here." But her tormentors could not allow themselves so much insight into who they were becoming. They must have had moments of doubt. But a mind captivated by a fixed idea such as racism cannot tolerate incertitude. Indeed anyone who questions or argues with such a dogma will be perceived as the author of doubt itself, an enemy who is all the more dangerous since his or her doubt mirrors an inner doubt the true believer has felt and tried to repress.

The few whites who helped the nine children understood that if they defended them openly, they would be targeted too. Though she intervened when she could, Mrs. Huckaby, the girls' vice principal, was cautious. She did not state publicly that she approved of integration. Even so, because she had suspended Sammie Dean Parker, one of the ringleaders of the assaults, Sammie, together with her mother, set upon Mrs. Huckaby, grabbing her glasses off her face, threatening to hit her. And there was a white boy who helped Melba more than once. He loved his nanny, the black woman who had raised him, and this allowed him to see beyond the racism he had been taught. But he too was careful never to be seen at the high school speaking in a friendly way with Melba.

There were some among the white students who realized later that they had done wrong. One, Hazel Bryan, a close friend of Sammie Dean Parker, was right behind Elizabeth Eckford during her terrifying walk past the Arkansas National Guard, which had prevented her from entering the high school. You can see her face, contorted with rage, in the photograph Ira Wilmer Counts took of Eckford's courageous walk that has become an icon of American history. Perhaps it was that photograph that helped Hazel to realize that she had done something terribly wrong. It was a reflection she had to live with for a long time. Five years later, she would apologize to Elizabeth Eckford. And on the fortieth anniversary of the event, she did so publicly. The two women formed a friendship afterward and began to give lectures together in the service of civil rights.

Both hatred and fear are isolating; they create seemingly impassable distances between us, building hierarchies of being that undermine equality. To survive, democracy requires the equality it promises, not just because it is a basic principle but also because equality sustains the process. I am thinking now of Hannah Arendt's idea that "the trustworthy company of equals" is a precursor to every kind of understanding. Without it, she writes, "self and world, capacity for thought and experience are lost at the same time," and along with this, I would add, the insight that is needed by citizens who are participating in self-governance.

MAY

Sense of defeat some feel after the president's veto. Many are saying that it doesn't matter what the people want, that we no longer have a real democracy.

Yet if equality is to be achieved, the only remedy is courage. It seems fitting that democracy, which was won with courage, would be sustained by it too. This was another great legacy that the civil rights movement gave to the nation, one example after another of stunning bravery. Such courage cannot be contained. It ripples out in every direction, feeding tributaries that move in unpredictable directions. It was not just a deeper understanding of equality I was given by the civil rights movement. Because the courage I witnessed became part of me, I was able to change my own life.

In the late sixties, following the example of the civil rights movement, a different kind of courage arose in women. We were not battling bullets or attack dogs. Yet, on a more subtle level, we were also facing considerable fear. Over time, we came to see that the same intricate system that sustained us was also destroying us from the inside out. Many of the injunctions against us were not as blatant as the violence that was perpetrated by segregationists. But the signs telling a woman she is inferior and warning her to stay in her place were ubiquitous, from demeaning jokes to the clothing she was urged to wear, the absence of her own sex from certain histories or professions, and even, if she married, the erasure of her name. Such expressions of prejudice, many of which, after all, often come from family members, husbands, lovers, and even sons, engender a particular kind of fear. Amorphous, partially concealed, wrapped in habitual routines, hidden by depression or bitterness, this trepidation may seem less urgent but, as a means of control, it is no less effective. If some women had been beaten by their husbands or raped by strangers, sexually abused or harassed, many of us suffered a less visible but insidious fate, a collapse of self-confidence, a failure to own our own thoughts and perceptions, a denial of the disappointment and anger we felt, as through our silence we collaborated with our oppression. A line from the poet Muriel Rukeyser seemed to predict both our fears and what was about to occur despite them. "What would happen, if one woman told the truth about her life?" she asked, and before answering, "The world would split open."

Now, against every prohibition and personal risk, we began to tell the truth. We were well aware that had any of us done this alone, we might have been ostracized, called mad, or even incarcerated. But we were not alone. The earliest and most lasting strategy of the movement for women's liberation was to meet. And the meetings we attended were not designed simply to plan political actions. They were powerful, catalytic events in themselves.

Since the earliest days, when the founders of the American Revolution met at the Raleigh Tavern, it has been crucial to the workings of democracy to gather and discuss common causes. Such meetings are necessary so that different goals and opinions can be aired and negotiated. But over and above practical needs, meetings also summon up the courage to stand by the truth. This is especially true whenever fear is used to intimidate. Where terror produces segmentation and even enmity within a community, meeting allows diverse people to confront the fears they share as one body.

MAY

Story about a seventeen-year-old girl in a village in Northern Iraq stoned to death, probably because she was a Yazidi, in love with a Sunni boy. Many reports saying life for women in Iraq has become so much worse since the 2003 invasion.

The meetings we held were different from all the political gatherings I had participated in before. They were kept small so that every woman would have time to speak and no one would be intimidated by a crowd. For the same reason, we rejected the procedures of *Robert's Rules of Order,* which had given me so much comfort as a child. We were not debating so much as revealing ourselves to one another. Instead, we formed circles and went around the circle until every woman had spoken. Because we wanted to protect what were new and still fragile insights into the nature of our lives, taking a page again from the civil rights movement, which had been excluding whites from certain organizations, we excluded men from these meetings. This created a safer atmosphere for more intimate disclosures. Just as we had done in friendships all our lives, as the trust grew among us, women could acknowledge things we had never said before, admitting unhappiness in a marriage, exhaustion with child rearing, disappointments at work.

Even the atmosphere itself was revealing. Though we had gathered socially without men before in kitchens and living rooms, few of us had had the experience of entering serious discussions exclusively with women. While not all women are adept at relationship, most women have been socialized to be better and more sensitive listeners than men. Most of us have been taught how to encourage expression and to read the subtler terrain of feelings. As the theologian Nelle Morton wrote of this process, *We heard each other into speech.*

JUNE

Hundreds of corpses of men kidnapped, tortured, and killed by warring militias being found all over Baghdad. The great irony is that we were supposed to bring democracy to Iraq, not terror.

We began to question the notion that analytical thought is superior to sensual and emotional knowledge. Though I was rarely intimidated in debates with men and could think and speak analytically, these meetings opened me to new understandings within myself that many of the logical arguments I had learned had served to hide. By validating emotional insights—fragments of perception that seemed like fleeting shadows, vague impressions, feelings at the border of awareness—we were reclaiming ourselves. Since so many of us had a high quotient in what Daniel Goleman has called emotional intelligence, in the reason of the heart that reason fails to understand, we began to look now at the way women think, a manner for which many of us had been ridiculed, as less a liability than a strength.

The transformation was alchemical. A stunning lucidity arose, almost as if by magic, from the stark discomfort and pain we expressed. The resonance was so thick it was almost palpable. As woman after woman reclaimed her voice, we were giving the right of assembly a new meaning. But of course it was not the revelation of secrets or the expression of feelings by themselves that was transformative. As we spoke and listened, we were bringing a new framework to the discussion. Suddenly we could delineate a political meaning linking our stories together. We realized how many subjects considered personal had political significance. We began to see that even the trivialization of our concerns was a political act, depriving us of dignity and insight. One by one, as our secrets were revealed, a new picture of our lives was emerging, and with this a new way of seeing society. As we placed our own lives and the issues we faced at the center of the national debate, we were creating a new vision of the entire political landscape.

JUNE

It may be that what we need to preserve democracy in America is to extend respect and compassion beyond our own borders.

The women's movement would go on to question the categories of both masculinity and femininity, exploring the ways that they confine the minds of men and women alike. Among the most lasting contributions we made to the common ground of consciousness was to augment and refine the concept of the meeting. It remains an important gift to democracy as it is practiced throughout America, in and out of government. Instead of acting simply as arenas for debate, with the practice of breaking larger assemblies into smaller groups, and allowing everyone present to say something about her (or his) life, meetings have encouraged a deeper level of connection between all the participants and at the same time have become more democratic.

Accepting and knowing the self does not end with the self but moves, in a natural arc of development, toward others. If democracy arose from a new vision of reality, in turn self-government leads to a democracy of visions. When other women mirrored back to me what I felt and perceived, I could place myself in the story and see with my own eyes. As a small girl, when I had tried to write a novel about war and the project failed, the problem had not been that I made the protagonist a man but that I had rejected my own angle of vision. Decades later, I would be able to write about war again as a woman. And when I stood on my own ground, I found that I could also imagine myself as a soldier, as a girl who was abused and the man who abused her, as a boy and a girl trying to survive an atomic explosion and as the pilot who flew the plane that dropped the bomb.

Only now can I see that this has all proceeded from the way my father talked with me that day in the kitchen when I was just short of six years old and angry because I could not join my sister. He did not try to talk me out of what I felt. But he gave me the chance to see my sister's point of view too. And with this gift, he was offering me not only reason but participation, a way I could play a role in the larger decisions that were to affect the course my life took.

And as I ask now who I would have become had there been no movement for women's rights, because that movement sprang from the movements for abolition and civil rights, I wonder too who would I be were it not for these histories? Thomas Jefferson and Jefferson Thomas, Sally Hemings, John Muir and Ralph Waldo Emerson, Major Ridge, Rose Schneiderman, Jelly Roll Morton, Allen Ginsberg, Angelina Grimké, Rosa Parks, Melba Patillo Beals. Countless lives have shaped my life. Were it not for American democracy, including all its flaws and failures, I cannot imagine being who I am today.

JUNE

It is perhaps what democracy is in the end: a meeting. It is a metaphor too for the turning point we have reached now, a crossroads between fear and understanding. What will we do in the twenty-first century as we face the choice?

6

ROUND

June 2007

The vice president's former chief of staff, Lewis Libby, has been sentenced to thirty months in prison for obstruction of justice, perjury, and lying to federal officials.

WHEN I WAS YOUNG, I was taught that what we called then the "discovery" of America led to the understanding that the world is round.

Everyone fears that Bush will pardon him. Hoping against hope that doesn't happen. Why? I want to see at least one of the men who planned and sold this war behind bars.

The notion was popularized in a novel written by Washington Irving in 1828 called *The Life and Voyages of Christopher Columbus*. But in the public mind, it served a larger mythology; the "discovery" of the Americas symbolized a new vision, a modern view of reality inspired by geographical and scientific discoveries.

Yet even more than seeing anyone behind bars I'd like to see a repudiation of the policy and the thinking that led to the war. It's so often treated in the media as if the Libby case revolved around issues of character alone. But so much more is at stake here. The grand plan, in which Libby's perjury played a minor role, has been riddled with deception.

But the fact that the world has a spherical shape had been known in Europe since the first century. Ptolemy drew his maps from a curved globe.

There is the lie, for instance, that led to Libby's perjury, the contention that Iraq bought uranium from Niger, which was used as evidence that Iraq had nuclear weapons and thus to justify the war. And then there was the absurd contention that Saddam Hussein was in league with Al Qaeda and thus tied to the terrorist attacks on 9/11.

What did surprise Columbus, however, was to find something beyond the curve of the earth that had not been seen before. At that time, it was believed in Europe that everything on earth was already known.

But the biggest lie has been the continual claim of omniscience and infallibility.

I imagine it would be comforting to believe that you or your king or queen knows everything in the world there is to know. This is why Galileo was imprisoned after proving Copernicus's theory that the earth travels around the sun. In demonstrating this, he was also showing the fallibility of the church.

In this vein, I suspect all the lies are part of a larger psychological state. The neocons and the group that planned the war have fallen under the spell of a fixed idea. And when such an obsession occupies the mind, no evidence to the contrary makes any difference. Reality ceases to matter. Or rather the idea becomes the only reality.

In his preamble to the *Diario,* the journal kept by Christopher Columbus from 1492 to 1493, during his first voyage to America, he addresses the volume to the "Most Christian and Very Noble and Very Excellent and Very Powerful Princes, King and Queen of Spain and of the islands of the Sea." The language seems preposterously pompous to us today. But in that period, it would have been crucial for a monarch to create the impression of omnipotence as well as omniscience. It is by creating the illusion of power that such displays actually maintain power.

And there is this too driving the disaster, since the followers of every fixed idea are driven by unconscious fears, a strong element of the irrational.

But clearly the King and Queen of Spain did not know everything. That was why Christopher Columbus sailed west. The Spanish monarchs hoped the great navigator might be able to find a new route to India.

It must be a formidable fear that is driving this plan. It is based on so many unreasonable assumptions, even logical contradictions, the notion that democracy can be imposed on anyone by force.

There were many reasons for this search. Violence had broken out between Christians and Muslims along the shifting borders between the east and the west, which to some degree hindered trade. And though the Ottoman Turks, who occupied Constantinople and much of Asia Minor, wanted and allowed trade to continue, they were levying expensive tolls.

A fixed idea also creates a false sense of safety. In this bargain, thought is replaced by belief, logic by allegiance. So in this state of mind, to invade and occupy another nation can be perceived as a form of self-defense.

Then there was the prospect of being able to trade exotic products; things that are hard to get become more valuable. The Portuguese had already found a way to sail east around Africa. Despite victory against the Moors in Granada, in the late fifteenth century Spain was losing the battle over commerce.

In fact the original lie, that the White House could prove Iraq was building weapons of mass destruction, has a chilling internal consistency. The grand plan the neoconservatives designed, which they called the New World Order, hinged on occupying Iraq. Thus the true believers would have seen the war as necessary to survival.

And there would have been other motives too, less material, the general malaise Europe suffered in this period. Waves of the plague still striking various cities. Famine. The church corrupt. A widespread belief that the world was coming to an end. And the need simply to be able to draw a more impressive map of Spain's possessions.

It is a great psychological temptation. To hope and even believe that all misfortune, loss, death, or any form of evil can be mastered by one idea, one grand plan, in the hands of one infallible leader.

None of these however are among the stated purposes of the voyage. In the preamble to the *Diario,* after praising the king's victory over the followers of Muhammad and the expulsion of the Jews from Spain, Columbus announces the reason for his journey to India was to "see the said princes and peoples of the lands ... and to see how their conversion to our Holy Faith might be undertaken."

> *Democracy, of course, requires another psychology altogether. To doubt, question, reason, to criticize leaders. And along with this to accept the unpredictable nature of life on earth.*

And in that regard there is this too. In one of the letters he had written to Isabella a few years before his voyage, Columbus promised that with the great profits he expected to bring back from his voyage he would take Jerusalem back from the Muslims.

> *It seems hopeful to see the approval for the president drop so far in the polls for more than one reason. Perhaps democracy is reviving now, at least in the capacity among citizens to place an inner sense of authority above loyalty to any leader.*

While I was still a child, whenever I imagined Columbus discovering America, I pictured him as startled and amazed, as if he knew immediately what he had found.

> *The real issue concerning character in this case is that Libby did not think for himself, that he was a follower and did not question the orders he was given but instead placed loyalty above ethics or even a respect for the law.*

But Columbus cannot see past what he has been taught. He does not realize where he is when he approaches the Bahamas. He does not know yet that the Americas constitute a separate continent. He thinks of this land as the easternmost portion of Asia.

> *Despite all the neoconservative rhetoric about democracy, Libby's behavior was more like that of a courtier in the court of King George III than an American citizen.*

The first sight that tells the sailors they are close to land is a white bird, which they recognize as tropical. Columbus takes this as a message from God.

> *The same can be said of the soldiers who tortured prisoners of war at Abu Ghraib, who did what they were told instead of what they knew to be right, morally and legally.*

Columbus tells us almost nothing about what he thought or felt when his ships landed. Perhaps this is because he knows so little. Uncertainty is difficult for anyone, much less a commander, and certainly not a state of mind one would want to convey to a monarch.

> *Reports now in the news of suspicions that the CIA taught military personnel abusive tactics of interrogation. All this goes on secretly, in subterranean realms, the undermining of democracy at home.*

Throughout his account of his exploration Columbus records his sense of marvel. There are so many kinds of trees, they are the most beautiful he has ever seen, he says. The air is so full of birdsong that this too is a marvel. The valleys so green, the fruit so plentiful, the fertility wondrous, he reports.

Perhaps because he is afraid of offending the king and queen, Columbus is careful to add that the verdure reminds him of the beauty of Andalusia. And then there must have been his own desire to remind himself of home, if not Andalusia, certainly southern Europe. He notes finding a fish that can be found in the Mediterranean, and trees that are well known to him. Again and again you can almost feel him reach out for the touch of the familiar.

> *Now it seems that Vice President Cheney too knew all about the torture and not only authorized but was in of favor it.*

On October 12, 1492, Columbus and his crew row ashore. He carries the official banner of the king and queen, and his captains carry two flags with green crosses. He asks those who have come ashore to bear witness that he has taken possession of the island for Spain and that he had made all the required declarations.

> *There are some who have stood up to authority, among them General Taguba who reported on "numerous incidents of sadistic, blatant and wanton criminal abuses . . . systemic and illegal" committed at Abu Ghraib.*

When the inhabitants of the island come to greet him, Columbus gives them small gifts, red caps and glass beads. He is impressed by their gentle manners, and later will note their effective method of agriculture.

> *At one point during the investigation he conducted, Taguba had the uncomfortable feeling that Rumsfeld and the Department of Defense*

were more worried about his efforts to reveal the torture than the torture itself. As he put it, "I'm now the problem." In fact he was soon given a minor assignment and then forced into early retirement.

Though the indigenous people Columbus meets in the Bahamas are actually called the Taino, still laboring under the illusion that he has reached Asia, he calls them "Indians."

Libby's lawyers have petitioned the courts to delay the time when he will begin serving his sentence.

When Columbus leaves he captures a few of the Taino men and takes them home with him as slaves.

The evasion of justice finds an inner ally in denial. Libby does not want to admit his guilt. Nor do we as a nation really want to face the implications of the fact that we have been torturing prisoners.

On his way home Columbus writes to Ferdinand and Isabella boasting of the "great mines of gold," the spices and aloes and cotton and "a thousand other things" that promise great profit and an endless stream of trade.

An article today claims that Libby, together with Cheney's lawyer, David Addington, actually physically cornered another man, as yet unnamed, who was an opponent of war and proceeded to intimidate and threaten him. Perhaps Libby is less a follower than a true believer. Though, these roles go together. The true believer is usually loyal to his leader. It's all of a piece. The fixed idea in the face of any evidence to the contrary, the brutalization of anyone who does not agree.

In the same letter Columbus describes the Taino as having a "keen intelligence," adding that they are simple and untainted, artless and free with their possessions, and that "they all go naked as their mother bore them."

Slowly the public is becoming aware of what we have been doing to the men we imprisoned at Guantánamo, too. They have been labeled "enemy combatants," which means that when they are questioned, they will supposedly not be protected by the Geneva Conventions that prohibit torture.

But despite his admiration, because Columbus's promises have put him under a great deal of pressure, on his second voyage he will force every

Taino man over the age of fourteen into slave labor, panning for gold. If any man fails to produce the ration of gold required, Columbus has commanded that his hands be cut off.

Whatever you do to others will always come home.

Contrary to what I was told when I was a child, Columbus was not the first European to reach America. But because he recorded the latitude and longitude as he went, his voyage would make it possible for others to come after him. This is the real significance of his accomplishment. His journey begins a round of voyages, conquests in which European nations would colonize and exploit the continent's resources and people.

> *Now the U.S. Court of Appeals for the Fourth Circuit, a very conservative court, has ruled against the notion that one of the prisoners at Guantánamo, a resident of Qatar, can be held as an "enemy combatant." The decision has great significance both for those who are being held as prisoners without charge and for American democracy, in which the right of habeas corpus is crucial.*

In still another voyage, Columbus finally begins to realize where he is.

> *Judge Walton has denied Libby's appeal to delay his sentence. This is small but still it feels like another victory. Some small measure of justice.*

As he goes ashore in a place called Paria, in what is now Venezuela, he finds a large stream, which can only flow from a large landmass. This must be a continent he tells himself. *I must have found a new continent.*

> *A new justification for continuing the war launched this week. Just as he leaves office, the chair of the Joint Chiefs of Staff, General Peter Pace, argues that we are using the wrong metric to determine whether or not the war is successful. He claims that the right measure for success is not the number who are dying but whether or not the Iraqi people feel more optimistic about their future.*

How does he take such a discovery into himself? How will he fit something so large into the map he carries in his mind?

> *The general's argument leaves me speechless. I do not know where to begin. Is he not capable of imagining what it would be like to try to*

conduct a life or raise children in the midst of unceasing violence? To
live with the constant threat of danger and continual loss, a husband,
a wife, a child, killed or injured, the loss of an arm or a leg, your eye-
sight, your home.

At one point Columbus tells himself that what he has found must be the
earthly paradise described in scriptures, the area supposed to exist just
beyond the Garden of Eden.

It is well over four years ago now, since the generals started to talk
about how they would attack Iraq with a plan called "Shock and
Awe." They spoke of a massive bombing campaign they would aim at
Baghdad. Even to hear this idea was chilling.

Either from this speculation or simply disorientation, his journals become incoherent for a period, a babbling mixture of theory, religious
zeal, speculation, fantasy, hope, and bombast.

The plans to attack Baghdad were couched in a strange tone of unre-
ality, as if there would be no people under those bombs.

Columbus will regain his equilibrium. Though he was accused of atrocities during his reign as governor of the colony and sent back to Spain
in chains, he would be released and allowed to conduct a fourth voyage
before he retired, a wealthy man.

Demonstrations against the war were occurring everywhere, in Lon-
don, Rome, Madrid, New York, Washington, and here, across the bay
in San Francisco where the trains were so crowded with demonstra-
tors they finally had to let us all ride for free.

But the condition of Columbus's soul when he first apprehended what
he had seen will prove contagious.

As so many came out to protest, hundreds of thousands in New York,
Washington, and San Francisco, a million in Rome and London, I
began to hope the war might be prevented.

As Columbus's journals are published, and books by other explorers and
commentators follow, European culture is flooded with excitement
about the unknown realms that lie to the west.

Yet the president and his administration seemed indifferent to the
massive public response.

At the beginning of the sixteenth century, Pietro Martire publishes a book called *De Orbe Novo,* making the phrase "the New World" popular.

On International Women's Day, March 8 of 2003, just before the war began, I went to Washington, D.C., to speak at a rally and join a march to Lafayette Park, just in front of the White House.

As various explorers bring back descriptions of the freedom they observe in the Indians in America and the new forms of government they practice based on greater equality, the subjects of European monarchies begin to dream of freedom and equality for themselves.

Those who spoke at the rally, many of us writers, walked in the front of the parade, which stretched out more than a mile through the capital.

In 1611 at Whitehall a play called *The Tempest* is performed before the king of England. "O brave new world!" a character called Miranda declares, "that has such people in't." The play shows the clear influence of accounts of the founding of Jamestown.

But when we reached the park, we discovered it was surrounded by a police barricade. For the first time in American history, demonstrators were prohibited from entering the public area in front of the White House.

Meanwhile in Virginia, the seeds for another story are being sown as Pocahontas rescues Captain John Smith from her father's wrath.

"Will we risk arrest and cross the barricades?" the organizers ask us. Yes, I say, almost without hesitation. It is not so much an impulse I follow, as it is a state of mind that propels me, one that has evolved within me over most of my life.

The story of a love affair between Captain Smith and Pocahontas will captivate the American imagination for years to come. The romance is symbolic.

For several hours, as we stand in front of the fence that encloses the White House lawn, swaying, singing, various police officers come to threaten us with arrest. And all the time we are there we can see the silhouette of a soldier of the roof of the White House.

It evokes the struggle within the American consciousness that continues even today. The erotic pull between these two, a mirror of an inner conflict, the woman we have imagined to be a noble savage, the Englishman, drawn to his own natural desires, who wants to be free and equal, and yet is pulled in another direction: his ambition, loyalty to his monarch.

> *The soldier carried a high-powered long-range rifle. And from time to time he would stop and aim this weapon down at us. It would make sense to feel powerless at such a moment. But strangely I did not feel that at all, not even when they finally put handcuffs on us and took us all to jail.*

There is the white bird Columbus saw. A sign of hope. And then there is the white whale.

> *Of course we were not able to stop the war. And even now, though the great majority of the public is opposed to it, the violence only increases while democracy seems to diminish.*

The captain who fell in love and the captain who doomed himself and his ship with his desire for revenge.

JULY

> *Lewis Libby was ordered to begin serving his sentence immediately today. But just a few hours later, the president commuted his sentence.*

Even now we are wrestling with the angel of democracy.

> *Which direction will we choose? I cannot say. No one knows.*

> *No one can possibly know.*

BIBLIOGRAPHY

I am not a historian, nor is this book a history, yet I relied on the research of many other scholars, historians, and curators. I want to thank the Tenement Museum in New York and the New York Historical Society (for the exhibit, Slavery in New York) and the Women's Rights National Historical Park in Seneca Falls. The primary sources I made use of include Thomas Jefferson's *Autobiography*, his *Notes on the State of Virginia* and other writings, and his correspondence; Emerson's essays and his journals; John Muir's books; recordings made by Jelly Roll Morton and recordings of the interviews with him conducted by Alan Lomax; a lecture by the dancer Frankie Manning; and the documentary *That's What Swingin' Is*, filmed by Robert Albers and Amol Pavangadkar, featuring a jazz master class taught by Wynton Marsalis. Beyond these, the books that were most helpful to me are listed below.

CHAPTER ONE

Alfred Owen Aldridge. *Franklin and His French Contemporaries*. New York: New York University Press, 1957.

Bernard Bailyn. *To Begin the World Anew: The Genius and Ambiguities of the American Founders*. New York: Vintage, 2003.

William L. Beiswanger, Peter J. Hatch, Lucia Stanton, and Susan Stein. *Thomas Jefferson's Monticello*. Chapel Hill: Thomas Jefferson Foundation with the University of North Carolina Press, 2002.

R. B. Bernstein. *Thomas Jefferson*. Oxford: Oxford University Press, 2003.

Natalie S. Bober. *Thomas Jefferson: Man on a Mountain*. New York: Simon & Schuster, 1997.

Claude G. Bowers. *The Young Jefferson 1743–1789*. New York: Houghton Mifflin, 1945, 1969.

Noble E. Cunningham Jr. *In Pursuit of Reason: The Life of Thomas Jefferson*. New York: Ballantine, 1987.

Phillip Dray. *Stealing God's Thunder: Benjamin Franklin's Lightning Rod and the Invention of America*. New York: Random House, 2005.

Joseph J. Ellis. *American Sphinx: The Character of Thomas Jefferson*. New York: Vintage, 1998.

Jay Fliegelman. *Declaring Independence. Jefferson, Natural Language, and the Culture of Performance.* Stanford: Stanford University Press, 1993.

Eric Foner. *Tom Paine and the Revolutionary America.* Oxford: Oxford University Press, 1977.

Terry Golway. *Washington's General: Nathanael Green and the Triumph of the American Revolution.* New York: Henry Holt, 2005.

E. M. Halliday. *Understanding Thomas Jefferson.* New York: Harper Perennial, 2002.

Christopher Hitchens. *Thomas Jefferson: Author of America.* New York: Harper-Collins, 2005.

Richard M. Ketchum. *Victory at Yorktown: The Campaign That Won the Revolution.* New York: Henry Holt, 2004.

Jan Ellen Lewis and Peter S. Onuf, eds. *Sally Hemings and Thomas Jefferson: History, Memory, and Civic Culture.* Charlottesville: University of Virginia Press, 1999.

David McCullough. *1776.* New York: Simon & Schuster, 2005.

Dorinda Outram. *The Enlightenment.* Cambridge: Cambridge University Press, 1995.

Alexis de Tocqueville. *Democracy in America.* New York: Alfred A. Knopf, 1994.

David Watkin. *The Architect King: George III and the Culture of the Enlightenment.* London: Royal Collection Publications, 2006.

Gordon S. Wood. *The Radicalism of the American Revolution.* New York: Vintage, 1991.

CHAPTER TWO

Henry Adams. *History of the United States (1801–1817).* New York: Library of America, 1986.

Carlos Baker. *Emerson Among the Eccentrics: A Group Portrait.* New York: Penguin, 1996.

H. W. Brands. *The Age of Gold: The California Gold Rush and the New American Dream.* New York: Doubleday, 2002.

Edward S. Casey. *Representing Place: Landscape Painting and Maps.* Minneapolis: University of Minnesota Press, 2002.

Susan Cheever. *American Bloomsbury: Louisa May Alcott, Ralph Waldo Emerson, Margaret Fuller, Nathaniel Hawthorne, and Henry David Thoreau: Their Lives, Their Loves, Their Work.* New York: Simon & Schuster, 2006.

Vine Deloria Jr., et al., eds. *Spirit and Reason: The Vine Deloria, Jr., Reader.* Golden, Colo.: Fulcrum Publications, 1999.

John Ehle. *Trail of Tears: The Rise and Fall of the Cherokee Nation.* New York: Anchor Books, 1989.

Bonnie Johanna Gisel, ed. *Kindred and Related Spirits: The Letters of John Muir and Jeanne C. Carr.* Salt Lake City: University of Utah Press, 2001.

Kenneth L. Holmes, ed. *Covered Wagon Women: Diaries and Letters from the Western Trails, 1840–1849.* Lincoln, Neb.: University of Nebraska Press, 1995.

Helen Hunt Jackson. *A Century of Dishonor: The Classic Exposé of the Plight of the Native Americans*. Mineola, N.Y.: Dover, 2003.

Gloria Jahoda. *The Trail of Tears: The Story of the American Indian Removals, 1813–1855*. New York: Wings Books, 1995.

Jerry Mander. *In the Absence of the Sacred: The Failure of Technology and the Survival of the Indian Nations*. San Francisco: Sierra Club Books, 1992.

Wilma Mankiller and Micheal Wallis. *Mankiller: A Chief and Her People*. New York: St. Martin's Griffin, 1999.

Sally M. Miller, ed. *John Muir: Life and Work*. Albuquerque: University of New Mexico Press, 1993.

Gary B. Nash. *The Unknown American Revolution: The Unruly Birth of Democracy and the Struggle to Create America*. New York: Viking, 2006.

Robert D. Richardon Jr. *Emerson: The Mind on Fire*. Berkeley: University of California Press, 1996.

Michael Paul Rogin. *Subversive Genealogy: The Politics and Art of Herman Melville*. Berkeley: University of California Press, 1985.

Vicki Rozema. *Voices from the Trail of Tears*. Winston-Salem: John F. Blair, 2003)

Lillian Schlissel. *Women's Diaries of the Westward Journey*. New York: Schocken Books, 1992.

Thomas Bryan Underwood. *Cherokee Legends and the Trail of Tears*. Cherokee, N.C.: Cherokee Publications, 2002.

Howard Zinn. *A People's History of the United States: 1492–Present*. New York: Harper Perennial, 2005.

CHAPTER THREE

Paul Buhle and David Wagner. *Radical Hollywood: The Untold Story Behind America's Favorite Movies*. New York: The New Press, 2002.

Blanche Wiesen Cook. *Eleanor Roosevelt: Volume 1, 1884–1933*. New York: Viking, 1992.

David von Drehle. *Triangle: The Fire that Changed America*. New York: Grove Press, 2004.

Benita Eisler, ed. *The Lowell Offering: Writings by New England Mill Women (1840–1845)*. New York: Harper Colophon, 1977.

David Halberstam. *The Fifties*. New York: Villard Books, 1993.

Eric Homberger. *Mrs. Astor's New York: Money and Social Power in a Gilded Age*. New Haven: Yale University Press, 2002.

Theresa S. Malkiel. *The Diary of a Shirtwaist Striker*. Ithaca, N.Y.: Cornell University Press, 1990.

Bill Morgan and Nancy J. Peters, eds. *Howl on Trial: The Battle for Free Expression*. San Francisco: City Lights Books, 2006.

Jacob A. Riis. *How the Other Half Lives*. New York: Penguin Classics, 1997.

Rose Schneiderman with Lucy Goldthwaite. *All for One*. New York: Paul S. Eriksson, 1967.

Leon Stein. *The Triangle Fire*. Ithaca, N.Y.: Cornell University Press, 1962.

James Sullivan. *Jeans: A Cultural History of an American Icon.* New York: Gotham Books, 2006.

Bruce Watson. *Bread and Roses: Mills, Migrants and the Struggle for the American Dream.* New York: Penguin Books, 2006.

CHAPTER FOUR

Miles Davis with Quincy Troupe. *Miles: The Autobiography.* New York: Simon & Schuster, 1989.

Ralph Ellison. *Living with Music: Ralph Ellison's Jazz Writings.* Robert G. O'Meally, ed. New York: Modern Library, 2002.

Samuel A. Floyd Jr. *The Power of Black Music: Interpreting Its History from Africa to the United States.* New York: Oxford University Press (USA), 1996.

Henry Louis Gates Jr. *The Trials of Phillis Wheatley.* New York: Basic Civitas, 2003.

Ashley Kahn. *Kind of Blue: The Making of the Miles Davis Masterpiece.* Cambridge, Mass.: Da Capo Press, 2001.

Bill Kirchner, ed. *The Oxford Companion to Jazz.* New York: Oxford University Press (USA), 2000.

Alan Lomax. *Mister Jelly Roll: The Fortunes of Jelly Roll Morton, New Orleans Creole and "Inventor of Jazz."* Berkeley: University of California Press, 2001.

Albert Murray. *The Blue Devils of Nada: A Contemporary Approach to Aesthetic Statement.* New York: Vintage, 1997.

Howard Reich and William Gaines. *Jelly's Blues: The Life, Music, and Redemption of Jelly Roll Morton.* Cambridge, Mass.: Da Capo Press, 2003.

Studs Terkel. *Giants of Jazz.* New York: The New Press, 2006.

CHAPTER FIVE

William L. Andrews and Henry Louis Gates Jr., eds. *Slave Narratives.* New York: The Library of America, 2002.

Melba Pattillo Beals. *Warriors Don't Cry: A Searing Memoir of the Battle to Integrate Little Rock's Central High.* New York: Washington Square Press, 1995.

Melba Pattillo Beals. *White Is a State of Mind. A Memoir.* New York: G.P. Putnam's Sons, 1999.

Taylor Branch. *Parting the Waters: America in the King Years 1954–63.* New York: Simon & Schuster, 1989.

Douglas Brinkley. *Rosa Parks: A Life.* New York: Lipper/Penguin, 2000.

Clayborne Carson, ed. *The Autobiography of Martin Luther King, Jr.* New York: Warner Books, 2001.

Eleanor Flexner. *Century of Struggle: The Woman's Rights Movement in the United States.* New York: Atheneum, 1973.

Larry Gara, Brenda E. Stevenson, and C. Peter Ripley. *Underground Railroad.* Official National Park Handbook 156. Washington, D.C.: National Park Service, U.S. Department of the Interior, 1998.

Elizabeth Jacoway. *Turn Away Thy Son: Little Rock, the Crisis That Shocked the Nation*. New York: Free Press, 2007.

Kathryn Kish Sklar. *Women's Rights Emerges within the Antislavery Movement 1830–1870: A Brief History with Documents*. Boston: Bedford/St. Martin's, 2000.

CHAPTER SIX

Oliver Dunn and James E. Kelley Jr., trans. *The Diario of Christopher Columbus's First Voyage to America 1492–1493*. Abstracted by Fray Bartolomé de las Casas. Norman, Okla.: University of Oklahoma Press, 1989.

J. H. Elliott. *Empires of the Atlantic World: Britain and Spain in America 1492–1830*. New Haven: Yale University Press, 2007.

Kirkpatrick Sale. *The Conquest of Paradise: Christopher Columbus and the Columbian Legacy*. New York: Plume, 1990.

John M. Thompson, ed. *The Journals of Captain John Smith: A Jamestown Biography*. Washington, D.C.: National Geographic Adventure Classics, 2007.

ABOUT THE AUTHOR

Writer, poet, and cultural critic, Susan Griffin is the author of nineteen books including *Woman and Nature* and *A Chorus of Stones: The Private Life of War,* which was a *New York Times* Notable Book and a finalist for both the Pulitzer Prize and the National Book Critics Circle Award. Named by *Utne Reader* as one of a hundred visionaries for the new millennium, she has received an NEA grant, a MacArthur Grant for Peace and International Cooperation, and an Emmy award (for her play *Voices*). She has also published several award-winning volumes of poetry including *Unremembered Country* and *Bending Home.*

Wrestling with the Angel of Democracy: On Being an American Citizen is the third volume of what she calls a social autobiography, the first volume being *A Chorus of Stones* and the second *What Her Body Thought* (an account of the experience of illness that explores the fear of the body and neglect of the ill). She is currently editing an anthology entitled *Transforming Terror: Remembering the Soul of the World.* Ms. Griffin lectures widely in the United States and abroad and teaches at Pacifica Graduate Institute, the California Institute of Integral Studies, and privately at her home in Berkeley.